FAT TALK

VIRGINIA SOLE-SMITH

FAT TALK

VIRGINIA SOLE-SMITH

ITHAKA

A list of resources, notes, sources, acknowledgements, and an index can be found at
https://virginiasolesmith.com/

First published in the UK by Ithaka Press
An imprint of Bonnier Books UK
4th Floor, Victoria House,
Bloomsbury Square,
London, WC1B 4DA

Owned by Bonnier Books
Sveavägen 56, Stockholm, Sweden

Trade Paperback – 978-1-80418-310-6
Ebook – 978-1-80418-311-3

A CIP catalogue of this book is available from the British Library.

Designed by Alex Kirby
Printed and bound by Clays Ltd, Elcograf S.p.A.

1 3 5 7 9 10 8 6 4 2

Ithaka Press is an imprint of Bonnier Books UK
www.bonnierbooks.co.uk

For Beatrix, who imagines a better world.

As I float,
I spread out my arms
And my legs.
I'm a starfish,
Taking up all the room I want.

—Lisa Fipps, *Starfish* (2021)

CONTENTS

Fat Talk: An Initiation

ONE summer day, when my daughters were five and not yet two, we went out for ice cream and ran into Barbara, an old family friend who hadn't seen either of them since they were both much tinier. When adults see children, we have a seemingly uncontrollable urge to comment on how they've grown and changed; to mark the passage of time, yes, but also to scrutinize their bodies for clues about the people they are becoming or might someday be. So, a part of me wasn't surprised when Barbara looked my girls up and down. "Oh, I love Violet's long ballerina legs," she said. Then Barbara looked down at her own body. "Hmm, let's see, do I have ballerina legs? I think I have Beatrix legs! Short and chunky!"

"I think . . . they both have great legs?" I offered. It felt awkward. The girls sprawled in the grass, dripping chocolate ice cream everywhere, their legs stretched out in front of us. Violet's, indeed, long and delicate. Beatrix's, much shorter and rounder, with deliciously squishy toddler thighs. We started talking about vacation plans and nobody said anything further about my kids' bodies or their own. But I wondered: *How much had that one comment sunk in?*

Since Beatrix was just starting to put sentences together, I wasn't too worried that she'd pick up on Barbara's despair about chunky legs. This time. But I wasn't at all sure about Violet. Studies dating back to the 1950s have shown that when children are presented with pictures of various body types, they rate the fat body as the one they like the least. More recent research suggests that kids as young as three years old already associate fat bodies (including fat legs) with negative traits. At "five and a half," as she would emphasize, Violet was old enough to understand this.

Of course, Violet was also the kid receiving the compliment. So, what's the harm? She had the "right" kind of legs, in the eyes of this friend, and the world. But I was a thin kid once, too. I remember reveling in the knowledge that adults in my life envied my body, which, until college, I felt mostly good about. And then my body changed. It was the late '90s, heyday of Britney Spears's exposed torso, of the Delia's catalog, of Kate Moss and heroin chic, of halter crop tops and low-rise jeans. I remember standing in an Abercrombie & Fitch changing room trying to understand why my waist curved out over the waistband where other girls' seemed to curve in. Suddenly, this body part I'd taken for granted for so long looked wrong.

This happens with waists. And arms. And collarbones. And all parts of legs. Bodies, by definition, are ever-changing. But our culture, dominated as it is by whiteness and patriarchy, slices bodies (especially girl bodies) apart into a series of discrete, idealized shapes—all smooth, taut, hairless, and, most of all, thin. We are taught to have clear expectations for how each of these body parts should look, and for the fact that they should always look this way. We teach our children to equate their worth with their body size, ignoring how we know, from our own firsthand experience of growing up, that body size is mercurial. And so, growing up to have a different shape from our childhood body becomes a personal failing. It makes our bodies alien, unruly, the enemy.

Complimenting a thin child also reinforces the idea that thin bodies are better than fat bodies. And this was what kept me from saying more in the moment to Barbara—because that belief is planted deep in our collective psyche. We want our children to love their bodies. We don't want them to diet or develop eating disorders. And yet, once they're past toddlerhood (or sometimes, even before)—we also want them to be thin. I could probably explain to Barbara why it wasn't good for

Violet to receive excessive praise about her appearance, why it might reduce her understanding of her worth to how she looked. I could articulate why I want my child to think bigger and live larger than that. But it would be much harder to explain why I just as fervently want Beatrix to love her thighs, should they stay squishy past early childhood. Or how damaging it is for kids of all sizes to know that grown-ups think this way about bodies. Or why Barbara shouldn't have to hate her own legs.

Unlearning this core belief about the importance of thinness means deciding that thin bodies and fat bodies have equal value. To do this, you have to know that humans have always come in a variety of sizes; that body diversity is both beautiful and necessary. You have to believe that being fat isn't a bad thing. And that means you have to challenge a lot of what you thought you knew about health, beauty, and morality.

THE WRONG EPIDEMIC

What most of us think we know is that thin bodies are not only healthier but also more attractive and more virtuous than fat ones. And because we've tangled health, beauty, and morality all together in this way, preventing or reversing fatness has become our culture's passion project, our spiritual calling, and our most popular national pastime. Our global weight management market, on track to be worth over $298 billion by 2030, thrives on our surety that we don't want to be fat and we don't want our children to be fat. Our healthcare system makes preventing and correcting fatness its primary means of managing health. Our schools teach kids how to read food labels in first grade and to count calories by middle school so they can write their own diets in high school. And on social media, influencers post "before" and "after" photos so we can celebrate how much prettier a small, taut body is than a soft, round one. All of this is anti-fat bias: the hatred of fatness that results in the stigmatization of fat people in almost every realm of society. Research shows that four out of five Americans hold some level of anti-fat bias and that our implicit dislike of fatness is increasing, even as our other biases hold steady or decline.

Activists also use the terms "fatphobia" and "anti-fatness," and you'll see me use these interchangeably throughout the book, with a slight preference for "anti-fat bias" because, as fat activist and author Aubrey Gordon writes: "Oppressive behavior isn't the same as a phobia. Phobias are real mental illnesses and conflating them with oppressive attitudes and behaviors invites greater misunderstanding of mental illnesses and the people who have them." I agree with Gordon, but still use "fatphobia" because I appreciate that "phobia" also means "fear"—and in talking to parents, especially, I think it's important to name how much fear and fearmongering about our children's health, well-being, and future success drives this conversation. As we'll see, it's very often a manufactured anxiety, taught to us by biased institutions and systems. But parents experience their fatphobia as a kind of terror, nonetheless, because anti-fatness goes well beyond an aesthetic bias. We see staying thin, especially if you do it via a plant-based, locally sourced, whole-foods diet, as the same kind of virtuous, socially responsible act as limiting your child's screen time or saving for college.

We arrived at this intersection thanks to decades of public health policies, diet culture messaging, food advertising, and other forms of public discourse that are all rooted in this same bias, that thin is better than fat. I'll trace the history of this belief system in Chapters 1 and 2, but what's important to understand now is that there is a chicken-and-egg-style conundrum underpinning every part of it. We don't have concrete data showing that a high body weight causes health problems like diabetes, heart disease, and asthma. This is, at best, a correlating relationship. And even when weight does appear to be a root cause of disease, there isn't much we can do about it because we have even less data to show that changing how you eat or exercise will change your weight in any safe or permanent way. But we do have decades of science rooted in anti-fat bias, which impacts the questions researchers ask and don't ask, the studies that get funded, and the conclusions we take away from that work. And most people raising kids today grew up in these same systems, absorbing the same advertisements, learning the same nutrition lessons, and stepping on the scale at every doctor's appointment. We do not question "fat is bad" because that is the premise built into everything we do.

It is also, increasingly, a premise of how we parent. This wasn't always the case, but as diet culture has intensified and made "healthy eating" an increasingly unattainable prospect for adults, it has also complicated our beliefs about how our kids should eat and what their bodies should be. We want desperately to get this right; to have the kids who love beets and kale and hummus, and who fall precisely in the middle of the body mass index at every pediatrician visit. Our kids' weight has become a measure of their current and future health and happiness, as well as our own success or failure as parents. Weight is racialized and has also become a marker of class. We associate the "obesity epidemic" with processed foods, too much TV, and Walmart sweatpants. We assume people get fat—or worse, let their children get fat—out of laziness and ignorance. And these negative stereotypes about the motives and morals of people in larger bodies reinforces our repulsion.

But there is a further push-pull of anxieties around our children's weight right now. Somehow, even as we've become so fixated on our kids' spot on the body mass index, we're also striving to teach them to love their bodies just the way they are. This message of body positivity originated with second-wave feminism and early fat rights activism but went mainstream in the past decade or so thanks in large part to social media, where body positive influencers began to champion the idea that we get to define beauty on our own terms; that we can and should embrace our flaws and wear the bikini. Thanks to their efforts, as well as the adoption of these ideas by major corporations like Dove Beauty and Old Navy, "body positivity" has become almost as ubiquitous as the hand-wringing around processed food and sugar, and "dieting" is now a dirty word. But all of this has contributed to a rebranding of diet culture rather than its dismantling.

Instead of dieting, we "eat clean" or cut out meat, dairy, or sugar. And we tie our weight-loss goals to "wellness" or "feeling healthy," or even to some larger sense of social justice. We don't want our children comparing themselves to the celebrities and influencers they see on social media. We don't want them worrying about whether their thighs touch or if they have too much belly fat. We understand that when some kids fall down the rabbit hole of dieting, they land in an eating disorder like anorexia or bulimia and never climb back out. We just want them to be able to avoid all these evil disorder-y things and yet stay effortlessly thin at the same time.

This was never going to work. And we can see, quite clearly, how much it hasn't. For the past forty years, we have treated childhood obesity and eating disorders as discrete issues: Thin kids need to worry about anorexia. Fat kids need to worry about fast food, soda, and getting diabetes. We also see fatness as the far bigger problem: One in five twelve- to nineteen-year-olds are classified as obese on the body mass index scale. The prevalence rates for individual eating disorders in the same age range are much lower: less than 1 percent for anorexia nervosa, 2.6 percent for bulimia. Eating disorders just don't happen that often, we think. And when they do, they happen only to a certain type of white, wealthy, overachieving, thin girl.

But eating disorders do happen to kids of all genders, races, socioeconomic statuses, and body sizes. They are the deadliest of all mental illnesses: A young adult aged fifteen to twenty-four with anorexia is ten times more likely to die during these years than their unaffected same-age peers. And these numbers don't account for what researchers call "subthreshold" disordered eating, where the disorder doesn't rate a diagnosis but still derails your life. When we take this wider view, we see that just over 13 percent of teenagers develop some form of disordered eating. "Obesity" may still be more common, but this is a false equivalence. A high body weight is not, in and of itself, a disease. Kids with eating disorders are truly sick. And when a higher-weight child gets the message that their body is wrong, they become even more vulnerable to this sickness precisely because the behaviors that raise red flags when thin kids engage in them will be praised and reinforced. We've spent four decades in a public health panic about rising childhood obesity, and we've not only failed to solve that "crisis"—we've stoked another fire.

WHY EVERY PARENT NEEDS TO TALK ABOUT FAT

In titling this book *Fat Talk*, I've borrowed a term used by body-image researchers to describe the way we engage in collective body shaming as a form of social currency. A more precise term (but much clunkier book title!) would be "anti-fat talk," because these conversations are always rooted in fatphobia. When your friend says she hates her thighs and you respond, "Your thighs are fine, but what about my chin," you're both agreeing that fat, on these body parts and in general, is what makes them objectionable. When we have these conversations around our kids, as Barbara did, they learn this, too. But fat talk isn't limited to our own self-derision. If your six-year-old points out a fat man's big belly in the grocery store, your instinct may be to rush in with, "That's not nice!" If your eleven-year-old asks if she looks fat in her new swim-suit, you might respond, "You're not fat. You're beautiful!" We say these things because we don't want our children to be rude, and we don't want them to hate their bodies. But what they hear is that fat is the worst way a body can be. And that's a problem not only because it's false, but also because lots of our kids are—or may someday be—fat.

What we need to do instead is to redefine fat talk—to stop making fatness the worst-case scenario and start reclaiming it as a perfectly good way to have a body. Instead of "That's not nice," we can say, "Isn't it cool that bodies come in different shapes and sizes?" Instead of "You're not fat, you're beautiful," we can try, "You look great—is 'fat' something you're worrying about right now?" I know those shifts sound hard. In this book, I'm going to ask you to talk and think about fat quite differently than maybe you ever have before. We'll start by untangling fat from health. In Part 1, we'll explore how decades of anti-fat bias engineered our current public health conversation about "obesity prevention" and the "childhood obesity epidemic." We'll look at how anti-fat bias harms the health of fat people, as well as the health of kids of all sizes. And we'll consider what it would look like to treat physical and mental health without the scale, an approach most refer to as Health at Every Size or weight-inclusive healthcare. In Part 2, we'll look at how diet culture shows up for parents and infiltrates our family life. We'll rethink what "healthy eating" might mean, if you aren't trying to teach kids to eat in the pursuit of thinness. And in Part 3, we'll explore how anti-fat bias intersects with racism and misogyny when our kids perform their bodies in public, as when they go to school, play sports, go through puberty, and navigate social media.

Throughout this book, we're going to get comfortable saying the word "fat" a lot. That may feel scary, especially if the word "fat" has been weaponized against you in the past. And indeed, the scientists who study anti-fat bias tend to call it "weight bias" and "weight stigma," to stay neutral and avoid harming research subjects who might feel stigmatized when described as fat. (You'll see me use these terms when referencing such work.) But if we stop equating "fat" with all its negative connotations, it becomes a neutral descriptor, like hair color or height. And this is important because when we don't say "fat," we're not fully seeing fat people—and that's no better than when we use "fat" as a slur.

Activists for fat justice (many of whom also use the term "fat liberationists") have been working to reclaim "fat" since the 1960s, and more recently, to find language for the full spectrum of fatness: I identify as "small fat," as someone who wears a mix of straight and plus sizes (anywhere from an XL to 2X or size 16 to 20, as of this writing). Folks who can wear only plus sizes and may have trouble fitting in airplane seats and other public spaces often identify as "midfat" or "large fat." The author Roxane Gay has referred to this whole range of small to larger fat people as "Lane Bryant Fat," because we can shop in plus-size clothing stores (which typically go no higher than size 28) and, as she told Ira Glass in a 2016 episode of *This American Life*: "You have multiple places where you can buy clothes and feel pretty and move through the world." Gay belongs to a different category of fatness, known as "superfat." Members of the National Organization of Lesbians of Size Everywhere (better known as NOLOSE) coined this term in 2008 to represent "the fattest of us, those of us whose body size isn't considered acceptable *even by most other fat people*," as fat activist Cherry Midnight wrote for *Medium* in 2020. (On Instagram, the term "infinifat" is also popular with this community.) Superfats can only order clothes online from a few specialty retailers; they cannot fit into the standard chairs offered in most restaurants and healthcare waiting rooms; they require special equipment (exam tables with higher weight capacities, larger gowns, and larger blood pressure cuffs) to undergo routine medical care. Talk shows, tabloids, and other media have long portrayed superfat people as grotesque spectacles or tragic cautionary tales. But what if we instead considered all the ways in which our world is built to exclude fat people and to deny them dignity and basic human rights?

Meanwhile, the term "straight-sized" is used to refer collectively to people who can find their clothing size in mainstream stores. Of course, thinness is also a spectrum, and a woman who wears a size 12 may have a very different experience of her body in public spaces than a woman who wears a size 2. When I wore a size 10 in my early thirties, and spent several months reporting on Hollywood celebrities, I did not identify with the term "thin" because by the standards of that world, I wasn't. But I was guaranteed equal access to clothing, except when shopping in high-end designer stores (which often run significantly smaller than your average American mall brand) and felt safe and welcome in public spaces. And straight-sized folks are unlikely to have their weight be a determining factor in their paycheck or access to medical care. We'll talk more about this concept of thin privilege in Chapter 4. For now, it's important to remember that the harm caused by anti-fat bias occurs on a spectrum related to body size. And yet, the solution is not to be anti–thin people. "Just as Kurt Cobain of Nirvana (1993) sang, 'everyone is gay,' in a fat-hating society, everyone is fat. Fat functions as a floating signifier, attaching to individuals based on a power relationship, not a physical measurement," wrote the iconic fat activist Marilyn Wann in *The Fat Studies Reader*, published in 2009. "If we imagine that the conflict is between fat and thin, weight prejudice continues. Instead, the conflict is between all of us against a system that would weigh our value as people."

One important note about these terms, and the concept of reclaiming fat in general: It's never our job to label other people, and especially not people who live in bigger bodies than we do. As a journalist, I make it my practice to ask sources which terms they identify with and use that language when writing about them. Throughout this book, you will see "fat" used as a generic descriptor and in reference to sources who identify with it. But you'll also see terms like "higher-weight," "larger-bodied," and "plus-size," when those felt more comfortable or accurate to a source. To protect their privacy and body autonomy when discussing fraught issues like eating disorders, dieting, and experiences of anti-fat stigma, I've changed many names and some identifying details, including for sources under eighteen and their adults, unless they'd already gone on public record with their story.

What you won't see in this book: me describing any human as "overweight" or "obese." The word "obesity" is rooted in the Latin word *obesus*, meaning "has eaten itself fat," so a crude stereotype of fat people as gluttons has been embedded into this term from its start. Nevertheless, the American Medical Association designated obesity as an official medical diagnosis in 2013. They argued that conceiving of body size as a disease would improve health outcomes and remove stigma by making people understand that high body weight is mostly beyond an individual's control. As a result, "obese" and "overweight" have become ubiquitous in doctors' offices and the scientific literature, as well as in our casual conversations around weight, whether we're talking about adults or children. And they are both synonymous with a flawed, unruly body. Surveys show that people of all sizes find the "o words" demeaning and offensive. And making obesity a medical diagnosis didn't change that. Instead, it pathologized and further stigmatized fat bodies, allowing people who don't like fatness to dress up their disgust in concern for our health. Scientists who identify themselves as "obesity researchers" argue that this stigma doesn't originate with the word itself. "I think the stigma is unavoidable no matter what you call it," says William Dietz, MD, PhD, a former director of the division of nutrition, physical activity, and obesity at the Centers for Disease Control and Prevention. He doesn't deny that obesity "is a pejorative term as it's widely used" but insists that "on the medical side, it's not a negative term. It's a diagnosis." I don't think you can have it both ways.

In recognition of the backlash against these terms, Dietz and other obesity researchers have made a push for "person-first" language, such as "person with obesity." During my first interview with Dietz, I used the phrase "obese people" in reference to his own research, and he interrupted me: "Wait a minute, let me hold you right there," Dietz said. "You used the term 'obese.' And I don't know whether you've had this conversation, but we're very sensitive to that. I would hope that you would do a word search and eliminate the term 'obese,' because that's an identity when you talk about an obese person, or an obese child, rather than a person or a child *with* obesity."

This concept has roots in the disability rights community. It's controversial there, too. Many "people with autism" prefer to identify as autistic or neurodivergent; many in the deaf, blind, and otherwise disabled communities feel similarly. They reject "person-first" language in recognition of the fact that these conditions shape their experiences of the world, become inextricable and important parts of their identities, and require visibility to achieve equal rights.

Proponents of "person-first" language argue that we should identify people as people first, and then mention their condition, "so the disease doesn't identify the person," as Dietz explained to me. "We talk about people with cancer, we don't talk about cancer people. This is a critical concern for people in the field." But it's not, as it turns out, a critical concern for many fat people. "Person-first language increases stigma because nobody uses it with other adjectives that describe our bodies," says Ragen Chastain, a fat activist and blogger who specializes in medical fatphobia. "We don't say 'a woman with thinness.' Person-first language suggests that accurately describing a higher-weight person's body is so awful that we have to find a way to talk around it." And in conversations around health, person-first language cites a person's struggle in the size of their body, not their experience of the world *in* that body. For these reasons, I don't use "person with obesity," or the even more awkward "person with overweight," unless a source specifically requests it. And you will only see me use "o words" when referencing research on weight and health, or when quoting scientists and others who continue to use those terms.

I also do my best to avoid language that stigmatizes or triggers in other ways. But talking about fatness, diet culture, and parenting inevitably involves discussions of eating disorders, weight loss, suicide ideation, and trauma. I have sometimes needed to include numbers pertaining to body weight or clothing sizes, as well as details of disordered behaviors, so that I can accurately convey someone's narrative. If those details will be uncomfortable or dangerous for you, please take care.

To rethink our cultural relationship to fat talk, we need to listen to fat people, and especially fat kids. In reporting this book, I've interviewed sixty-five parents and forty-five kids from all over the United States and Canada. I've also had extensive and often ongoing conversations with at least eighty researchers, doctors, therapists, activists, and other thinkers in this space (many of whom are parents themselves and reflected on that experience or their own experiences of being parented around their bodies). Around half of all these sources identify as fat. And every week on the *Burnt Toast* newsletter and my social media platforms, I hear from thousands more. Not every fat person thinks alike, of course. We each bring our own context, our own set of privileges or other intersecting identities, and our own unique experiences of our bodies and the world's treatment of those bodies. In reporting this book, I sought to talk not only to folks deeply embedded in fat activism, but also to folks very much enmeshed in diet culture, and lots of people somewhere in the middle. This holds true both for the personal narratives you'll read and the researchers, doctors, and other experts represented.

But there is one through line: Listening to fat people and believing what we say about our bodies will very likely mean you have to question a lot of your assumptions about weight and health, diet, and exercise, and what it means to be a good person, with a good body. Reporting this book helped me to unlearn many of my own assumptions around weight, health, and morality, and there are certainly more questions to be worked through than I can address here. But my goal isn't to present final answers to every dilemma you might have relating to body size; it's to help parents (and anyone who cares for children) understand the impact of anti-fat bias on kids. Because once we can do that, we can name it when it happens—and start to think more critically about what we can do to make the world a safer and more weight-inclusive space for kids of all sizes.

Something else I've learned while doing this work: Fatphobia doesn't happen in a vacuum. Discrimination against fat bodies is rooted in, and constantly intersects with, racism (especially anti-Blackness) and misogyny. Virtually every culture throughout history has held its own rigid standards about good and bad body sizes, but in the United States we can trace the rise of modern anti-fatness to the end of slavery, when it became more important than ever for white people in power to marginalize and discriminate against Black people. Modern diet culture arose in the 1970s, just as we gained the right to birth control and legal abortions. Policing marginalized bodies and keeping everyone focused on the importance of thinness helps ensure that we take up less space, both literally and in terms of our cultural power.

I'm writing this introduction in June 2022, just days after the Supreme Court struck down *Roe v. Wade*, once again banning or restricting abortion in at least twenty-one states. The decision grants state governments control over the bodies of millions of Americans, including many of our children as they reach puberty. It's part of a concerted and ongoing effort to strip body autonomy from anyone who isn't a cisgender white man, but especially from people of color and people living in poverty. And it's a decision that will disproportionately impact fat people, both because we make up significant portions of those two groups and because Plan B, the most easily obtained form of emergency contraception is less effective for people who weigh over 155 pounds. (Just how much less effective is a matter of some debate, but one 2011 study found that women with a body mass index over 25 were more than three times as likely as women in the "normal weight" BMI range to experience a Plan B failure. A 2017 study found that women with BMIs over 30 had eight times higher odds of becoming pregnant while using Plan B compared to women in lower BMI categories.) Proponents of overturning *Roe v. Wade* argue that women should be held responsible for our choices; that if we have unprotected sex (even as a minor, even against our will), we should be denied healthcare and forced to live with the consequences of that experience no matter how it impacts our physical safety, mental well-being, or ability to make other choices about our lives. As we'll see in Part 1 of this book, there is a strong parallel narrative in how we approach healthcare for fat people; in who we think needs to "take responsibility" versus who we think "deserves" to make their own care decisions or to access care, period.

We are also watching state governments around the country pass laws that limit the rights of trans people, especially trans children and their parents. In October 2022, the *Washington Post* reported that 390 anti-trans laws have been introduced in statehouses around the country since 2018; over 150 of them in 2022 alone. These laws would ban trans girls and women from playing on female sports teams and prohibit all trans youth from using the bathrooms and locker rooms that correspond to their gender identity. And in Texas, Governor Greg Abbott directed child welfare agents to investigate gender-affirming medical procedures as child abuse. As of this writing, a federal judge had partially blocked that directive, but the intent of anti-trans legislation is clear: to deny trans people, especially trans kids, access to healthcare and body autonomy. Again, we'll see many parallels and intersections with anti-fatness, which is also about controlling and dehumanizing bodies. That's why it's applied most intensively to the largest bodies and to the bodies of people who are marginalized in other ways.

When we teach our kids that their bodies need to be small to be good, we are also teaching them that their bodies need to be controlled. They learn that left to their own devices, bodies are untrustworthy, unpredictable, and dangerous. This has consequences for how they explore their gender and sexuality, and for how safe they feel in their bodies. It informs how much they can even expect to have body autonomy. This is not what we want any of our kids to grow up knowing. But we can't edit or rewrite every cultural message our children get about gender roles and control, because the onslaught will never stop. Instead, we must teach them how to recognize and reject these messages—even when they hear them from us.

I don't blame Barbara for saying her fatphobia out loud. That kind of fat talk has long been accepted in our culture and even required; it's a way that women, especially, learn to perform our bodies for others; to apologize for the space we take up. But in hearing Barbara say the quiet part, I realized my kids were already learning how hard it is to just exist in our bodies, without thinking about those bodies in terms of how they look to the world. What if, instead, we just let our kids' bodies be? What if they could take unbridled joy in their appetites, without someone commenting on how that will impact their body size? What if they could play sports, wear clothes, and go through puberty without worrying about the emotions their bodies elicit in other people? What if they could see doctors who saw them as whole, complex people instead of numbers on a BMI growth chart? What could true body autonomy look like for them?

Answering those questions is only possible if we reject the premise that fat is bad, and instead identify diet culture and anti-fat bias as our common enemies. And this work is essential, because, to quote Marilyn Wann once more: "If we cannot feel at home in our own skins, where else are we supposed to go?" Changing this conversation starts now.

FAT TALK

PART 1

. . .

"WHAT ABOUT HEALTH?"

CHAPTER 1

The Myth of the
Childhood Obesity Epidemic

ANAMARIE Regino is a twenty-five-year-old in Albuquerque, New Mexico, who looks a lot like every other twenty-five-year-old on Tik-Tok. She posts videos of her dogs and her tattoos. She lip-syncs and tries out new ways to wear eyeliner. And she participates in sassy memes: "Soooo . . . this whole meme that's going around with 'decade challenge'?" she says in a video from 2019. "I just want to say: I think I won that." Then Anamarie's current lipsticked smirk is replaced by a photo of her from 2009. In both shots, Anamarie is fat. In fact, in other recent TikTok videos and Instagram posts, Anamarie proudly describes herself as fat, affectionately calls out her double chin, and uses hashtags like #PlusSize and #BBW (short for "big, beautiful woman"). But this video is also tagged #WeightLossCheck, because in the 2009 photo, Anamarie is significantly larger than her adult self. Twelve-year-old Anamarie has a half-hearted smile, but her dark bangs are swept over most of her face. It is the classic awkward "before" shot.

It's not, however, the most famous photo ever taken of Anamarie. That photo, shot by Katy Grannan when Anamarie was just four years old, first ran in a 2001 *New York Times Magazine* story and is now archived in the National Portrait Gallery's Catalog of American Portraits. Anamarie's body became part of our historical record when she was removed from her parents' custody by the state of New Mexico because she weighed over 120 pounds at age three, and social workers determined that her parents "have not been able or willing" to control her weight.

The case made international headlines, with Anamarie's parents telling their story to *Good Morning America* and to Lisa Belkin of the *New York Times Magazine*, for the article that accompanied Grannan's portrait. Anamarie's mother, Adela Martinez-Regino, had long been concerned about her daughter's appetite and her rapid growth, and then, her delayed speech and mobility. She sought help from medical professionals repeatedly from the time Anamarie was just a few months old, and multiple tests ruled out any known genetic cause, such as Prader-Willi syndrome, a rare chromosomal disorder that causes children to never feel fullness. But Anamarie continued to grow. And doctors grew frustrated by what they perceived to be a dangerous pattern: Anamarie would lose weight when undergoing their intensive medical regimens, including prescription liquid diets that provided her no more than 550 calories per day. But she would regain the weight when the protocol ended and she was once again left in her family's care. To the doctors, the risks to Anamarie lay not in their use of aggressive weight loss tactics on a toddler but in what happened when her family let her eat. "They treated her for four years, doctor after doctor. Not one of them could help. Then they took her away for months, and they still couldn't tell me what was wrong," Martinez-Regino told Belkin. "They've played around with her life like she was some kind of experiment. [. . .] They don't know what's wrong, so they blame us."

Martinez-Regino also reported that when Anamarie was taken from her parents, they had to listen to their daughter screaming for them as a nurse wheeled her away. During her months in foster care, Anamarie lost some weight and got new glasses but also stopped speaking Spanish (her father's native language) and was understandably traumatized by the separation from her parents. The state's decision to take custody of Anamarie was immediately controversial: "If this were a wealthy, white, professional family, would their child have been taken away?" Belkin asked in her piece, noting how often doctors and social workers perceived a language barrier with the Regino family, even though English was Anamarie's mother's first language. As a nation, we debated the question in op-eds, on daytime talk shows, and at water coolers: Should a child's high body weight be viewed as evidence of child abuse?

Anamarie Regino wasn't the first or the last child to be removed from parental custody due to her weight. In 1998, a California mother was convicted of misdemeanor child abuse after her thirteen-year-old daughter, Christina Corrigan, died weighing 680 pounds. A handful of similar cases popped up in Indiana, New York, Pennsylvania, and Texas over the subsequent decade, according to a report published in *Children's Voice*, a publication of the Child Welfare League of America. And in 2021, a British case made international headlines when a judge ordered two teenagers into foster care because their parents had failed to make them wear their Fitbits and go to Weight Watchers meetings. A 2010 analysis published in the *DePaul Journal of Health Care Law* by a legal researcher named Cheryl George summarizes one prevailing cultural attitude on such tragedies:

> Parents must and should be held accountable for their children's weight and health. Parents can be a solution in this health care crisis, but when they are derelict in their duties, they must be held criminally responsible for the consequences of their actions.

George acknowledged the "fear and anxiety" caused when a child is removed from parental custody but quickly dismissed that as a priority, quoting an earlier article on the subject: "If a child remains with his or her parents in order to affirm the 'attachment,' we may be overlooking the looming morbid obesity problem," she wrote. Never mind that removing custody in an effort to address this "morbid obesity" overlooks a child's emotional and developmental needs, as well as several basic human rights.

A New Mexico judge dismissed charges against Anamarie's parents after a psychiatric evaluation of Martinez-Regino found no evidence of psychological abuse. But the family was left to sort through the wreckage of those harrowing months, while continuing to seek answers that doctors could not provide to explain Anamarie's accelerated growth.

And Anamarie's story embedded itself in our national consciousness. She became a kind of "patient zero" for the war on childhood obesity. Even Belkin's piece, which is largely sympathetic to the family, frames Anamarie's body as the problem. Belkin makes sure to emphasize how this toddler's weight made her unlovable, describing Anamarie's "evolution from chubby to fat to horrifyingly obese" in family photos, and noting that Martinez-Regino "knows that the sight of her daughter makes strangers want to stare and avert their eyes at the same time." Having a fat child was framed as the ultimate parental failure. Anamarie's story confirmed that our children's weight is a key measure of our success as parents, especially for mothers.

Nowhere in the public conversations around Anamarie's early childhood was there ever any attempt to understand what Anamarie herself thought of her body or the treatment she received because of it. Today, her social media makes it clear that she's proud to have lost weight but also proud to still identify as fat, and maybe also still working it all out. (Anamarie—quite understandably—did not respond to my interview requests.) But in the late 1990s and early 2000s, our anxiety about the dangers of fatness in children far outstripped any awareness of their emotional health.

Today, this conversation has evolved, but only so far: We want our kids to love their bodies, but we also continue to take it for granted that fat kids can't do that. A child's high body weight is still a problem to solve, a barrier to their ability to be a happy, healthy child. This thinking is the result of a nearly forty-year-old public health crusade against the rising tide of children's weight. We've been told—by our families, our doctors, and voices of authority, including First Lady Michelle Obama—that raising a child at a so-called healthy body weight is an essential part of being a good parent.

But when we talk about the impossibility of raising a happy, fat child, we're ignoring the why: It's not their bodies causing these kids to have higher rates of anxiety, depression, and disordered eating behaviors. Even when high weight does play a role in health issues, as we'll explore in Chapter 2, it's often a corresponding symptom, a constellation point in a larger galaxy of concerns. The real danger to a child in a larger body is how we treat them for having that body. Fat kids are harmed by the world, including, too often, their own families. And our culture was repulsed by fat children long before we considered ourselves amid an epidemic of them. "It is easy for us to assume today that the cultural stigma associated with fatness emerged simply as a result of our recognition of its apparent health dangers," writes Amy Erdman Farrell, PhD, a feminist historian at Dickinson College, in her 2011 book, *Fat Shame: Stigma and the Fat Body in American Culture*. "What is clear from the historical documents, however, is that the connotations of fatness and of the fat person—lazy, gluttonous, greedy, immoral, uncontrolled, stupid, ugly, and lacking in will power—preceded and then were intertwined with explicit concern about health issues." To understand how we've reached this anxious place of wanting our kids to love their bodies, but not wanting them to be fat, we have to first go backward and understand the making of our modern childhood obesity epidemic. And we need to see how it has informed, and been informed by, our ideas about good mothers and good bodies.

A SHORT HISTORY OF FATPHOBIA

Just as we think of childhood obesity as a modern problem, we often frame fatphobia as a modern response and wax poetic about the days of yore when fat was seen as a sign of wealth, status, and beauty. But when historians dig back through old periodicals, newspapers, medical records, and other historical documents, they find plenty of evidence of anti-fat bias throughout Western history. The ancient Greeks celebrated thin bodies in their sculptures, art, and poetry. By the 1500s, corsets made from wood, bone, and iron were designed to flatten the torsos of the European aristocracy. And early novels like *Don Quixote* and the plays of Shakespeare are full of fat jokes and fat characters played as fools. For the purposes of understanding our modern childhood obesity epidemic, it's most helpful to see how Western anti-fatness intensified at the end of the late nineteenth century and then strengthened in the early decades of the twentieth century. This happened in response to the end of American slavery and increasing rights for women and people of color, as Sabrina Strings traces in her seminal work, *Fearing the Black Body*. In *Fat Shame*, Farrell notes that for much of the nineteenth century, fatness was attached to affluence and social status "and as such, might be respectable [. . .] but also might reveal gluttonous and materialistic traits of specific, unlikeable, and even evil individuals. By the end of the 19th century, fatness also came to represent greed and corrupt political and economic systems." Around the same time, advances in medicine and sanitation led to a decrease in infant mortality and infectious disease death rates. This meant that by the early 1900s the scientific world could begin to consider the ill effects of high body weight in a more concerted way. And scientists brought their preexisting associations of fat with sloth and amorality to this work.

The template for our modern body mass index was first designed as a table of average heights and weights in the 1830s by a Belgian statistician and astronomer named Lambert Adolphe Jacques Quetelet. Quetelet set out to determine the growth trajectory of the life of the "Average Man," meaning his white, Belgian, nineteenth-century peers. He never intended his scale to assess health. But in the early 1900s, the American life insurance industry began using his work to determine what they called an "ideal weight" for prospective clients based on their height, gender, and age. How closely you matched up to this ideal determined whether you qualified for a standard life insurance policy, paid a higher premium, or were denied coverage. And as the medical world was connecting these first dots between weight and health, we see the unmistakable presence of anti-fat bias. "A certain amount of fat is essential to an appearance of health and beauty," wrote nutrition researchers Elmer Verner McCollum and Nina Simmonds in 1925. "It is one indication that the state of nutrition is good. [. . . But] we all agree that excessive fat makes one uncomfortable and unattractive." Health and beauty were synonymous to these researchers, and many other medical experts of the late nineteenth and early twentieth centuries.

Much of the early scientific work around weight was rooted in the racist belief that fat bodies were more primitive because they made white bodies look more like Black and immigrant bodies. Black women, in particular, were (and still are) stereotyped as a "mammy" (a fat and asexual maternal caretaker of white families), a hypersexual "Jezebel," or, more recently, a "welfare queen" (a fat, amoral, single mother whose existence endangers the sanctity of the white family). The almost exclusively white and predominantly male fields of medicine and science were eager to find "proof" of white people's superiority to other racial groups and made broad generalizations about racial differences in body size and shape (as well as facial features, skull size, and so on) to build their case.

In 1937, a Jewish psychiatrist named Hilde Bruch set out to challenge the theory of fatness as a sign of racial inferiority by studying hundreds of Jewish and Italian immigrant children in New York City. She examined their bodies (with a particular focus on height, weight, and genital development). She visited their homes to observe children eating and playing, and she interviewed their mothers extensively. And Bruch determined that there was nothing physically wrong with the fat kids in her study—which could have been a huge breaking point in our cultural understanding of weight and health. But although she disputed the notion that fat white immigrants and fat people of color were biologically inferior to thin white Americans, Bruch still framed fatness as a matter of ethnicity: "Obesity occurs with greater frequency in children of immigrant families than in those of settled American background," she declared in a 1943 paper. And instead of blaming physiology, Bruch blamed mothers. Her papers on childhood obesity explain the children's fatness as "a result of the smothering behavior of their strongwilled immigrant mothers," writes Farrell. "These mothers simultaneously resented and clung to their children, trying to make up for both their conflicting emotions and poor living conditions by providing excessive food and physical comfort. Bruch described the fathers of these fat children as weak willed, often absent, and 'yearning' for the love that their wives devoted to the children."

Bruch's description of immigrant parents of fat children is a neat precursor to the treatment the Regino family received during Anamarie's custody case. Anamarie's father, Miguel, goes unquoted in the *New York Times Magazine* feature and most other media, while her mother is required to defend herself as a parent and assert herself as an American repeatedly, in the media and with doctors and social workers who assume she can't understand them. "There were so many veiled comments which added up to, 'You know those Mexican people, all they eat is fried junk, of course they're slipping her food,'" the Regino family's lawyer told Belkin. The social worker's affidavit recommending that Anamarie be placed in foster care concluded by saying, "The family does not fully understand the threat to their daughter's safety and welfare due to language or cultural barriers." Martinez-Regino said such comments showed her that "they decided about us before they even spoke to us."

So anti-fatness, racism, and misogyny have long intersected with and underpinned one another. Even when a researcher like Bruch set out to challenge one piece of the puzzle, she did so by reinforcing the rest of our cultural biases. The immigrant children she studied weren't diseased—but their weight was still a problem, and their mothers still held responsible. It would be decades before anyone thought to question either assumption. In 1969 the nascent "fat acceptance" movement took off with the establishment of the National Association to Advance Fat Acceptance (NAAFA). In 1973, two California activists named Judy Freespirit and Aldebaran wrote the first "Fat Manifesto" for their organization, the Fat Underground: "We believe that fat people are fully entitled to human respect and recognition," they began. A later clause specifies:

> We repudiate the mystified "science" which falsely claims that we are unfit. It has both caused and upheld discrimination against us, in collusion with the financial interests of insurance companies, the fashion and garment industries, reducing industries, the food and drug establishments.

These early activists created spaces where fat people could find community and support and begin to understand the way they were treated as a form of chronic oppression. Along with disability rights activists, they operated on the fringes of feminism and queer activism, and their ideas were far from any mainstream conversations about weight.

But around the same time, a handful of researchers began studying fat stereotypes as a way of understanding how we learn and internalize biases. In several studies from the 1960s, researchers showed children drawings of kids with various body types (usually a disabled child, a child with a birth defect, and a child in a larger body) and found that they consistently rated the fat child as the one they liked least. In a 1980 experiment, a public health researcher named William DeJong found that high school students shown a photo of a higher-weight girl rated her as less self-disciplined than a lower-weight subject unless they were told her weight gain was caused by a thyroid condition. "Unless the obese can provide an 'excuse' for their weight [...] or can offer evidence of successful weight loss, their character will be impugned," he wrote. In 2012, researchers revisited the picture-ranking experiment from the 1960s with a group of 415 American fifth and sixth graders and found that anti-fat bias had only intensified. They noted, "The difference in liking between the healthy and obese child was currently 40.8 percent greater than in 1961." So, the farther we come in claiming to understand and care about the health of fat children, it seems, the less we like them. As Anamarie's mother said in the *New York Times Magazine* story: "They decided about us before they even spoke to us."

THE MAKING OF THE MODERN OBESITY EPIDEMIC

In 1988, Colleen was ten years old, living in Highlands Ranch, Colorado. She had never heard of fat acceptance or the Fat Manifesto or early research on anti-fat biases. But she experienced fatphobia every day. At home, family members would make comments like "You look like you're going to have a baby with that belly" and remind her to suck in her stomach and stand "like a lady," with her hands clasped in front of her middle, especially when she went up to receive Communion at church. At school, kids teased her mercilessly, calling her "Tank" when she played four-square at recess. When everyone got weighed in her gym class, Colleen recalls stepping on the scale in front of all her classmates and then having to put her weight on an "About Me" poster that was hung in the school hallway. Highlands Ranch is a mostly white, affluent suburb of Denver also known as "The Bubble," and Colleen thinks its lack of diversity played a role in her experience. "There was a sense of perfectionism and I didn't fit that 'perfect' or ideal body type."

When the bullying reached a breaking point, her parents called a psychologist—and put Colleen on the popular '90s weight loss plan Jenny Craig. "I remember my mom saying, 'You need to nip this in the bud right now,'" says Colleen, who is now a forty-two-year-old physician's assistant, still living in a larger body, and still living in Highlands Ranch, with her husband and eleven-year-old son. "I think she felt that if I was fat at that age, I'd be fat for the rest of my life, and live this horrible life where everyone would make fun of me, and I'd never be accepted." There was no discussion of consequences for the kids bullying Colleen at school. Her family is white and now upper middle class, but having a fat child still subjected Colleen's parents, who grew up working class themselves, to stigma and scrutiny. Colleen's weight was their problem to solve, and her mother, especially, was determined to fix it.

Indeed, by the 1990s, fixing everyone's weight had become a national project. In 1997, a Boston pediatrician named William Dietz, MD, PhD, joined the front lines of the fight, as director of the Division of Nutrition, Physical Activity, and Obesity at the Centers for Disease Control and Prevention. "I took the CDC job because I thought that obesity needed to be a national concern, and I couldn't really do that much about it in an academic setting," he tells me. Dietz and his colleagues had been warning about a rise in body size for both children and adults since the mid-1980s, based on data collected in the National Health and Nutrition Examination Survey, known as NHANES, which is executed every two years. Data collected beginning in 1971 showed that just 5.2 percent of kids aged two to nineteen met the criteria for obesity then. By the survey begun in 1988, that percentage had nearly doubled, and the 1999–2000 NHANES showed a youth obesity rate of 13.9 percent. That rate has continued to climb, reaching 19.3 percent in the 2017–2018 NHANES. A similar rise in body size was documented for adults: Data collected from 1976 to 1980 showed that 15 percent of adults met criteria for obesity. By 2007, it had risen to 34 percent. The most recent NHANES data puts the rate of obesity among adults at 42.4 percent.

The statistics alone were startling, but Dietz wanted to find an even more effective way to communicate to Americans the scale of the obesity epidemic. One day early in his CDC tenure, while chatting with staffers in a hallway, Dietz suggested they plot the NHANES findings across a map of the United States, to designate which states had become "obesity hot zones," using a green to red color-coded system. "Those maps, more than anything else, I think, began to, well, transform the discussion of obesity," Dietz tells me. "Nobody argued thereafter that there wasn't an epidemic of obesity because those maps were so compelling."

Dietz's maps, which are updated every year, and the NHANES numbers are dramatic, unprecedented, and, to some extent, indisputable. Americans are, on average, bigger than we were a generation ago. And our kids are bigger, on average, than we were as kids. We'll look more at explanations for this rise in body size in Chapter 2. But what I want to note about these numbers now is how they continued to climb even as public health officials were printing their maps and assembling this evidence of their epidemic; even as weight loss became our national pastime. One conclusion we can therefore draw is that the weight loss industry and public health messaging have failed, quite spectacularly, in their quest to make anyone smaller. They may even have had the opposite effect. But it's also worth looking at these statistics in a little more detail, to see what else they tell us.

The NHANES researchers determine our annual rate of obesity by collecting the body mass index scores of about five thousand Americans (a nationally representative sample) each year. BMI is a blunt tool, never developed to directly reflect health. But it's useful for tracking populations in this way because it's easy to calculate by dividing a person's weight in kilograms by the square of his or her height in meters. From there, researchers can sort people into the categories of underweight, normal weight, overweight, or obese, depending on where they fall on the BMI scale. This entire project of categorizing people by body size— and determining that there is only one "normal" weight range—is flawed and loaded with bias. And to make matters more confusing, the cutoff points for those categories haven't stayed fixed over the years. A major shift happened in 1998, when the National Institutes of Health's task force lowered the BMI's cutoff points for each weight category, a math equation that moved twenty-nine million Americans who had previously been classified as normal weight or just overweight into the overweight and obese categories. The task force argued that this shift was necessitated by research. But just a few years later, in 2005, epidemiologists at the CDC and the National Cancer Institute published a paper analyzing the number of deaths associated with each of these weight categories in the year 2000 and found that overweight BMIs were associated with fewer deaths than normal weight BMIs. (Both the obese and underweight groups were associated with excess deaths compared to the normal weight group, but the analysis linked obesity, specifically, with less than 5 percent of deaths that year.)

Rather than revisiting the cutoff lines for BMI weight categories after this research came out, many researchers objected to that study being published at all. "There was a lot of criticism that our finding was very surprising," the study's lead author, Katherine Flegal, MPH, PhD, told me in 2013. "But it really wasn't, because many other studies had supported our findings." These included studies that the Obesity Task Force had reviewed while debating BMI cutoffs—so many studies, in fact, that in 2013, Flegal and her colleagues published a systematic literature review of ninety-seven such papers, involving almost three million participants, and concluded, again, that having an overweight BMI was associated with a lower rate of death than a normal BMI in all of the studies that had adequately adjusted for factors like age, sex, and smoking status. They also found no association with mortality at the low end of the obese range. This review was also met with criticism and fury by mainstream obesity researchers. The Harvard School of Public Health held a symposium to discuss all the ways that Flegal's work made them mad. "I think people will be endlessly surprised by these findings," is how Flegal put it to me then, while she was still employed by the CDC and presumably felt required to be circumspect about the criticism her work received.

But in 2021, years after retiring, Flegal published an article in the journal *Progress in Cardiovascular Diseases* that details the backlash her work received from obesity researchers:

Some attacks were surprisingly petty. At one point, Professor 1 posted in a discussion group regarding salt intake that JAMA had shown a track record of poor editorial judgment by publishing "Kathy Flegal's terrible analyses" on overweight and mortality. Similarly, again using a diminutive form of my name, Professor 1 told one reporter: "Kathy Flegal just doesn't get it."

After her paper was published, former students of the obesity researchers most outraged by Flegal's work took to Twitter to recall how they were instructed not to trust her analysis because Flegal was "a little bit plump herself." The most depressing part is how well these personal attacks, rooted in fatphobia and misogyny, worked: For years, Flegal's findings have been all but ignored by doctors and other healthcare providers, for whom using BMI to determine health has remained accepted practice.

Doctors use BMI to determine health for kids, too, using a similar calculation, and then plotting that number as a percentile on a BMI-for-age chart, which shows how they are growing compared to same-sex peers of the same age. BMI doesn't take a child's muscle mass or level of pubertal development into account, both of which influence body composition. And the BMI-for-age chart used in most doctors' offices today is based on what children weighed between 1963 and 1994. "It's true that the demographics of the population have changed," says Dietz, noting that obesity rates differ dramatically by racial identity. Black kids, especially, tend to be bigger than non-Black peers and start puberty earlier, which impacts their growth trajectory. But Dietz stops short of acknowledging that maybe we should use a different scale to assess the weight/health relationship of these kids, pointing to research done by the World Health Organization, which found the growth curves of upper- and middle-income, healthy children in six different countries to be similar. "You know, you need to draw the line somewhere," he says.

Dietz drew that line in 2010, when categories on the pediatric growth charts were renamed. Kids who were previously identified as "at risk of overweight" were relabeled "overweight," and kids who had been classified as overweight were now designated as "having obesity." This decision, along with the earlier 1998 reshuffling of the adult BMI scale, was controversial. "There was a feeling at the time, from a conservative faction, that obesity was too drastic a diagnosis [for kids]," says Dietz, who pushed hard for the change. He stands by it a decade later, though he does acknowledge that the "overweight" range, defined as the 85th to 95th percentiles on the growth chart, is more of a gray area. "There are a lot of misclassifications there because you find kids who just have a large frame or are very muscular," Dietz says. "Whereas body weights in excess of the 95th percentile are almost invariably fat."

I want to point out here that there is anti-fatness even in how Dietz (and Flegal, in her work on adult BMI categories) make allowances for bodies who are "just overweight," or on the low end of obesity versus the higher end. Such distinctions still rank different kinds of fatness in ways that silo and stigmatize people at the top of the scale and ignore that they have just as nuanced and complicated a picture of health as anybody else. Or would, if anybody bothered to study their health in non-stigmatizing ways. In fact, kids' body weights above the 95th percentile vary tremendously in composition—we just don't have a good tool for measuring them. A child in the 99th percentile might have a BMI of 29 or 49, but they're plotted along the same line because the chart doesn't go any higher.

The debates within research communities over how to define obesity rarely make headlines—only the resulting scary statistics, which is how those numbers bake into our collective subconscious as truth, even though they cannot tell the full story. A particularly dangerous one is the claim that "obesity kills 300,000 people per year!" This figure is used by doctors, the media, and for years by Jillian Michaels, the celebrity personal trainer and host of the TV show *The Biggest Loser*. But where did we get this number? From a 1993 study by researchers at the United States Department of Health and Human Services titled "Actual Causes of Death in the United States." These scientists combed through mortality data from 1990 and attributed 300,000 American deaths due to heart attacks, strokes, and other medical issues to "diet and activity patterns." The only contributor with a higher death toll was tobacco (400,000). The researchers made no mention of weight, and they also analyzed data for only one single year. Nevertheless, in 1994, former surgeon general C. Everett Koop joined forces with then First Lady Hillary Clinton to kick off their "Shape Up America" campaign, citing that 300,000 figure as proof of the need for a "war against obesity." Other researchers also referenced the figure often enough that in 1998, the study's authors published a letter to the editors of the *New England Journal of Medicine* saying, "You [. . .] cited our 1993 paper as claiming 'that every year 300,000 deaths in the United States are caused by obesity.' That is not what we claimed." But the "epidemic" was already underway.

What motivated researchers and public health officials to hype their "war on obesity" in this intense way? Many operate from a place of deep concern for their fellow humans. Dietz, for example, struck me as personable and passionate about helping children during both of our conversations. But he has also been financially entangled with the weight loss industry for much of his career. After his tenure at the CDC, Dietz served on the scientific advisory board of Weight Watchers. And even before joining the CDC, Dietz was a member of the group then known as the International Obesity Task Force. Now known as the World Obesity Federation, this task force began as a policy and advocacy think tank "formed to alert the world to the growing health crisis threatened by soaring levels of obesity," according to the organization's official history. The task force was framed as an independent alliance of academic researchers—but many of these researchers, including the organization's founder, a British nutrition scientist named Philip James, were paid by pharmaceutical companies to conduct clinical trials on weight loss drugs; James even hosted an awards ceremony for the drug manufacturer Roche. In 2006, an unidentified senior member of the task force told a reporter for the *British Medical Journal* that the organization's sponsorship from drug companies "is likely to have amounted to 'millions.'" And in the years around that first shift in the BMI cutoffs— the one that resulted in twenty-nine million more Americans in the overweight and obesity categories—the Food and Drug Administration approved a flurry of weight loss drugs: dexfenfluramine (sold as Redux) in 1996, sibutramine (sold as Meridia) in 1997, and orlistat (sold as Xenical and Alli) in 1999. More overweight and obese Americans meant a larger potential market for the makers of those drugs. In America's "war on obesity," the weight loss industry had just negotiated its arms deal.

While both Redux and Meridia were later recalled due to concerns about heart damage, the FDA approved several more weight loss drugs in 2012, 2014, and 2021. Today the US weight loss market is valued at over $70 billion. Dietz is now the director of the Strategies to Overcome and Prevent (STOP) Obesity Alliance at the Sumner M. Redstone Global Center for Prevention and Wellness at George Washington University. Like IOTF before it, the STOP Obesity Alliance looks like an academic think tank but actually comprises "a diverse group of business, consumer, government, advocacy, and health organizations dedicated to reversing the obesity epidemic in the United States," according to its 2020 annual report, which further discloses that in that year alone, the alliance received $105,000 from corporate members including Novo Nordisk, a pharmaceutical company that manufactures liraglutide and semaglutide, two recent weight loss drugs to get FDA approval, and WW, the brand formerly known as Weight Watchers. They also received an additional $144,381 from Novo Nordisk to sponsor a research project on primary care obesity management.

Dietz is perfectly up-front about all of this when I ask him about the role of corporate sponsorship in obesity research. "We would not have been able to do this work without that kind of support," he tells me. "Does that bias my judgment about medication? I don't think so. But, you know, that's an external kind of thing." It doesn't feel problematic to Dietz to be funded by drug companies because he views weight loss medication as "the biggest thing that's been missing in obesity care"—a silver bullet that's going to transform people's lives—because he doesn't question the premise that fat people must need their lives transformed. "Companies and practitioners have the same goals. And that's to treat obesity effectively and to be reimbursed for that care," he tells me. "Those go hand in hand. So, there's no way of avoiding that conflict of interest." The bias is baked in.

Almost thirty years later, Colleen can't even remember if she lost weight on that first diet, though she does recall going to her brother's Cub Scout camp out in the mountains of Colorado and watching all their friends eat hot dogs while she ate her Jenny Craig meal. "It was always, 'Come on, Colleen, you know that French fry is not on your diet,'" she says. Dieting became an ever-present feature of her tween and teen years. Colleen gave up on expecting her body to fit in; she channeled all her energy into being "the smart one, the sweet one, the people pleaser," as she puts it. "I had a lot of friends, I was part of the 'popular clique,' but I felt like, I had to conform in those ways," she explains. "Everyone else was the same physical body type, and pretty soon they were all kind of going out with each other. But boys weren't interested in me."

So, Colleen excelled at being a good friend and being good at school. When she got to college, she decided to major in nutrition. "I was so, so sick of people telling me what to eat, how to eat, how to do anything," she explains. "I wanted to go find out for myself what the truth is behind all of this." But Colleen studied nutrition from 1999 to 2003, the same years when the 300,000 deaths figure and the state maps were making headlines. "It was a very weight-centric education, to say the least," she says. When a guest lecturer came to campus to give a talk on how we can be both "fat and fit," Colleen recalls her professors telling students to completely disregard it. They were sure it couldn't be true—after all, our own government research had told them everything they needed to know about weight and health.

MODERN MOTHER BLAME

Elena, forty-one, grew up in New York City and New Jersey and has her own list of childhood diets prescribed during the war on obesity's early years: Richard Simmons's Deal-a-Meal, Weight Watchers, and "Get in Shape, Girl!" a workout video series marketed to tween girls, which involved a lot of pastel leotards, ankle weights, and side ponytails. "I remember my mom taking me with her to this twelve-week weight loss group she was doing, and at the end of it, we all went out for pizza to celebrate, which seems so absurd now," says Elena. Her mom dieted steadily, but it's Elena's dad who took it even further. "He was in the Air Force Reserves and he'd have to hit certain weights every so often, so I remember him, like, not eating or eating and puking and eating," she says. Nobody suggested this was a good idea, but it certainly communicated to Elena that her own "chubby" body was not okay.

Her extended Afro–Puerto Rican family reinforced that narrative: "My grandmother would make comments, and I remember one of her friends would always say, 'You're fat!' to me. But in Spanish, so she would say, 'Ahhh, gordita!' and it's like, a term of endearment and a term of criticism all in one," Elena says. "You were not supposed to be fat. But also, my grandmother would fry a chicken for me, for like, a snack. It was very convoluted." Elena isn't sure if her grandparents and their friends were measuring her by Puerto Rican or white American beauty standards, but she knows which metric she used on herself. "I compared myself to the typical teen and fashion magazines of the 1980s and 1990s, which were very white and thin," she says. "My friends were of varying races, but they were almost all thin, so I also compared myself to them. I knew my weight was different from what was mostly around me. And I hated that."

Like Colleen, Elena was also teased constantly at school and didn't date in high school. But some of her most intense trauma came from pediatricians. "I remember one doctor just berating me in front of my mother, telling me, 'You have to stop eating fast food!'" Elena says. She was nine years old. She liked fast food but ate it only rarely. "Getting to go out to eat at all was kind of special," Elena says. "She made all these assumptions about me, and I remember being so crushed." Elena told her mother she'd never go back to that doctor. "And probably from the time I was twelve, until I needed a physical for college, I just didn't go."

Elena is now a public health nurse—finding her way into a version of the profession that so stigmatized her, just as Colleen did with nutrition—and lives with her husband and two children in Philadelphia. She spends her workdays making home visits to low-income, expecting, and new mothers. Elena weighs the babies after they're born, but she never asks a mother to get on a scale. "I never talk about my clients' health through the lens of weight. Never," she says. "The health impacts they face are due to racism and poverty, not weight. So, I approach it that way: How can we get you money and resources? How can I radically listen to and accept you? That's my role."

Elena parents carefully around weight, too; her kids never hear her discuss diets or body size. If they hear someone described as "fat," Elena never says, "Don't say that!" because she doesn't want to reinforce that fat is bad. "I say, 'Yes, fat people exist, and I am one of them, and there's nothing wrong with being fat. But we don't need to comment on everyone's body because that might make people uncomfortable,'" she explains. "But none of this has stopped my brain from saying, 'Oh my God, please don't let my kids be fat.'" And even while she speaks so positively about bodies to her children, Elena has also done everything she can to prevent their early weight gain. "I breastfed each of them for three years; we eat vegetarian, rarely drink juice, and never set foot in McDonald's," she reports. "The motivation for all of this was 'no fat kids.'"

And yet. When her now-eight-year-old daughter reached kindergarten, Elena noticed her "chunking up a little." The same thing has happened in the past year for her five-year-old son. "It was just this realization of, 'Oh man, genetics are real,'" she says. "I've never said anything about this to my kids. I would never say that to anyone. But I think about it every day." Part of what Elena is struggling with is the intense desire to spare her kids the anxiety she felt around weight as a child. She's already told their pediatrician not to discuss weight loss in front of them. But she also worries how their weight reflects on her as a mother. "All of their friends are stick thin. Like, it's a striking difference. And so, I wonder, do people look at them and think I'm a bad parent?"

When I follow up with Elena more than a year after our first conversation, that fear of being a bad parent, of being to blame for her children's bodies has escalated. "My son gained forty pounds over COVID and has high cholesterol and fatty liver," she writes in an email. "I really fucked him up. And it's really awful. I feel terrible." We'll talk more about the links between weight gain and health in the next chapter, but whether Elena's son's bloodwork is related to his body size or not, I know one thing is true: Elena did not fuck him up. She loved her child and kept him safe during a global pandemic, which has left scars on all of our bodies, hearts, and minds in complex ways. Subjecting him to the same kind of perpetual weight anxiety that Elena experienced as a child is unlikely to help, as we'll see in Chapter 3. But I am not surprised that this is the solution she reaches for: "We're going to a healthy weight clinic in January and I'm back on Weight Watchers."

Elena is responding to the same cultural narratives that judged Anamarie Regino's mother before her, Bruch's Italian and Jewish immigrant mothers before both of them, and Black mothers from the time they were enslaved. These narratives predate the modern obesity epidemic, which is to say, they've also shaped it. As the first data on the rise in children's body size was unfolding, doctors, researchers, and public health officials immediately turned the conversation to parental responsibility: how to make parents "aware" of their children's weight, and how to get parents to make better decisions about the family's food and activity habits. "The researchers in this camp suggest that we need to educate mothers about how to determine whether their children weigh too much," noted Natalie Boero, PhD, a sociologist at San Jose State University, in an essay for *The Fat Studies Reader* published in 2009. "Implicit in this critique of American culture is a blame of working mothers for allowing their children to watch too much television, for not having their eating habits more closely monitored, and for relying on convenience foods for meals."

Research began to pile up pinpointing links between children's higher body weights and these kinds of poor parenting decisions. And this has resulted in tangible limitations on how fat people, especially fat women, are allowed to parent. As comic storyteller Phoebe Potts explores in her 2021 one-woman show *Too Fat for China*, many countries ban fat parents from adopting. In addition to China (where Potts was rejected for having a BMI of 29.5), BMI has also been a deal breaker for adoption proceedings in South Korea, Taiwan, and Thailand as well as parts of Australia, the United Kingdom, and the United States. And, as I reported for the *New York Times Magazine* in 2019, it has become a common practice for infertility clinics to deny in vitro fertilization and other treatments to mothers above a certain body weight.

It's easy to classify stories like Anamarie Regino's as rare and exceptional, the sad, salacious stuff of daytime talk shows that blow up in brief Twitter storms and then become memorialized in internet memes but don't factor into our everyday lives. But every time we put a mother on trial for making her child fat, we put all mothers on trial for the size and shape of their children's bodies. For moms like Elena, it's nearly impossible to separate out her fear of judgment from her fear of fat because we've always dealt with these as one and the same in our culture. It's also incredibly difficult to separate her experience of anti-fat bias from her fear for her child's health, because what we know about kids, weight, and health has been informed and shaped by that same stigma. This is why, in almost every interview I do with someone who has lived with an eating disorder, they tell me about what their mother said or did about their weight and how it contributed to their struggle. The "war on childhood obesity" of the past forty years has normalized the notion that parents, but especially mothers, must take responsibility for their child's weight, and must prioritize that responsibility above their own relationship with their child as the ultimate expression of maternal love. And almost nobody pushed that message more fervently than the most famous mother ever to take on this fight: former First Lady Michelle Obama.

DIET CULTURE IN THE WHITE HOUSE

In November 2008, it was then president-elect Barack Obama who gave an interview to *Parents* magazine where he explained how "Malia was getting a little chubby." He described how he and Michelle got serious about the problem and made changes to the family's diet. According to Michelle, the result "was so significant that the next time we visited our pediatrician, he was amazed." When the Obama family arrived at the White House, First Lady Michelle Obama made fighting the war on childhood obesity her central mission, perhaps at least in part because it felt like a safe issue for the nation's Mom in Chief to take on as she battled extreme levels of scrutiny and misogynoir as the first Black First Lady. She told the story about Malia and the pediatrician repeatedly when promoting her "Let's Move" initiative, which ran from 2010 to 2016. "The thought that I was maybe doing something that wasn't good for my kids was devastating," she said of that doctor's appointment, in a 2016 speech to a group of parenting bloggers. "And maybe some of you can relate, but as an overachiever, I was like, 'Wait, what do you mean, I'm not getting an A in motherhood? Is this like a B-? A C+?'"

In another speech, Obama spoke more directly to parents' failings, saying, "Back when we were all growing up, most of us led lives that naturally kept us at a healthy weight," before describing her own idyllic childhood as full of healthy habits like walking to school, playing outside, eating home-cooked meals with green vegetables, and saving ice cream as a special treat, all because her parents imposed such policies whether kids liked it or not. "But somewhere along the line, we kind of lost that sense of perspective and moderation," implying that kids' weights are rising because parents have become too lax and indulgent. Obama also painted a grim picture of what kids' lives had become, thanks to this loss of parenting standards: "Kids [. . .] are struggling to keep up with their classmates, or worse yet, they're stuck on the sidelines because they can't participate. You see how kids are teased or bullied. You see kids who physically don't feel good, and they don't feel good about themselves," she said in a 2010 speech to the School Nutrition Association. Later in the speech, she added: "And by the way, today one of the most common disqualifiers for military service is actually obesity." References to military readiness are sprinkled throughout Obama's "Let's Move" speeches, reinforcing the "war" rhetoric around weight first popularized in the 1990s by Koop and Clinton, but this time placing kids on the battlefield.

By 2013, Obama was putting the responsibility for childhood obesity even more squarely on parents:

> When it comes to the health of our kids, no one has a greater impact than each of us do as parents. [. . .] Research shows that kids who have at least one obese parent are more than twice as likely to be obese as adults. So as much as we might plead with our kids to "do as I say, and not as I do," we know that we can't lie around on the couch eating French fries and candy bars and expect our kids to eat carrots and run around the block.

The "Let's Move" campaign often portrayed the physical activity part of fighting obesity as fun; Obama hosted dance parties at public schools and went on TV for a push-up contest with Ellen DeGeneres and to dance with Big Bird. Nutrition activists were frustrated that Obama often seemed more interested in dance parties than in holding large food corporations to higher standards. "'Move more' is not politically loaded. 'Eat less' is," wrote Marion Nestle, PhD, a professor of nutrition, food studies, and public health at New York University in a 2011 blog post. "Everyone loves to promote physical activity. Trying to get the food industry to budge on product formulations and marketing to kids is an uphill battle that confronts intense, highly paid lobbying."

Meanwhile, although anti-hunger activists mostly supported Obama's goals of reforming school lunch programs, there was some quiet resignation in that community that she had chosen to focus on childhood obesity, which accounted for 19.7 percent of kids aged six to seventeen when Barack Obama was elected in 2008, instead of food insecurity, which was arguably the bigger issue, impacting 21 percent of all American households with children. But the relationship between hunger and fatness has long been fraught with stigma: In the early 2000s, conservatives began to argue that the United States Supplemental Nutrition Assistance Program (SNAP, formerly known as food stamps) and other federal food programs should be abolished because, they claimed, poor Americans couldn't be hungry when so many of them were fat. "We're Feeding the Poor as if They're Starving," ran the headline of a 2002 *Washington Post* column by Douglas Besharov, director of the American Enterprise Institute's Social and Individual Responsibility Project. "Today the central nutritional problem facing the poor [. . .] is not too little food, but too much of the wrong food," he wrote.

In fact, as we'll see in Chapter 3, it's possible to be both fat and not eating nearly enough food. But rather than clarify this misconception, anti-hunger organizations, pediatric health, and nutrition organizations, as well as journalists like Michael Pollan and Eric Schlosser, and public health researchers like Nestle, set out to document how our modern "toxic food environment" represented an immediate threat to the health of all children. Very quickly, fighting childhood obesity became a progressive cause deeply intertwined with protecting SNAP and other social safety net programs. But when Obama had to pitch a legislative agenda, she needed to pick an issue that would spark outrage among liberals and conservatives alike. And framing kids' weight as a matter of good parenting and personal responsibility was easier to sell across the aisle. "I do think the administration cared about fighting hunger, but it's definitely not what they led with," one anti-hunger advocate told me. "I'm not sure what political calculations they made around that. Part of it is that I think people just have a really hard time understanding the intersection of obesity and hunger."

Obama did talk openly about the fact that poor children of color tended to weigh more than wealthier white children. But by zeroing in on their weight, she steered the conversation away from dismantling oppression or shoring up social safety net programs. Instead, Obama championed an in-depth overhaul of school nutrition standards, which culminated in the Healthy, Hunger-Free Kids Act of 2010. That piece of legislation is now hailed as a centerpiece of Obama's progressive legacy; it's the reason you see whole grains on school lunch menus and fewer vending machines in schools. It also expanded after-school programs' supper offerings around the country and brought free school lunch and breakfast to over thirty thousand schools nationwide, both of which were huge wins for the anti-hunger community. But what progressives discuss less often is the fact that those school initiatives were paid for by pulling funds from SNAP, ending a temporary increase in food stamp funding five months earlier than expected. The original bill took money from a different pot, but when the Senate Committee on Agriculture, Nutrition, and Forestry marked up the bill, they quietly shifted the funding source. Money that low-income families had been using to pay for dinner now covered their kids' tab for lunch.

Over a decade later, the question of the Healthy, Hunger-Free Kids Act funding is still a sore spot with many food and hunger activists, all of whom declined to go on record to discuss what happened. "We believe that kids deserve the healthiest meals possible. There are lots of good things in that act, but paying for it through SNAP just didn't make any sense to us," an anti-hunger activist who worked on the bill told me. Indeed, over 50 percent of SNAP recipients are children, and several studies have shown that when you cut a household's food budget, the nutritional quality of family meals drops fast. Anti-hunger groups lobbied Democrats to block votes on the bill for several months, leading to bitter disagreements with the child nutrition organizations they had previously considered allies. The anti-hunger groups worried about families falling off a financial cliff, but the nutrition groups were focused on achieving their nutrition standards overhaul. "An additional five months of the temporary increase in SNAP funding is a price worth paying for a lifetime of reforms and ten years of resources to address childhood hunger and obesity," argued Margo Wootan, who was then director of nutrition policy at the Center for Science in the Public Interest, in a piece by TheHill.com. "This bill wasn't a Sophie's Choice. It was more like choosing between your child and your pet fish. Like the temporary increase in SNAP funding, goldfish never live long anyway."

However Michelle Obama herself felt about the funding decision, the Obama administration sided with the nutrition advocates to get the bill passed. And it's clear that Obama's own passion for nutrition and health meant she viewed dieting as a necessary evil for both parents and kids. "I have to tell you, this new routine was not very popular at first," Obama told the parenting bloggers in 2016. "I still remember how the girls would sit at the kitchen table and I'd sort out their lunches, and they would sit with their little sorry apple slices and their cheese sticks. [. . .] They'd have these sad little faces. They would speak longingly of their beloved snack foods that were no longer in our pantry." Obama also spoke longingly of her own beloved, banned foods: "I could live on French fries," she told the *New York Times* in 2009, explaining that she doesn't because "I have hips." Instead, she follows a strict diet and exercise routine.

I want to stop here and note just how much scrutiny Obama has faced personally about her body size and shape. In her latest book, *The Light We Carry*, she talks about becoming aware of her "differentness" as a tall Black woman when attending Princeton, and that experience only intensified during her husband's first presidential campaign and throughout their time in the White House. I remember watching her wave on television from some early campaign stop and noticing that her upper arms jiggled a little; a few months later, the jiggling had stopped, and it seemed like everyone was talking about Obama's sheath dresses and toned biceps, which were nicknamed "Thunder" and "Lightning" by *New York Times* columnist David Brooks, who thought she should "cover up." And much of the public discourse about Obama's body was racialized, because she was our first Black First Lady and therefore was in a position "to present to the world an African-American woman who is well educated, hardworking, a good mother, and married," noted the feminist historian Amy Erdman Farrell, PhD, in *Fat Shame*. Obama's job was to reject the mammy, the welfare queen, and every other derogatory stereotype about Black women, and thinness was a part of how she did that. Depriving her kids and herself of French fries was "an ideological lesson, teaching the girls how to survive in a world that will scrutinize their bodies unmercifully for signs of inferiority and primitivism," writes Farrell. "Fatness is one of those signs, this lesson teaches, one too dangerous to evoke."

It's impossible to say how conscious Obama was (or is now) of the potential downsides of taking such a restrictive, even authoritarian, approach to food for herself and her children. She acknowledges in *The Light We Carry* that her "fearful mind" "hates how I look, all the time and no matter what," and recalls envying smaller girls like the cheerleaders at her high school: "Some of those girls were approximately the size of one of my legs." But she also makes frequent casual references to the joys of vigorous exercise and bonding with friends through "spa weekends" that include a punitive schedule of three workouts a day. And while she argues that the way out of anxiety and fear is to celebrate our differentness as a strength, Obama never names a larger body as one of hers.

In terms of her public agenda, it's worth noting that her speeches also frequently included disclaimers that "this isn't about how kids look, it's about how kids feel." But her office ignored the lobbying efforts of fat activists and even mainstream child nutrition experts like Ellyn Satter, a therapist and nutritionist who developed the "Division of Responsibility" framework for feeding children that we'll discuss in Part 2. "Don't talk about childhood obesity," she implored in an open letter to Obama. "Research shows that children who are labeled overweight or obese feel flawed in every way—not smart, not physically capable, and not worthy. [. . .] Such labeling is not only counterproductive, it's also unnecessary." Satter also wrote an opinion piece for the *New York Times*, which ran alongside several other critiques of "Let's Move," including one from Alwyn Cohall, MD, a professor of sociomedical sciences at Columbia

University and director of the Harlem Health Promotion Center, who argued, "Public health interventions that address the real reasons why people gain weight and suffer from chronic diseases will not ostracize or discriminate because they are not focused on the surface level symptoms, but rather on the more profound reasons why they occur."

Obama never appears to have addressed this criticism directly, though she did begin to add lines like "I don't want our children to be weight-obsessed," to her public talking points and in her 2021 Netflix show *Waffles + Mochi*, she takes the focus off weight entirely to instead teach kids how to have fun trying new foods (mostly vegetables). But the "Let's Move" rhetoric around parents taking responsibility for their kids' weight tied in nicely with our larger cultural narrative of weight as a matter of personal choice. And the way she downgraded herself as a mom when Malia's weight became a problem made Obama relatable to other mothers taught to judge themselves by this same standard.

Today's generation of parents grew up embedded within the war on childhood obesity. Some of us were its direct victims, like Anamarie, Colleen, and Elena. The rest of us represent a kind of collateral damage—even if we were thin kids, even if we didn't feel pressure to diet ourselves, we still internalized its key lessons: Fat people can never be healthy. Fat people can never be happy. Fat children are less lovable. And parents, especially mothers, of fat children, are doing something wrong unless they are fighting that fatness relentlessly with apples, cheese sticks, and a "take no prisoners" mindset. "To her mother, she is beautiful," Lisa Belkin wrote of four-year-old Anamarie in the 2001 the *New York Times Magazine* piece, before hastening to add that "Martinez-Regino is not so blind that she does not see what others see." Reading that, I paused to consider how much harm happens when parents must define their children, and their own parental success, by body size in this way. What was lost, in those three months of forced separation but also through-out Anamarie's childhood, and Colleen's, and Elena's, and those of so many others? What if Anamarie's mom had just been allowed to see her child, and love her for who she was? What if all parents got to do that with and for our kids?

CHAPTER 2

Separating Weight and Health

WHEN Lizzy was eight years old, she began vomiting often. Her mom, Stella, is a family medicine doctor in Seattle, and she wasted no time getting Lizzy checked out. But it still took several months of constant illness, near-daily doctor's appointments, and frequent emergency room visits to figure out that Lizzy had developed type 1 diabetes. In the process, Lizzy lost a lot of weight. And that's what everyone noticed.

"She was getting so many compliments on her body," says Stella, "not just from people who knew her, but from strangers, too." She remembers taking Lizzy and her younger sister, Phoebe, to their favorite clothing store and standing awkwardly by as the salesperson made a fuss over Lizzy's "cute little body" that would fit "so perfectly" into their clothes. And she remembers Phoebe, who was then five years old, quietly taking in the scene. She was three years younger, but already easily sharing clothes with her big sister. In fact, some of Lizzy's clothes were too small for Phoebe.

The first time I talk to Stella and Phoebe, it's about six years after that clothing store visit, but Phoebe, now eleven years old, remembers it, too. "It was so weird how people would just stop us to say, like, 'Oh my god, she looks wonderful!'" she tells me.

We're all on Zoom; Stella is speaking to me from a sun-filled home office and Phoebe is curled up with her laptop in another, darker nook in their house. She's soft-spoken, and her mom keeps reminding her to lean forward so we can hear her. But Phoebe knows what she wants to say. "Even though I was too young to understand why it was wrong, I could see how sick and uncomfortable Lizzy was," she tells me. "And so, I didn't understand why her being thin was such a good thing."

Stella smiles at her younger daughter through the camera. "You know, Phoebe, you've always had this ability to see through to the truth and you knew that Lizzy wasn't okay," she says. "And even though [you were] at that age, and when none of us knew what was wrong with Lizzy, you knew it was really weird that people were saying her body looked good when she was literally dying."

Stella was still exclusively breastfeeding Phoebe the first time their pediatrician referred them to a dietitian because of Phoebe's high weight. Today, Stella says that both she and Phoebe consider "fat to be both a neutral descriptor and an identity we claim." But back then, Stella did not think fat was good, or even neutral. She had also been big as a kid and began dieting in childhood. When her own girls were young, Stella was obsessed with her own weight, and always either dieting or falling off a diet. But the idea that an infant's weight could be a problem before she had even begun to eat solid food struck Stella as patently absurd. "I remember talking to that dietitian and just being like, 'But this is all she eats? What can we do?'" she says.

It was a moment of reckoning for Stella. She began to wonder if her long-held assumption that a thin body was a healthy body was correct. Clearly, her big baby was destined to be a bigger kid, just as other children seemed destined to be thinner. Why would one body size require investigation, explanation, and the intervention of experts, while the other was heaped with praise? Stella didn't put baby Phoebe on a diet. But that meant that Phoebe's weight continued to come up as a problem to monitor, if not correct, at every pediatrician appointment thereafter. By the time the girls were eight and five, Phoebe's status as a fat kid had been firmly cemented, and Stella was anxious about it. While Lizzy's frail body was admired by total strangers, Phoebe's healthy body—despite her love for dancing and playing outside—was the one the family was told to worry about.

To see this dynamic play out within one family is jarring, but also probably familiar to anyone who grew up fat with a thin sibling, or vice versa. Kids have always come in different sizes because body diversity is a necessary part of the human experience. But our modern "war on childhood obesity" has taught parents that the least healthy thing your child can be is fat. We assume that a high body weight in childhood is a one-way ticket to diabetes, heart disease, and other health issues. And while we mostly think of these as concerns for when kids grow up, we are told increasingly that they could also happen *right now*. This is why almost any parent who has ever put their child on a diet will say it wasn't about looks—it was about health. It's uncomfortable to acknowledge you're unhappy with your child's appearance. Nobody wants to admit that the sight of his double chin or her stomach spilling over a waistband fills you with revulsion. And so most parents don't, even though we all carry some level of disgust around fat bodies. Instead, we talk about their energy levels (remember Michelle Obama worrying about the kids who can't keep up at recess), their athleticism, and those looming future health risks. And virtually every pediatrician, as well as the public health officials behind school BMI screenings, "Let's Move," and other childhood obesity interventions back us up.

But as we've seen, our culture's pervasive anti-fat bias both predated and continues to inform our scientific understanding of the relationship between weight and health. And kids know what parents mean when we say we're concerned about their health. "When I ask families what they hope to achieve [through weight loss treatment], the parents all talk about 'I don't want them to get diabetes like their grandmother and lose a leg at age forty-five,'" says Sarah Armstrong, MD, who is the director of the Children's Healthy Lifestyles Program, a weight management program for children and teens at Duke University School of Medicine. "But when I ask the kids, for the most part, it is a lot of social stuff, like 'I just want to be able to shop at Forever 21 with my friends.' I think if Forever 21 just had clothes that fit their body, then maybe this social piece wouldn't be such an issue."

You might argue that kids focus on such aesthetic concerns because they don't think about long-term health. But I read it as proof that kids know what grown-ups don't want to admit: that we're mostly shrink-ing their bodies to make life easier. To make everyone around them more comfortable. To reassure ourselves that this isn't our fault. And this leads us to treat kids in all body sizes in ways that can worsen their health. And yet, I know, you're still worrying: What *about* diabetes and heart disease? We need to unpack a lot of our assumptions about how a child's weight impacts their health, to understand how to put these risks into perspective. It sounds counterintuitive, but one of the most important things parents can do to benefit their children's health is take weight out of every health-related conversation.

WHAT MAKES KIDS FAT

To understand how and why we need to separate weight and health, we first need to understand why some kids end up bigger than oth-ers in the first place. I want to acknowledge the implicit bias of that statement, though. For one thing, as the fat activist and author Aubrey Gordon writes in her book "*You Just Need to Lose Weight*," these are not questions on which the science is decided: "We simply *do not know* why some people are fat and others are thin. And the closer we get to an answer, the more complex the picture becomes. [. . .] It is straight-forwardly judgmental to look at a fat person and invent a story of how our bodies came to be, how they must be a result of our broken brains, broken willpower, broken lives." This is why you and your child don't owe the world an explanation for their body size.

And yet, if you have a bigger kid, you're likely asked to justify their body (as well as explain how they eat and how much they move) because the most common misconception, as we saw in Chapter 1, is that fat kids are the result of bad parenting. When Armstrong interviews new staff for her clinic, "Why do you think children get obese?" is one ques-tion she asks every applicant. Not because she expects them to have a deep and research-based answer, but "because I want to know what's in their heart," she tells me. "Nine times out of ten, they say, 'It's the parents' fault.' Because they know it's wrong to blame the child, but they feel like it has to be somebody's fault." Yet nothing about modern parenting practices has changed so dramatically that it could explain why today 19.3 percent of kids aged two to nineteen meet the criteria for obesity, while in 1971, just 5.2 percent of kids did. Your child's body size is not your fault.

Before we get into what's causing more kids today to grow up in bigger bodies, let's talk about how a child's growth is determined in the first place. Or at least, let's talk about how little we know about that process. I've highlighted the ways in which the pediatric BMI chart used to track growth between the ages of two and nineteen fails to capture the body diversity of kids today. If BMI data tells us anything, it's that we need to stop holding Black and Brown kids' bodies to a dated standard. And yes, your white kid can be fat, too. It's also a problem that we pathologize the bodies of everyone at or above the 85th percentile, instead of recognizing that one aim of a growth chart is just to capture the full range of normal human body diversity.

Before age two, the CDC recommends that pediatricians use a World Health Organization chart to track growth; and this, too, is based on a narrow and non-inclusive data set. The WHO chart was constructed using data from healthy children who were all breastfed through at least six months of age, and growing up in economically stable environments. "You can already see how this doesn't necessarily reflect the experience of all infants in the United States," explains Charles Thomas Wood, MD, MPH, an assistant professor of pediatrics at Duke who studies weight gain in early childhood.

Further, Wood points out that the curves on both growth charts are meant to demonstrate measures of "appropriate growth" across populations—they don't represent any individual's expected growth pattern. "Children can vacillate between percentiles for a variety of reasons that we don't consider abnormal," says Wood. He says he does pay attention to very dramatic shifts in either direction—an infant who started at the 50th percentile and by six months jumps up to the 97th percentile, or down to the 10th. But for the most part, he doesn't want parents or clinicians to worry about shifts in percentile nearly as much as we do. "We have a ton of unaddressed questions about what the actual clinical meaningfulness of [these changes] is."

So, the tools we use to measure how kids grow have serious limitations. And while we know that children's growth trajectories are a product of both genetics and environment, researchers are much less sure
about how big of a role each of these factors might play. My husband,
for example, is tall, thin, of Irish descent, and looks exactly like his siblings, his father, his father's brother, and his paternal grandfather. We
can assume that genetics play a significant role in that because the food
and many other aspects of the environment of Dan's upper-middle-class
1980s childhood looked different from his dad's, growing up working-
class in the 1950s, and differed even more from his grandfather's, who
grew up poor in the 1930s. "Everything is certainly a mix of genetics
and environment, in varying proportions that we are still working to
understand," says Wood. "The consensus tends to be that if a child stays
on a stable growth trajectory as they get older, we'll say, 'Well, that's
genetically predetermined.'"

I'd argue that our culture's anti-fat bias means we're more comfortable assigning genetics as the explanation of a family's body type when
they are all thin, because we don't pathologize thin bodies; we consider
thinness to be our natural, healthy state. On the other hand, when
researchers look at families with multiple generations of fat people, they
start to talk about epigenetics (how your behavior and environment
influence how your genes work) and look for behavioral and environmental factors to explain what they perceive as an intergenerational
abnormality. Research on the Dutch famine of 1945 found that babies
gestated during that time were more likely to live in larger bodies as
adults than babies born to non-starving mothers. More recent research
on the genetics of pregnant women in the United Kingdom suggests
that pregnant women who diet or, for other reasons, consume few carbohydrates during pregnancy may send a "starvation signal" to their
developing fetuses' DNA, essentially turning up the volume on genes
that influence appetite and fat storage. Such genetic tweaks might help
an offspring survive in a food-scarce environment but "puts children
out of sync with the high-calorie world," as the author of a 2011 *Science*
magazine article put it. In other words, a fetus primed to survive food

scarcity by a malnourished mother may become a child with a larger appetite and tendency to store more fat once they're out of the womb and eating on their own.

These findings are fascinating, but the language of epigenetics research on childhood obesity reinforces the idea that a fat child born to a thin parent is a sign something went "wrong" in utero (and if we can blame it on a conscious decision Mom made, all the better!). If you're a mother who dieted while pregnant and now have a child in a larger body, you may be reading this research summary with some simmering sense of *So it is all my fault.* First, remember that humans are always a mix of our genetics and environment—no one thing you did or didn't do can ever be singled out as the cause of anything about your child's body or health. Then, consider how it might feel to reframe these findings: What if we saw the fetus's ability to turn up the volume on appetite and fat storage genes as a quietly brilliant survival strategy? What if the problem isn't that their body is now "out of sync with the high-calorie world" but rather that their growing and thriving body is unnecessarily demonized by our fatphobic world?

Because even more often, we hear parents in larger bodies shamed for "passing down" a tendency toward weight gain to their kids: Having a fat parent more than doubled the odds that a child will also grow up to be fat in one 2009 evidence review. A 2017 analysis of the heights and weights of one hundred thousand parents and children in six countries concluded that around 35 to 40 percent of a child's BMI is inherited but noted that this "parental effect" was much stronger for kids in larger bodies than for kids in smaller ones. Of course, from there, we make assumptions that the fat parents programmed their kids to be fat by eating too much and not exercising. But remember Stella: Lots of fat parents diet, too, and so did their parents. Some of this handing down of fatness could be a product of the same epigenetic starvation signaling seen in the research on famine survivors. And some of it is just body diversity at work. Your family of bigger bodies is replicating its genes just as steadily and successfully as my husband's thin family.

Indeed, some studies suggest that as much as 60 to 80 percent of the variation we see in human body weight can be accounted for by inherited factors. Researchers have identified hundreds of genetic loci that are potentially involved in body weight regulation, through more than one hundred different interactions. These genes influence hormonal and neural pathways in our bodies that in turn shape our appetites and our bodies' response to energy input and output, among other processes. Genes can also influence weight in ways that are not inherited: Spontaneous genetic changes that occur during the formation of reproductive cells or early in embryonic development can also lead to complex chromosomal disorders like Prader-Willi syndrome, a hallmark symptom of which is an inability to feel fullness. Prader-Willi syndrome is very rare, occurring in just one out of every ten thousand to thirty thousand births, but some researchers argue that there may be many other conditions and genetic predispositions to larger bodies that we haven't identified yet. As I write this, pharmaceutical companies are even starting to market genetic tests that claim to detect whether your child has a genetic variant in one of the neuropathways that regulates hunger.

Thinking of weight as genetically determined removes blame and certainly challenges our long-held myth of weight as a matter of personal responsibility. But it's not helpful to chase a "genetic condition" explanation for every child in a larger body, both because the science just isn't there yet and because this pathologizes and stigmatizes so many otherwise healthy kids. Non-pathological human body diversity exists and has always existed. Why would we find fat jokes in the writings of Shakespeare and the ancient Greeks if they didn't have any fat people to make fun of? And Wood notes that this human diversity will continually assert itself in a child's growth pattern. "Let's say a baby's genetically predetermined weight at six months old is the 75th percentile, but their growth was constrained for whatever reason in utero. That child is probably going to reset a little bit, and that may look like they're gaining weight too rapidly," he explains. He points to research suggesting that when children cross one or two percentiles during the first year of life, it increases their risk of having a higher-weight body in childhood and adulthood. "But that does not mean that growth was not genetically predestined."

What genetics cannot explain, however, is the group of kids today who are bigger than their parents and grandparents were at the same age. Again, let's note the underlying anti-fatness that compels us to find explanations for this shift. If kids today had gotten thinner, would we be on the same quest to understand what happened? And yet: "Something happened, or is happening, or was happening forty years ago because genetic changes don't happen that fast," says Wood. One common explanation for "what happened" is: Our food environment changed. School lunches became "more and more industrialized," says Marlene Schwartz, PhD, who is director of the Rudd Center for Food Policy & Health at the University of Connecticut. The National Soft Drink Association won a lawsuit that kept the sale of soda from being banned in schools, and other food manufacturers started packaging pizza, chicken nuggets, and other processed fare for cafeterias. Of course, the Healthy, Hunger-Free Kids Act of 2010 led to a major overhaul in the nutritional quality of school lunches in the last decade. Based on a recent analysis, one Tufts University researcher pronounced that "schools are now the single healthiest place Americans are eating." But other changes in the food environment have been harder to reverse. Americans also started spending a larger share of our money at restaurants (which meant largely fast food) than at home. By 2010, Americans spent 50 percent of our food budgets on food eaten away from home, up from 41 percent in 1984; by 2012, meals eaten out accounted for 34 percent of our energy intake, up from 17 percent in 1978. Schwartz also points to how food manufacturers began to target children directly with advertising; studies from the 1970s through 2000 found that anywhere from 48 to 87 percent of the television ads seen by kids were for food products, though this number appears to have dropped since then and has not continued to track along with kids' rising body sizes. Still, "[the] food industry, changes in the family structure—all of these forces combined to work against parents who are trying to raise healthy children," Schwartz says.

Another popular "what happened" theory is our increased environmental exposure to endocrine-disrupting chemicals, a class of chemicals (including phthalates, bisphenol A, and many others) used in consumer products like shower curtains, plastic bottles, and couch cushions. These chemicals have been shown to mimic estrogen and other naturally occur-ring hormones in the human body, and some research suggests that they also influence weight gain. But this relationship is not well understood, as I'll discuss further in Chapter 12.

Schwartz and other researchers studying such large-scale environ-mental changes don't dispute the role of genetics in determining body size; they see the families most prone to larger bodies as the ones who are also most vulnerable to environmental impacts. "If you look at your family and see a lot of obesity among your parents, your in-laws, and other relatives, then there's more risk [that your food environment will exacerbate that]," Schwartz says. She and other obesity researchers frame this relationship as "Genetic background loads the gun, but the environ-ment pulls the trigger." They use this rhetoric to justify weight loss inter-ventions, because they aren't fighting the fatness that nature intended us to have, they're protecting these "most vulnerable" kids from a fatness that our modern environment has invented.

This strategy ignores the significant harm caused by subjecting kids to weight loss interventions, which we'll discuss in detail in the next chapter. And it reinforces the long-standing myth that a child's "food environment" includes mostly factors we can control through education and better parenting. It hasn't shaken out that way. "If you look at data from the early 2000s, there was a much smaller difference in the rate of obesity between Black and white kids," says Katie Loth, PhD, MPH, an assistant professor in the University of Minnesota's Department of Family Medicine and Community Health who studies the social and environmental influences on childhood weight and disordered eating. "But as we began to intervene with a variety of public health strategies, there was a widening in racial and socioeconomic disparities. We saw declines in the prevalence of obesity among affluent white kids, while rates continued to climb in other groups."

Loth argues that both the drivers of kids' increasing weight and our solutions to it have been rooted in existing systemic economic and racial inequities. "So many of our solutions, like the provision of individual diet counseling, or requiring schools to have health advisory committees, have not had the intended impact on communities of color because it wasn't developed with them in mind," she says. "Many of our efforts ignore existing systemic barriers that limit the ability of an individual or community to engage. Or we even require them to take responsibility for these systemic barriers rooted in white supremacy." Schwartz agrees that the racial and socioeconomic disparities in childhood obesity rates underscores a need to rethink how "controllable" a family's food environment truly is. "If you only have $20 to buy groceries for the week, you are not going to spend $5 of it on organic strawberries," she says. "It irritates me when we focus so much on nutrition education. These communities don't need education, they need more money." They also need public health strategies and supports that focus on their real problems—poverty, lack of healthcare, chronic experiences of oppression—instead of their weight.

These social determinants of health underscore just how much of a child's weight is out of their control, and irrelevant to their health and happiness. But it's our handling of the remaining "within our control" piece of the body weight puzzle that has done the most damage to kids. And this is arguably the most important answer to the question of "what's changed." Forty years ago, modern diet culture was just ramping up. It was not unheard of but still unusual to put children on diets, not just because there were fewer fat children but because we didn't think about children's diets with anything like the obsessive fervor that we do today. But public health policy that encourages restriction for fat kids is now the norm, along with our broader cultural messages that normalize dieting at every turn.

Dianne Neumark-Sztainer, PhD, MPH, who is the head of the Division of Epidemiology and Community Health at the University of Minnesota School of Public Health, says she first recognized the harm of dieting while running a weekly weight loss group in Israel back in the late 1980s. "One woman came in and said, 'I was really good this week, I didn't eat a piece of cake,'" she recalls. "And it just kind of struck me that that's not what I wanted. I did not want people not to be eating cake." Neumark-Sztainer set out to study the relationship between dieting, disordered eating, and weight through an intensive research undertaking called Project EAT. Beginning in 1997, Neumark-Sztainer and her colleagues have followed multiple cohorts totaling thousands of teenagers into adulthood, to understand their eating habits, weight, and weight-related health. "We saw that the strongest predictors of weight gain in kids were things like weight teasing and dieting," she explains. "Just as they were the strongest predictors for eating disorders."

Neumark-Sztainer's research has been replicated and expanded on by other researchers many times. A paper published in 2014 in *JAMA Pediatrics*, for example, found that being labeled "too fat" in childhood was associated with higher odds of having an obese BMI a decade later, no matter what kids weighed when they were so labeled. But for years when Neumark-Sztainer went to obesity and public health conferences to present her evidence that dieting led to weight gain, she knew that at some point during the talk, someone in the audience would stand up and say, "Something's wrong with your analysis." They would question her methodology or claim she'd forgotten to adjust for something. "And yes, I heard this from women and men," she notes. "But particularly, I would say, from men." They couldn't believe that trying to lose weight, let alone just feeling bad about your weight, would result so consistently in people weighing more.

WHAT MAKES KIDS UNHEALTHY

If kids are bigger today because of how their genetics interact with our changing food culture, changing environmental exposures, and (maybe most of all) modern diet culture—how does that impact their health? The standard "war on obesity" answer is: "Disastrously." But when we drill into the research, we see that the answer is something closer to "We don't really know—maybe to some extent, but not for the reason you think, and maybe not at all."

For starters, Wood notes that it's not uncommon to see children in the same growth percentile with remarkably different health profiles. A child with a BMI at the 97th percentile might have an elevated liver enzyme, but another child of the same age with an even higher BMI might have "no lab abnormalities whatsoever," he says. Here again, genetics may play a role in whether a child is at risk for one of the many health conditions that we associate with higher body weights, such as heart disease, diabetes, or asthma. A high BMI during adolescence is linked to a higher risk for adult diabetes and coronary artery disease, for example, but diabetes and heart disease are also themselves hereditary. What we don't understand is whether a genetically predisposed large body weight is what causes you to be genetically vulnerable to these conditions, or if these are mere correlating factors in your family history.

This causation versus correlation question also comes up when a child's weight is more likely the result of their environment. It's easy to blame both a high BMI and a child's future diabetes risk on a diet heavy in processed foods, for example. But we don't know if it's the elevated weight itself that causes any resulting health concerns, or if the child's weight is just one by-product of their family's inability to access healthier food, and their diabetes is another. It's also possible that an environmentally induced health condition is the cause of a child's high body weight rather than the reverse. One recent study showed that while a high weight in childhood predicted asthma during adolescence, a history of wheezing during childhood also predicted adolescent weight gain. "I think this is just really complicated to tease apart," says Wood. "We certainly know there is a stepwise relationship with BMI and cardiometabolic health. I hope at some point in the future, we have enough information to understand the health risks more precisely for each individual independent of their BMI."

In the meantime, not knowing exactly how weight influences health means we also don't know that lowering the child's weight is necessary to reduce their disease risk. Addressing racism, poverty, and other inequities within their environment is likely to do much more to improve their health, regardless of whether their weight changes. Kenisha Campbell, MD, who specializes in the medical treatment of eating disorders in her work as director of Adolescent Medicine Outpatient Clinical Services at the Children's Hospital of Philadelphia, worries much more about the harm caused by weight loss interventions in kids than she does about weight itself. "Most kids in bigger bodies don't have any complications yet. And if you focus just on weight loss, we know that they'll lose it, but then gain it back if they haven't made any long-term lifestyle changes," she says.

Indeed, a large body of research now documents how much more important it is to focus on those long-term lifestyle changes to improve health than it is to focus on weight loss—and confirms that these benefits hold up regardless of whether lifestyle changes also achieve weight loss. In a 2012 analysis of data from the CDC's National Health and Nutrition Examination Surveys, researchers found that regardless of weight class, people lived longer when they did not smoke, drank alcohol in moderation, ate five or more servings of fruits and vegetables daily, and exercised more than twelve times per month. "If you're obese and you have a healthy lifestyle, you are no more likely to die early than a person of normal weight," said Eric Matheson, MD, an associate professor at the Medical University of South Carolina in Charleston when I interviewed him for *Scientific American* in 2019. His work was later backed up by an analysis of data on 22,476 Americans aged thirty to sixty-four published in 2020, which found that being physically active was associated with a larger reduction in a person's ten-year heart disease risk than having a normal BMI.

This is not to say that weight itself never contributes to or even causes a health concern. "Obesity causes changes in the body that in turn increase risk factors, which in turn lead to diseases," explains Kelly Brownell, PhD, a former director of what became the Rudd Center for Food Policy & Health and now a professor of public policy at Duke University. These biological pathways look different for every health condition, and indeed, for every kid. And they're important to understand for disease prevention and treatment. But they do not tell the whole story of weight and health. "Every pathway [between weight and health] is exacerbated by the presence of weight stigma," Brownell adds. When Brownell told me this during an interview for *Scientific American* in 2019, I was surprised to hear him say it. By the time this book is published, I will have reported on weight and health for twenty years. When I asked mainstream obesity researchers if weight stigma was harmful to health a decade ago, or even more recently, while researching my first book, I was told that it was an interesting question that required further study. Nobody beyond fat liberationists and some Health at Every Size activists were prepared to acknowledge anti-fatness as the real and damaging form of oppression that it is.

But in the same decades that I've been reporting on these issues for mainstream women's magazines and other media outlets (all of whom subscribed to a weight-centric paradigm of health), the scientific field of weight stigma research has been piling up evidence to make its case. A 2016 analysis of data collected on over twenty-one thousand American adults with BMI above 25 in the National Survey of Alcohol and Related Conditions found a significant association between a person's experience of weight stigma and an increased incidence of heart disease, stomach ulcers, diabetes, and high cholesterol, even after researchers controlled for their subjects' socioeconomic status, physical activity level, and BMI. A 2014 analysis of 9,584 adults who participated in the Aerobics Center Longitudinal Study found that those who expressed "weight dissatisfaction" were at higher risk for type 2 diabetes than people who were satisfied with their weight, again even after controlling for BMI, according to results published in the journal *Health Psychology*.

Since I just told you that most research on weight and health shows correlation, not causation, it's important to acknowledge that these studies show the same; the authors of the latter paper described weight dissatisfaction as "a potentially important psychophysiological modifier" of the relationship between weight and diabetes risk. But the fact that the correlation stands even after controlling for body size is significant: "This tells us that it is stigma, rather than one's weight per se, that contributes to these adverse health outcomes," says Rebecca Puhl, PhD, who is the deputy director for the Rudd Center and a leader in the study of weight stigma and health.

Puhl and other weight stigma researchers have also begun performing experimental studies where they expose subjects to "weight stigma stimuli." In one such study, by psychologists at the University of California in Los Angeles, a researcher told unwitting volunteers that they couldn't participate in an exclusive shopping experience because they were too big and might stretch out the clothes. (They did later debrief with participants to mitigate lasting harm.) These experiments consistently show higher physiological stress responses, like increased cortisol levels, for subjects exposed to the stimuli compared with people assigned to non-stigmatizing experiences, which suggests weight stigma may trigger some portion of the poor health outcomes disproportionately seen in people in larger bodies. Put another way: Maybe fat people wouldn't get as sick if they weren't discriminated against for their size. "We know that physiological stress plays a role in body weight because higher levels of cortisol contribute to weight gain," Puhl told me. "Weight stigma is a form of chronic stress. So that has chronic health effects, both physiologically and in terms of how people cope with that stress."

Perhaps the most ironic risk of perpetuating anti-fat bias in a medical model dedicated to weight loss is the clear evidence that people who experience stigma tend to end up gaining more weight. For a 2017 study published in the journal *Preventive Medicine*, Puhl's team analyzed Project EAT data that followed 1,830 teenagers for fifteen years and found that the kids who experienced weight-based teasing at the start of the study were more likely to have an obese BMI, as well as poor body image, binge eating tendencies, and other related struggles, well into adulthood. Many other studies have replicated this finding, which flies in the face of a long-held belief in public health circles that shame motivates compliance. "Shame may have worked for smoking," notes A. Janet Tomiyama, PhD, an associate professor of psychology who studies the intersection between dieting, stress, and health at the University of California in Los Angeles. "But smoking and body weight are very different things; one is a behavior, and the other is a physical trait."

But the most dangerous way that anti-fat bias impacts the health of children, especially adolescents, is how it results in the missed diagnosis of eating disorders in kids in bigger bodies. Doctors know to look for eating disorder red flags in thin, white, teenage girls. But they are much less likely to notice these issues in other genders, other races, and in kids with higher BMIs—and even likely to praise disordered behaviors like skipping meals and overexercising when they do come up. "A good percentage of the kids I treat [for eating disorders] were actually overweight or 'obese' based on BMI to start out, and their pediatrician or family doctor always zeroed in on their weight," says Campbell, the doctor who specializes in eating disorder management at the Children's Hospital of Philadelphia. "And a lot of the time, these kids were actually very healthy, they were never in danger of anything, they just happened to be bigger, so the focus was always on their weight. And telling a kid to lose weight, especially if you're not telling them how much or how fast, can be all it takes for them to fall into the trap of an eating disorder."

The research backs Campbell up. One 2015 study on 179 patients aged nine to twenty-two seeking eating disorder treatment found that 36.7 percent of them reported a previous weight above the 85th percentile for their age and sex. Other research shows that teenagers in larger bodies engage in self-induced vomiting and laxative use more frequently than their thinner peers. In fact, researchers now suspect that eating disorders are even more common among kids and adults in larger bodies than they are in thin people, although this data is difficult to track because people with higher BMIs are so often denied treatment and excluded from studies on eating disorders. Classic anorexia nervosa is diagnosed in just 0.6 percent of Americans, in part because one of its diagnostic criteria states that patients must have reached a "significantly low body weight." But atypical anorexia, which was added to the fifth edition of the *Diagnostic and Statistical Manual of Mental Disorders* in 2013, is now used to diagnose patients who would otherwise meet criteria for anorexia but aren't underweight; by one recent estimate, 2.8 percent of twenty-year-olds would qualify for this diagnosis. Other research on eating disorders suggests that patients who develop them at higher weights are just as at risk for medical complications such as dangerously low blood pressure and slow heart rates. And they are often even sicker and have struggled longer by the time they access treatment because doctors ignore or misdiagnose their symptoms, or reinforce their disorder by praising their weight loss.

The data on the overlap between eating disorders and higher body weight is substantial enough that in 2016, the American Academy of Pediatrics published a report called "Preventing Obesity and Eating Disorders in Adolescents," in which they strongly advised pediatricians to limit their discussion of weight and avoid talk of dieting. "If the pediatrician only focuses on weight loss without identifying the associated concerning symptoms and signs, an underlying [eating disorder] may be missed," the report's authors warned, though they failed to acknowledge the inherent stigma in equating high body weights and eating disorders as diseases. "I'm not saying extreme obesity isn't a problem. But malnutrition will kill you quicker," says Campbell. "Restrictive eating disorders kill more kids than either diabetes or cancer." Even given the current issues with underreported data, eating disorders are one of the most common chronic conditions of adolescence, right behind asthma. ("Obesity" is usually at the top of the list—but that math requires us to accept the erroneous premise that high body weight is always evidence of disease.) In fighting one "epidemic," we've quietly created another one.

So, the fact that weight stigma impacts health is no longer in question. Even William Dietz, MD, the former CDC director who fought in favor of adding "obesity" to the pediatric growth charts, responded with an unhesitating "Yes, definitely" when I asked him if weight stigma played a role in weight-linked health outcomes. And yet, he added, "We know that if a clinician calls a patient's weight to their attention, that patient is much more likely to actively change their ways. I'm not sure we know if the same thing happens if a physician just talked to a patient about healthy living. But it's a good question." A good question that's hard to answer because of the way this stigma shapes the science that's getting done.

One giant challenge remaining for weight stigma researchers is to determine how much of someone's resulting health is a product of their weight per se, versus the oppression they experience in that larger body. "People come from different camps on this and say it's clear but it's really not clear," says Neumark-Sztainer, noting that a key reason for this lack of clarity is lack of research funding for stigma studies. Loth calls it "a sort of unanswerable question," because to answer it scientifically, you would need to compare people experiencing stigma to people who have never experienced stigma—and that second group doesn't exist. A better approach would be to include weight stigma as a variable on every other study about weight and health, since we know it's ever-present. And that means you would also have to factor stigma into any research claiming to show that making people smaller improves their health, because when you reduce someone's weight, you reduce their direct exposure to weight stigma too—for as long as the weight loss lasts.

Taking weight out of her understanding of her children's health was liberating for Stella, the family medicine doctor in Seattle. She felt like she could start to understand both her daughters as whole people rather than body types. Once Lizzy's diabetes was finally under control, she began to regain some of the weight she had lost while she was sick. Meanwhile, her younger sister, Phoebe, has continued to be a bigger—and physically healthy—kid. Even when weight does influence health, the relationship is so much more complicated than we've been told. And making weight loss the solution for every health problem reinforces an entire system of stigma that we know, in turn, brings its own health consequences. "I just keep coming back to the question of what will make us all more well," Stella says to me from her sunny office, in the cozy house where she fervently hopes her daughters can somehow just get to exist in the bodies they have. "Chronic dieting has not made us more well."

CHAPTER 3

When "It's Not a Diet"

WINTER, now fifteen, says she never even thought much about her body until the summer she turned twelve. She was at the sleepaway camp she's gone to every summer since she was eight, but it suddenly felt like she didn't fit in with the same old group of friends. Everybody's bodies had changed, but not all in the same ways. And although Winter has never been fat, she felt painfully aware of what she calls her "weight distribution," meaning that, like many girls on the cusp of puberty, she was rounder in the middle than she wanted to be. "I remember feeling like, 'These clothes don't fit me,' and then noticing that my friends were all thinner, and just being like, 'Oh, I want that,'" she tells me.

Then came her bat mitzvah: Winter had her dress fitted in the spring of her thirteenth year. A few months later, when it came time to wear it, "she had gained so much weight, the dress barely fit," says her mom, Elise. "It was just surprising because Winter had always been super little, like noticeably tinier than her peers up until then. And I could tell that she was starting to notice herself in a different way."

Winter is now the kind of poised, articulate fifteen-year-old girl produced by years of private schools, sleepaway camps, and expensive extracurricular activities. She needs no warming up to tell me her story, but rather launches in like she's already practicing for college interviews.

And while you may not be surprised to read that a white girl growing up on Philadelphia's wealthy Main Line is struggling with an eating disorder, it's worth noting that Winter does know not to believe what she sees on Instagram and TikTok. She explains to me at length about the harmful impact of "what I eat in a day" videos and influencer workouts. And she uses terms like "fatphobia" and "diet culture" with confidence. She also doesn't think she grew up in a dieting household; Winter describes her mom as "a pretty good intuitive eater" who never banned cookies or questioned the number of croutons on her salad, like she's seen many of her friends' moms do. "My friend's mom likes to say stuff like, 'You don't need to have carbs at every meal,'" Winter says, rolling her eyes. Another, even after her daughter's bulimia diagnosis, commented that she wouldn't waste calories on the Mallomar her daughter was eating. "It's just, like, these subtle comments, but they mean so much."

In contrast, Winter felt like she could talk to Elise about her anxieties and not face that kind of judgment. Elise had always talked a lot about "balance," but she didn't force vegetables or count calories in front of her kids. "My approach is, have some junk food, have some healthy food, and just always strive for the middle," Elise says. But when Winter got worried about her weight, Elise did, too. "I would say to my mom, like, 'I'm fat, I'm fat. What can I do?'" says Winter. "And she was trying to help, like, in the best way that she could, but what she did was give me meal plans."

Elise's plan felt to them both like a "strive for the middle" approach: She wanted Winter to eat one rice cake with peanut butter and a banana for breakfast; a salad with olives, avocado, and chicken for lunch; a protein bar or fruit and nuts for afternoon snack; and a protein or carb with vegetables for dinner, plus a small dessert. It's the kind of plan that women's magazines have run forever as "just a lifestyle change." After all, you're not cutting out any food groups and you can even still eat dessert! But when I emailed a description of that plan around to a few eating disorder experts, I could just about hear their horrified gasps through my laptop. "This is the kind of plan you get if you type your weight and height into an app like MyFitnessPal," wrote Anna Lutz, RD, MPH, a dietitian in private practice in Raleigh, North Carolina, who specializes in eating disorders and family feeding dynamics. Such low-calorie plans are too restrictive to adequately nourish most adults, Lutz noted. "But compared to what a growing twelve-year-old needs, they are way, way off." Kenisha Campbell, MD, the doctor who specializes in eating disorder treatment at the Children's Hospital of Philadelphia, highlights how dangerous calorie restriction can be for adolescents in particular: "Food is critical to life, and especially for teenagers because they are growing at the same rate as toddlers," she explains. "Would you starve your toddler? No. Growing brains and bodies need fat, protein, carbs, and calories."

Elise says that she can see now that the plan was too restrictive. "I think I sort of had her doing the diet of a thirty- to fifty-year-old woman, not knowing that it wouldn't be the safe and healthy approach for someone her age," she says. "Because this is how I eat. And I probably was thinking, 'Is there a way for her to navigate adolescence and not gain as much weight as I've seen the daughters of friends gain?' But it's like, I just shouldn't have been involved." For her part, Winter still doesn't consider that plan a diet. "I think I grew obsessed with like, fitting these meal plans, and eating the exact perfect way," she says. And that's because she was hoping to lose weight on it.

Winter also joined her school's swim team, which meant increasing her exercise from around ninety minutes a week to six hours or more without increasing her caloric intake. She stopped menstruating in January of her eighth-grade year. And by spring—which coincided with the start of the COVID-19 pandemic and all the isolation and added stress that brought, particularly for teenagers—she had gone way beyond rice cakes and chicken salad. She became pescatarian, then vegetarian, then vegan. She framed all these changes as environmental concerns and then about health. Elise says that Winter does have a lactose intolerance and what she describes as "a refined sugar intolerance," which is why initially, cutting those food groups seemed like a good idea. "I didn't understand how these kinds of behaviors can be damaging," she says. "I thought, she's a teenager, and she's so defensive and secretive—I can't say anything, or I'll make it worse. So, I just tried to be supportive." Finally in September 2020, Elise made an appointment with an endocrinologist because she was worried about Winter's lack of a period. The doctor diagnosed anorexia nervosa and referred them to an eating disorder treatment team. They were both shocked.

Some 38 percent of adolescents aged thirteen to sixteen have tried to lose weight within the past year, according to NHANES data collected between 2013 and 2016. And 28 percent of kids aged eight to fifteen made "persistent attempts" to change their weight between 2005 and 2014. "For some people, engaging in this sort of behavior can be harmless. But for people who are susceptible [to eating disorders], this can be an entry point to something that spirals out of control," explains Kendrin Sonneville, ScD, RD, an associate professor of nutritional sciences at the University of Michigan School of Public Health, who studies how to promote health and well-being among kids without inadvertently increasing body dissatisfaction and disordered eating.

The percentage of kids who go on a diet and then progress to a full-blown eating disorder is small, but the link is undeniable: Teenage girls who dieted "at a severe level" were eighteen times more likely to develop eating disorders than those who did not, according to a three-year study on almost two thousand kids published by Australian researchers in 1999. Even moderate dieters were five times more likely to progress to an eating disorder; subsequent studies have replicated these findings repeatedly. And on the spectrum from "healthy" to "eating disorder," there is also a large middle swathe who won't meet the diagnostic criteria for clinical eating disorders but will struggle and suffer, nonetheless. The problem with diets is that none of us have any idea where on that continuum our child might fall when we first buy the rice cakes.

MEAL PLANS AND LIFESTYLE CHANGES

Elise had hoped that by giving Winter the structure of what seemed like a sensible eating plan, she could help her avoid excess weight gain and steer clear of the eating disorder rabbit hole. But this is the needle that's impossible to thread. In offering the meal plan, she reinforced the message Winter was already getting from the rest of the world that fat is bad and affirmed Winter's worst fears about her body. "She kept saying all the time, like, 'You eat so unhealthy, you eat so unhealthy,'" says Winter. "She was trying to help me, but I felt guilty. And from then on, I never ate something without feeling guilt." Guilt wasn't the goal. I suspect comments like "You eat so unhealthy" were meant to inspire a kind of optimism or relief. Elise wanted Winter to understand that her body wasn't some sort of lost cause but, rather, a problem that could be readily solved with a few simple changes to her eating habits, if they just made a project of healthy eating the same way they had planned Winter's bat mitzvah together. Elise wanted Winter to feel a sense of control over her body, at a time in her life when everything about her body was changing. She wanted her daughter to be healthy.

In talking to Winter and Elise, I was reminded of another mom who rather famously put her daughter on a "meal plan" that turned out to be very much a diet. It's been over ten years since Dara-Lynn Weiss, a writer in New York City, was maligned on the internet in 2012 after writing an essay for *Vogue* about putting her then seven-year-old daughter on a diet. In her subsequent book, *The Heavy*, she wrote about canceling cupcakes and cooking vegetables without oil to get her daughter's caloric intake down. There was something undeniably "Mommie Dearest" about such tactics, and their *Vogue* fashion photo shoot. Especially when Weiss wrote in her book that she regretted that the photographer shot her daughter lying on her stomach, because the pose made her look thinner than she really was (even in this "after" shot), as if that's what inspired the backlash. Weiss also insisted that her daughter lost only a "healthy" amount of weight, and that she wasn't obsessed with thinness. My translation: If only people could have seen how fat her daughter had *really* been, they wouldn't have questioned the need for a diet.

In 2022, Weiss's now grown-up daughter Betty Kubovy-Weiss told her story to Today.com. It's a complicated piece. At eighteen, Kubovy-Weiss identified as "a body positive advocate, first and foremost." But she also disclosed that she's taking a prescription medication designed to curb her appetite. And she was eager to defend and forgive her mother: "At the end of the day, I know my mom had my best interests at heart," Kubovy-Weiss said in the piece. "She was worried about my health. She understood the social stigma of obesity and wanted to protect me."

I think Kubovy-Weiss is exactly right about her mother's motivations, as heartbreaking as it is to read her apologizing for the person who once dumped her Starbucks hot chocolate in the garbage because a barista didn't know the calorie count. And even as we critiqued her, I suspect that many parents expressing horror over "*Vogue* Mom" could also connect to the desperation Weiss felt for her child. We think putting a kid on a diet is the kind of thing only beauty-obsessed pageant moms do. But it happens more often than we think. And even in affluent, image-conscious enclaves like New York's Upper West Side, it most often happens because a parent is afraid for their child's health and happiness and has tangled both of those concepts up with weight. After all, everyone, including their own pediatrician, has told them to fear fat and to understand fat as the opposite of everything we want for our kids. We want our kids to be healthy. If their bodies remind us of our own, we want to spare them from suffering the way we suffered for having that kind of body at their age. We want them to find a peace with themselves, and with food, that we maybe haven't ever known ourselves. And a "meal plan" or "lifestyle change" is framed as the way to achieve all these goals, whether a child is in a bigger body or even just worried that she's getting bigger, as Winter was.

"It's not a diet, it's a lifestyle change" is textbook diet culture marketing, a refrain repeated by classic American weight loss brands like Jenny Craig and WW, as well as their hipper, Pilates-toned, wellness industry competitors like Goop and Paleo. One of the most popular diet brands of the last few years is Noom, an app that claims to "create long-term results through habit and behavior change, not restrictive dieting," but nevertheless relies on a strict calorie-counting model to achieve those promised results. We both know not to fall for this hype and forget that we know this when we're the ones desperate to lose weight. So, it makes sense that we can also know kids shouldn't diet, and yet not recall this when it's our own child's body causing concern—especially because we encounter that same "it's not a diet" rhetoric in so much of the public health discourse around childhood obesity.

The 2016 American Academy of Pediatrics report that I discussed in Chapter 2 neatly summarizes all the research showing how dieting can increase the risk for both eating disorders and higher body weight. It highlights one government analysis which found that from 1999 to 2006, hospitalizations for eating disorders increased 119 percent for children under twelve. The researchers also pointed out that kids in larger bodies may be more likely to engage in some disordered eating behaviors than thinner peers. The report's authors view dieting as so dangerous that they explicitly instruct pediatricians to discourage it: "The focus should be on healthy living and healthy habits rather than on weight," they wrote. And yet even here, the authors make frequent distinctions between "diets" and "obesity prevention and treatment," writing that the latter, "if conducted correctly, does not predispose to [eating disorders]. On the contrary, randomized controlled trials of obesity prevention programs have shown a reduction in the use of self-induced vomiting or diet pill use to control weight." One of the paper's lead authors, Neville Golden, MD, a professor of adolescent medicine at Stanford University, used familiar rhetoric when I asked him to explain this apparent protective effect: "In general, these programs attempt to address lifestyle changes; they don't only focus on weight," he told me. "So, if they're recommending three meals and two snacks, and involving the whole family, we know those behaviors can prevent the onset of an eating disorder."

I'm not convinced, and neither is Sonneville, who maintains that the claim that obesity interventions don't increase the risk for eating disorders is a function of the research's limitations. "If you give a group of kids a dietary intervention and follow them for one year, you likely won't find a heightened risk for eating disorders at twelve months because that is probably not the right time period to see that consequence," she says. Eating disorders still happen far more often in adolescents than in children under ten, so a weight loss intervention on, say, six- to eight-year-olds would need to follow those children for years to definitively establish any relationship with future eating disorder risk. "And we mistake the short-term improvement in body image that results from these programs as a step in the right direction—but if you're getting a lot of praise because you lost weight in the short term, of course you're going to have these improvements in body satisfaction," Sonneville notes. It doesn't mean that improvement will last or protect you against future disordered eating, especially if you later regain the weight you lost on the diet.

The AAP paper also notes that "some adolescents and their parents misinterpret obesity prevention messages and begin eliminating foods they consider to be 'bad' or 'unhealthy,'" which I read as doctors wanting to blame families for just not understanding the pure intentions of whatever "lifestyle change" they're prescribing. But what if, to a child's brain, it all feels like a diet? Is restriction really that different when it's a classic dieter's trick like Winter's breakfast rice cakes, versus a more diffuse message about lifestyle changes and maintaining a healthy weight? Or can it all be interpreted, and absorbed, in harmful ways?

The scientific literature on kids and dieting makes this question surprisingly hard to answer because most researchers themselves are so convinced that public health initiatives and even doctor-supervised weight loss programs are "not a diet" in the obsessive, celebrities-living-on-lemon-juice-and-cayenne-pepper sense of the word. "It's a sparse literature to begin with. And I think we make this false dichotomy around healthy versus unhealthy weight-control behaviors," says Sonneville. "If what you're doing is purging, well, that's certainly unhealthy. But if you're eating more fruits and vegetables with the explicit purpose of controlling your body weight, that's somehow a healthy behavior. Because everybody feels nice about trying to increase fruit and vegetable intake."

And yet, many a disordered relationship with food has begun with a so-called healthy behavior just like that, which suggests that the intention behind a behavior may matter as much as, if not more than, the behavior itself. "Separating intention from behavior is not a nuance you see in almost anyone's work," says Sonneville. She does point me to a 2007 analysis of Dianne Neumark-Sztainer's Project EAT data, which showed that girls who used both "healthy" and "unhealthy" weight control behaviors raised their future risk for binge eating compared to girls who did not try to control their weight. But when I check in with Neumark-Sztainer about that finding, she's less definitive: "The EAT study has not found consistent evidence that using only healthy weight-control behaviors will increase future risk for engaging in disordered eating," she writes. Nevertheless, how we define "healthy" matters here: Remember that Elise thought Winter's meal plan was healthy. And that Dara-Lynn Weiss thought she was doing the best thing for Betty's health.

One explanation for why weight control attempts can so quickly trigger this cascade of consequences is evolution. We evolved to survive in a food-scarce society, so our bodies are programmed to treat all caloric restriction as equal whether you're an early human who can only eat what you can hunt or gather, or a modern teenager going Paleo before prom. "Our bodies slow down our metabolism, and our brains change how they think about food and satiety so we are safe during this perceived famine," says Jennifer Gaudiani, MD, an internist who specializes in the medical management of eating disorders in Denver, Colorado. "Even if a child is put on a diet that is calorically adequate, I'm convinced that just the thought of restraining certain food groups can be enough to trigger these physiological and psychological reactions."

There is some evidence that just thinking about restriction can increase anxiety about bodies and food. A 2011 study of 121 female college students found that participants who were randomly chosen to count calories and record what they ate for three weeks, but *not* to eat any less than usual, still scored higher on a "perceived stress scale" than participants in the control group who weren't monitoring their intake. (A separate group that both monitored and restricted their intake experienced even more distress, not surprisingly.) Gaudiani sees restricting carbohydrate foods in particular as most likely to trigger this scarcity mindset, though it's hard to say if that's because glucose is so essential to children's growth and development, or because carbs are among modern diet culture's most feared foods. Either way, too much restriction at home—in practice or in perception—is often what leads kids to then be the one at the birthday party inhaling cupcakes. They're doing exactly what their bodies need them to do; eat, now that their "famine" has ended or at least paused. But when parents don't understand the role of that underlying restriction, this kind of birthday party binge will only confirm their fear that this is a child who just cannot control themselves around food.

WHY BANNING FOOD BACKFIRES

Phoebe, the now eleven-year-old from Seattle we met in Chapter 2, has often been that cupcake-inhaling kid at the party. "We'd go to the neighborhood picnic, and my kid would stand by the cupcakes and eat five of them," her mom, Stella, recalls. "I would feel horrified, and my husband would feel horrified, and maybe if we had been able to not be horrified by it, or to not monitor her eating, she could just take three and be happy with it. But here we are."

The year Phoebe turned six, the family's pediatrician referred her to a program "for learning how to eat," as Phoebe puts it now. Stella calls it "the wellness program" and describes it as a nutrition counseling center that offered a gentle-seeming approach to weight management for kids in bigger bodies. Stella was anxious about the whole idea from the get-go and never actually let Phoebe set foot in the place. "It was supposed to be something that the kid attended, but I knew that if we were going to be talking about Phoebe's body size and what she should be eating, I did not want her there," says Stella. "I wanted to be the one to filter that information. But that was unusual; I was the only parent attending without my child." Even though Stella was still dieting herself at the time, she was certain that she did not want to put her six-year-old on a diet. Still, she was worried, because the doctor was worried, about Phoebe's body size and the way she seemed to never turn down a snack, to never not be hungry. Like Elise, Stella wondered if they could address the problem of Phoebe's body through a sort of half measure—not a diet but a lifestyle change or two.

So, Stella implemented a few of the program's recommendations. She stopped serving their meals family style and started pre-plating everyone's dinner in the kitchen. "Only the salad bowl went out on the table," she says. "I was supposed to make sure that there just weren't seconds available for the pasta or rice, so if Phoebe was still hungry, she'd go back for more salad." Another strategy Stella used was to make sure Phoebe's after-school snack was more like a mini meal, to be consumed sitting down with a parent or babysitter. "It was hard to explain why she could no longer just go into the fridge herself and make her own snack, or how, if she grabbed an apple, she also needed some milk and crackers to balance it," Stella says. "These felt like such good ideas in principle; to make eating into a social activity, to ensure that every meal is balanced. But in practice they led to a lot of battles over these new rules."

Even though Stella introduced the new plan as something the whole family would do, Phoebe knew the new rules were just for her. She knew the rest of the pasta was still sitting in the kitchen, instead of on the dinner table. She knew her access to snacks had changed. And her rebellion was swift: At six years old, she started sneaking food to eat whenever her parents weren't around. "I got really good at it," Phoebe tells me. "Like, I could pick up on the cues when someone was going to leave the room. And then I would be like, 'Okay, they're in the bathroom.' So, I knew that when I heard the flush, I had to put the food away. And if we had just cleaned the kitchen, and there was nothing in the sink, I knew to put the bowl or the spoon somewhere else. I got really smart about it."

Power struggles and sneaking food are two of the most common, and most quickly reported, consequences when parents enforce any kind of restrictive feeding practice or diet. Given what we know about the body's physiological responses to restriction, this makes sense: You can't fight your child's appetite or metabolism, or the way her brain fixates on food more when she's eating less of it. And beyond biology, you're also navigating the larger social and emotional context of your child's relationship with food and their body. "Children are exquisitely attentive to what's my friend eating, what's my sibling eating," says Gaudiani. "If there are differences, that will be perceived as restriction and inadequacy." Stella remembers freezing with fear if the whole family was out somewhere and wanted to spontaneously stop for ice cream: "It wasn't 'Everyone can have ice cream except Phoebe' but it was, 'Oh wait, but Phoebe is supposed to have some fruit and fiber alongside her ice cream, so we can't get cones to eat here, we'll have to get a pint and bring it home,'" she recalls. "But of course, if I were out with just Lizzy, I wouldn't do that. It felt like we kept pointing out how Phoebe was different." It also felt like they were underscoring that there was something wrong with Phoebe's appetite; that her love of ice cream was an issue while everyone else was allowed to get excited about ice cream.

Although researchers are inconsistent in how they use the term "diet," we do have a strong body of evidence for the harm caused by what they call "restrictive feeding practices." In young children, we know from the work of the late developmental psychologist Leann Birch, PhD, that banning certain foods or requiring kids to finish a so-called healthy food to earn dessert only leads them to want the forbidden foods more and like the mandatory foods less. That happens even when parents are restricting with only a stated goal of, say, healthy eating or less food waste, maybe because kids know when that's not the whole story. It can happen as well when parents are simply uncomfortable with what they perceive to be their child's excessive appetite. Our culture has trained us to think in terms of "child-size portions": We buy individually wrapped granola bars, single-serving packages of chips or cookies, yogurt portioned out into plastic pots. Those serving sizes are determined by people who have never met your individual child, and who may be guided by the economics of food manufacturing as much as, if not more than, any nutrition standards. But parents are often alarmed when their child wants to eat three granola bars—or six—because we have these prepackaged, preconceived notions of what a "normal" appetite should be. And because we're worried that a child who loves food too much will gain too much weight.

"I think restrictive feeding practices are almost always about weight, because weight and health are so conflated in our culture," says Sarah Nutter, PhD, an assistant professor at the University of Victoria in British Columbia. Of course, once we layer in restricting for the express purpose of weight loss, things get even stickier. Nutter interviewed six women, ages nineteen to twenty-nine, for a qualitative study published in the journal *Eating and Weight Disorders* in 2020; the women's parents had put them on weight management diets as children. Nutter found that the experience had led several of the women to equate their self-worth with their weight and internalize negative stereotypes about larger bodies. Other research shows that when families put kids on diets, those kids tend to eat less healthfully; they are more likely to sneak food and binge eat, and over time to have a higher BMI than kids who weren't fed restrictively.

Not every child responds to restrictive feeding by sneaking food, of course. In Phoebe's case, restriction caused her weight to plateau for several months and triggered a scarcity mindset that caused her to fixate even more on the foods she wasn't allowed to eat freely. But for Winter, the combination of food restriction, increased exercise, and weight loss likely contributed to what eating disorder researchers call a "negative energy balance," when you expend more energy through movement and other activity than you consume in calories. A negative energy balance can happen to any of us briefly when we don't fuel up enough before a workout or we're swamped at work and skip lunch. And most of us respond by correcting the imbalance: We eat more at our next meal. But dieters don't do that, because they are trying to induce weight loss by chronically burning more calories than they consume. Living in negative energy balance in this way can trigger the rigid, restrictive mindset that is a hallmark of anorexia and causes someone to double down and eat even less.

It's important to say here: Neither of these response patterns—digging deeper into restriction, or "rebelling" against restriction with secret eating—is dictated by a child's body size but rather by a whole web of genetic predispositions, neurological responses, and environmental influences. A child in a bigger body can just as easily go the anorexia route—and will likely have their behaviors ignored or reinforced because their weight loss is seen as "progress." And a child in a smaller body can become food-fixated and prone to binge eating, though they may not be pathologized for this behavior unless it results in weight gain. And whatever a child's initial response, the more an eating disorder becomes entrenched, the more they may cross back and forth between the different pathways, hitting a wall with restriction that leads to binge eating, and then responding to that perceived failure with more restriction. "Eating disorders are brain disorders because the brain cannot function [without appropriate nutrition]. So once the 'eating disorder brain' is in control, patients can't make any decisions around eating," explains Campbell. "We have to feed the brain so the brain can be healthy enough to fight the eating disorder."

WHY DIETS DON'T WORK

By one measure alone, Elise's meal plan and Stella's new policies around portion control and balanced meals worked: Both of their daughters lost some weight, in the short term. This is the most common response to caloric restriction, after all, and the reason why so many diets, life-style plans, and other "obesity prevention programs" can claim success. Eating less will result in temporary weight loss. But diets don't achieve their stated goal in the long term, because virtually nobody can both lose weight and keep it off forever. According to an evidence review of common commercial weight loss protocols first published in 2007, and later updated in 2013: People lose some weight in the first nine to twelve months of any diet, but over the next two to five years, they gain back all but an average of 2.1 pounds. "The dieters had little benefit to show for their efforts, and the non-dieters didn't seem harmed by their lack of effort," says Traci Mann, PhD, the paper's co-author, who is now a professor of health and social psychology at the University of Minnesota. "Weight regain appears to be the typical response to dieting, not the exception." There is less evidence documenting the failure rate of dieting in kids, in part because researchers don't like to call what they do to kids "diets," and in part because they expect the actual pounds lost to be less in pediatric populations since kids are growing; they're more focused on whether a child can drop to a lower percentile on the growth chart. Most studies also don't follow kids long enough to determine the intervention's sustainability. But we do know that childhood dieting is a predictor of future weight gain, so it seems fair to say that a similar pattern emerges.

The kids who "fail" at dieting do so not because they lack discipline or willpower but because their bodies are responding exactly the way our bodies are supposed to respond to restriction. Their metabolism slows down, their hunger hormones increase, and they become preoccupied with food. The kids who "succeed" at dieting are kids like Winter who are predisposed to respond to restrictive feeding with more restriction; to override this physiological response, which kicks in any-time our weight drops below the range that some researchers call our "set point," or the place where our bodies are genetically programmed to function best. Set point theory originated in the 1940s with the now-infamous Minnesota Starvation Experiment, where researchers put thirty-six healthy young men on a six-month diet of 1570 calories per day (yes, they classified this as "semi-starvation"; yes, I know you've likely done a diet that required you to eat just 1,200 calories a day and claimed this was adequate nutrition; it wasn't). The men lost on aver-age, around 25 percent of their starting weight. The researchers then stopped the diet and spent three months helping the men recover, feed-ing them up to 10,000 calories per day. By the end of the trial, the men were up to 148 percent of their initial weight. But as their eating habits evened out over the next several months and years, they almost all set-tled back at their pre-starvation weight, or set point.

We don't starve people for science anymore, but further research has found that weight loss lowers our resting metabolic rate, which is the baseline rate at which our bodies burn energy when we're sitting still. This means that a 150-pound person who was once 200 pounds burns energy more slowly than someone who has always been 150 pounds—and so the dieter will only maintain that lower weight if they continue to eat less than their new same-size peers. Some of the most compelling research on this was conducted on former contestants from the television show *The Biggest Loser* (because we do still starve people for entertainment!). A 2016 study on fourteen show participants found that they all experienced a major decrease in their resting metabolic rate along with their dramatic weight loss—but also that this decrease in metabolic rate persisted for six years after the show. This was even true among those contestants who restored their weight to its pre-show level, so they could now only maintain that higher weight through a lower caloric intake.

Translating set point theory to kids is complicated, since kids are growing and therefore gaining weight regularly as a normal function of childhood. But kids likely have what we might call a set point trajectory, since their body size at any given stage of childhood, as well as their overall growth pattern, is so influenced by their genetics. And kids appear to respond to diets in similar physiological ways as adults. A handful of studies have shown that weight loss affects a child or adolescent's metabolism just as drastically; in a small 1990 study of eighteen children aged ten to thirteen, losing fifteen pounds in three weeks (after being fed just 700 calories per day) resulted in a 27 percent reduction in resting metabolic rate—and the effect persisted for eight months even among participants who regained some weight. Another study from 1999 on sixty-four teenagers found that even losing fourteen pounds over six weeks was enough to reduce their resting metabolic rate by 11 percent. "The evidence strongly suggests that kids establish their set point prior to adulthood," says Sonneville. "Since we don't know the potential adverse consequences of this kind of early metabolic disruption, it's unethical and inappropriate to pursue intentional weight loss for kids."

Of course, the diet industry sees pursuing intentional weight loss for kids as both ethical and essential. Joanna Strober is a technology executive in Silicon Valley who cofounded a health app for children called Kurbo after a pediatrician told her that her twelve-year-old son was obese. "She said, 'We have a big problem here!' It was really scary," Strober told me when I interviewed her for the *New York Times* in 2019. "It felt like we had very few options because there's such a stigma around this." By "this," I thought Strober meant the teasing or bullying her son was facing for his weight. But then I realized she meant the stigma she faced as a mom who wanted her child to lose weight. In Strober's elite community, everybody agreed that childhood obesity was a problem, but they were uncomfortable to discover it in their midst. "Nobody wants to talk about it," she said.

Strober worked with a behavioral health coach at Stanford University's Pediatric Weight Control Program to develop her app, which teaches kids to use Stanford's "traffic light" system for categorizing foods. In 2018, the diet industry veteran Weight Watchers (now known as WW) purchased the app for $3 million and, in August 2019, relaunched it under their brand. WW says the program is based on thirty years of research. Kids don't count points or calories; instead, they learn to rate foods as "green lights" (mostly fruits and vegetables, plus skim milk and condiments like vinegar), "yellow lights" (chicken, eggs, pasta), and "red lights." This last group includes cookies and chips, but also foods like bagels, peanut butter, avocados, and yogurt—healthy staples in many family meals. According to Kurbo, all of these are to be consumed in moderation: "5 or fewer" per day, the app advised me when I downloaded it. Strober believes that this system just teaches kids to think more critically about the foods they're offered. "Kids would tell us, I didn't even know that [food on my school lunch tray] was a red!" she said. Strober saw this as a victory, proof that Kurbo was teaching kids a kind of critical food literacy. She seemed unconcerned that it could leave kids—many of whom rely on school-provided meals—feeling like their lunch was too dangerous to eat.

Gary Foster, PhD, WW's chief science officer, who is also a clinical psychologist and adjunct professor at the University of Pennsylvania who previously led research and treatment centers on obesity and eating disorders there and at Tufts University, wanted to make sure I understood, of course, that Kurbo is not a diet. "We're not prescribing weight loss for kids, to be clear," he told me. "We wouldn't say to a kid or a family, 'What's your weight loss goal?' The goal is to live the traffic light system." But Kurbo's health coaches advise parents to keep their own soda and pretzels in the trunk of their car so the kids don't see them snacking on forbidden foods. They do intervene if they hear of parents going so far as to lock kitchen cupboards, Foster and Strober reassured me, though neither could quite explain why a locked kitchen cupboard is more traumatic for a kid to discover than a trunk full of secret food. They also felt strongly that parents should not feed the child on Kurbo differently from the rest of the family. And if a child reports losing more than two pounds a week, their health coach follows up to assess whether the child or parent is at risk for an eating disorder. But Kurbo coaches are not extensively trained in how to screen for eating disorders, perhaps in part because some common eating disorder red flags are the very behavioral changes they advise. They don't know how to deal with the underlying emotional issues that might cause a child to sneak food, and they certainly aren't prepared to address restriction-fueled binge eating, since their program teaches restriction.

Kurbo claims success, of course: A 2019 analysis of Kurbo found that it had a significantly lower attrition rate over up to twenty-four weeks compared with in-person weight management programs, and that the kids who participated in the most health coaching sessions reported the most weight loss. But their weight loss was entirely self-reported and not tracked long-term. The study also had no control group (of comparable kids not participating in Kurbo). And the researchers only examined their intended outcomes; they did not track unintended consequences like whether the kids began sneaking food or developed other disordered eating habits, nor did they evaluate the participants' body image or level of internalized weight stigma. "This is a classic example of 'you can only find what you're looking for,'" says Sonneville.

William Dietz, MD, the former CDC director and obesity researcher who has served on Weight Watchers' Scientific Advisory Board, tells me that WW is "the most effective community-based program that we know of," but he doesn't dispute that these kinds of diets fail to result in significant or durable weight loss. He argues that you can't measure Weight Watchers solely by their ability to help people lose weight: "I think there are other outcome measures that are quite positive," he tells me. "Like the support, like being in a safe place, which is often not available to people with obesity." But how can a program be safe for fat people (kids or adults) when it's rooted in the premise that fat people are not okay?

When Stella did finally realize what Phoebe was doing, she dropped out of the wellness program immediately. "I realize in retrospect that even though it was just 'lifestyle interventions,' Phoebe had experienced it as really restrictive," she says. "And it makes me so sad because I remember sneaking food when I was little. And that was one of the things I really did not want my own children to go through." When I talk to Phoebe and Stella together, they talk openly about Phoebe's food sneaking, in a way that makes it all feel very much in the past. Phoebe doesn't seem to remember her mom's own dieting. "When you were still believing in diet culture, I think I was too young to be affected by it," she tells her mom. But she remembers coming home from school in third grade and telling her mom that kids had made fun of her weight on the playground. "That's when she was like, there's this whole movement called Health at Every Size, fat isn't a bad thing, blah, blah, blah," Phoebe explains. "And then I guess I got pretty passionate about it." Which is an understatement: By sixth grade, Phoebe was giving presentations about body image, Barbie, and fatphobia to her school. When we talk, she's thinking about starting an anti-diet culture podcast for kids. I'm blown away by her confidence, her intelligence, her fearlessness.

And yet, Stella tells me later: Phoebe still sneaks food, even after years of no rules around food choices or portion control. "She can eat ten Oreos at lunch and ten Oreos at dinner, and I'll still find an empty sleeve and know she's sneaked them in between," Stella says in a second conversation without Phoebe on Zoom. Her solution for now is to lean into as much permission as she can: "Let's not call it sneaking, let's just say, 'Have Oreos when you want to have them.'" But she's not sure if that's right, either. "That drive hasn't decreased for her, the way I think it should, the way it did for me, when I stopped dieting and got treatment for my own binge eating disorder," Stella says. She knows that this expectation of how Phoebe's eating should change may be part of the problem; if we stop dieting but only give ourselves unconditional permission to eat with the hopes that we'll start eating less or get thinner, we're still living with a diet mindset. So Phoebe may, on some level, be continuing to pick up on her parents' anxiety about her hunger and eat more in response. Or maybe she's just now a kid beginning puberty, needing to eat more to fuel the phenomenal changes and growth her body is ready to undergo. Stella's husband says their experiment of no restriction hasn't worked. But he doesn't know what to do, either. "I know that the old way doesn't work; I won't put her on another diet," Stella says. "But I don't know what the new way is, either."

CHAPTER 4

Thin Kid Privilege

JESSICA, a mom of six in Southern California, is experienced in all the ways that siblings can gang up on each other. Her kids range in age from just turned one to almost fourteen, and navigating the dynamic between her two oldest boys, in particular, has always been a challenge. "They are just yin and yang to each other," she tells me of Jacob, her almost fourteen-year-old, and Sawyer, her twelve-year-old. And as soon as we get on Zoom, I can see what she means: Sawyer is round and friendly and jumps easily into chatting. Jacob isn't even in the room. "He said he had to go to the bathroom," Jessica offers. "We'll see if he joins us." Jacob finally pokes his head in a few minutes later, looks like he wants to back right out, and then begrudgingly takes a seat next to his brother. He's a beanpole kid, all ears and lanky limbs. And for most of our call, he sits with his body angled away from the camera. When I ask a direct question, he turns toward me and answers politely. But it's clear he would rather eat glass than have this conversation.

And I don't blame him because the conversation we're having is about how Jacob bullies Sawyer about his weight.

When the boys were small, Jessica says, they were both skinny. Jessica describes herself as small fat, but her husband, William, at almost six feet tall, weighed just 130 pounds when they got married. "For a

long time, I worried, 'Please don't let [my kids] get my body, please!'"
Jessica says. "I worried about all of them having to go through what
I've had to go through." Which is the familiar story: Years of dieting
and excessive exercise that only ever resulted in Jessica being "a little
bit thin," as she puts it. Her whole family is big; there was no mystery
to Jessica about her size, only why she was expected to try to change it.
"I always wondered: Why do I have to work so hard just because I was
born with a bigger body?" she says. "It's not fair."

Jessica hit the wall on dieting while she was pregnant with her
second-youngest child, Hugo, who is now three. "I read a book that
explained why women gain weight in our abdomens during pregnancy
because the body needs to put a ton of fat on the baby so it can be
healthy when it's born," she says. "I remember learning that and thinking, wow, the body is so cool. And oh: There's nothing wrong with
me." Jessica had never been one to ban cookies or make body-shaming
comments, but she began to talk much more directly with her kids
about how body size is determined by genetics rather than willpower.
She read books about intuitive eating, started to follow body positive
influencers on Instagram, and made them the subject of family dinner
discussions.

The conversations were well timed: A few months before he turned
nine, Sawyer hit a growth spurt, and it became clear that he took after
Jessica's side of the family. "He started to plump up more, and I went,
'Uh-oh, people are going to be mean,'" she says. She didn't expect "people"
to include her own children. But as Sawyer got bigger, Jacob, as well
as their next-oldest brother, Beckett (who is now ten), noticed—and
began to use it against Sawyer. So much so that when I ask the boys
where they see fatphobia in the world, Sawyer doesn't hesitate: "The
main place I see it is right here [at home]," he says. "Because Jacob and
Beckett, the first word they use when they're mad at someone is 'fat.'"
Especially if the person they're mad at is Sawyer.

Jacob doesn't say a word while Jessica and Sawyer explain that whenever Jacob gets mad, he lays into Sawyer with "You fat idiot!" or some
other similar slur. "I've started talking to them about how 'fat' is not an
insult. We are trying to neutralize the word, at least in our own home,"

Jessica says. She points out that Jacob also uses "skinny" as an insult when he's teasing Beckett, who is small for his age. "That's not great either," Jessica acknowledges. But we all know it feels different for one skinny brother to mock another skinny brother than for both to gang up on the one larger kid.

So, I ask Jacob: "Why do you call Sawyer fat?"

He untwists and looks at me. "It usually comes up when I just can't think of anything else to say or we're having an argument or something," he says.

I ask Jacob what he thinks about using "fat" this way. "It's like Sawyer said, it's not okay to use 'fat' as an insult because you're teasing someone for something they cannot control," he tells me. Yes, he's parroting his mom and brother here, but Jacob seems to get it. There's just a disconnect between what he understands, intellectually, about the word "fat" and the purpose it serves in the heat of a brotherly dispute. But I notice something else, as the boys talk—or rather as Sawyer talks, and Jacob goes back to staring at his knees. For Sawyer, having his mom explain that bodies come in all shapes and sizes has been liberating. It's enabled him to roll with his changing body in a remarkably drama-free way. When Jessica asks him how it feels to wear "husky" clothes, he says: "To be completely honest, it makes me feel proud because, wow, I'm bigger than Jacob."

But for Jacob, the weight talk has always felt more abstract. "I just didn't see the big deal about it when I was younger," he says. "I didn't think it was, like, a huge issue that I needed to focus on. So, I just kinda ignored it." As a thin kid, Jacob can use "fat" as an insult without acknowledging the full power of his words. His own insecurities feel more significant to him: "When Sawyer did start getting bigger, I was like, 'You get to wear husky clothes and huskies are like wolves,'" Jacob says. "I thought it meant he would be braver than me." But he also knows that the world will never hold his body against him. He doesn't need Jessica's concerted efforts to help him accept his body in the same way Sawyer does. Jacob can tease Sawyer for his weight and know that Sawyer will have no satisfying comeback because Jacob has thin privilege.

Thin privilege refers to the way our world is built to accept, support, and celebrate thin bodies. Thin privilege means never having to worry if you'll fit in the seat at a restaurant, on an airplane, or in your friend's dining room. It's knowing you can eat an ice cream cone in public, or skip a workout, and—whatever internal struggle you might feel around these decisions—you will not be judged or ridiculed for the choice by others. It's the fact that you can shop in any clothing store and be confident that they'll have your size. You have thin privilege when you mostly see people with bodies roughly like yours—tanner, maybe, and much better dressed, but not worlds apart in size or shape—in a magazine, in a movie, or on social media.

Thin privilege also means never worrying that a doctor will refuse to treat you until you lose weight, or will only prescribe weight loss, no matter what your symptoms. It means that other people, even health professionals, may assume that you have knowledge and expertise about health that you might not actually possess. "If you hear a thin, fit dietitian or sports professional talking about fitness and nutrition, you might be more likely to trust them implicitly than if you hear someone with the same credentials speaking to us from a fatter body," says Erin Harrop, PhD, an assistant professor at the University of Denver's School of Social Work, where they study eating disorders, weight stigma, and marginalized identities in healthcare. And thin privilege means safety: "Someone with more thin privilege than me might not have to worry about strangers on the streets, shouting 'Hey, fatso!' at them," says Aubrey Gordon, the fat activist who wrote for years under the anonymous byline "Your Fat Friend" to protect her safety and only began using her own name when she published her 2021 book *What We Don't Talk About When We Talk About Fat.*

For kids, thin privilege means not being a target of weight-based bullying, which research shows is the number one reason girls are bullied and the second most common reason for boys. It also means fitting, physically, into the chairs in a classroom and the swings on a playground. Gordon, who also cohosts the *Maintenance Phase* podcast, says that, as a fat teenager, "those desks with a chair attached were a special kind of hell." If she could fit in the seat, she couldn't flip down the desk. "I would just have to sort of sit in the chair with the desk flapped up, which was like a little flag

waving," she recalls. "It felt like, 'Hi, everybody! I'm the fat kid! Hello!'"
Gordon spent middle school and high school writing with her notebook
balanced on her knee. "My notes were kind of garbage," she says. "It was
nothing insurmountable, but it was more difficult, and there were more
things to navigate than there should have been."

Thin kids can also join a sports team or a dance class, without worrying if the uniform or costume will come in their size. And they can
join these activities just because they love them, not because anyone
thinks it will help them manage their weight. This changes how they'll
measure their success at the activity, as well as how much they can enjoy
it. Thin privilege can often mean the freedom to eat more candy or
other treats than kids in bigger bodies, or than dieting grown-ups. As a
former thin kid, I can remember how often the adults in my life turned
down the plate of doughnuts or the box of fudge on the grounds that
they were watching their weight. I ate as much as I wanted because I
already had the body they were trying to get.

Thin privilege—like white privilege and male privilege—is a slippery and often-controversial concept. It can be invisible to anyone who
has it and glaringly obvious to everyone else. That's because we're conditioned not to notice any form of discrimination that doesn't apply
directly to us, whether it's happening around us or we are directly perpetrating it. We might even think we're fighting against fatphobia and
nevertheless reinforce it. When we hold up pro athletes like Shaquille
O'Neal or the Rock as proof that the BMI system is flawed (because it
doesn't account for muscle mass), we're saying, "It's so terrible that this
measurement labels thin people as 'fat.'" And I often receive notes from
parents furious about a comment that someone else made about their
child's body or food preferences—and then they cap off their outrage
with some version of: "And he's not even fat!" These parents believe
they are angry because, like Jacob, they know it's wrong to shame someone for their weight. But they're actually angry that someone has put
their child in the fat kid club. Because they don't want a fat kid. They
don't want any proximity to fat. They believe that their thin child should
never be shamed or policed around food, but there comes a jeans size

where, of course, you have to get it together and stop eating the cookies. This is the double-edged sword of thin privilege. And it's damaging to kids of all sizes.

THE SPECTRUM OF THIN PRIVILEGE

One fascinating thing about thin privilege: You can have it even if you live in a body that doesn't perfectly conform to our culture's rigid beauty ideals. You can even have it if you're fat. Notes Gordon: "I actually have more thin privilege at 350 pounds than someone who is fatter than me." This is important to reckon with. As a "small fat" woman, I mostly can't shop in straight-sized clothing stores, but I can fit easily into the lowest size or two of every plus-size line. I have experienced doctors who focused on my weight in negative ways, but once I started refusing to be weighed at checkups, that stopped. And my refusal has never been questioned because I'm not at the level of fatness where doctors can't see past my size. On social media or on Zoom, depending on the angle of the camera, I might present as thinner than I am—and this certainly plays into why something I post on Instagram about fatphobia might perform better than a post from someone who cannot pass as thin.

Harrop notes that your body's weight distribution matters as well: "You could have a smaller fat body and still be fairly discriminated against based on how little your body represents the beauty ideals for your gender," they explain. "A small fat body with an hourglass figure experiences a different type of thin privilege than a small fat body with a round torso. But both would have thin privilege in terms of fitting into airplane seats or finding athletic shorts in their size, compared to folks in larger bodies."

And of course, thin privilege intersects with all our other identities. "It's not like we have one privileged group and one discriminated-against group," says Harrop. A very fat, cis, straight, white, able-bodied person will experience weight stigma. But it will manifest differently than someone who is thin, but also, say, Asian, queer, and/or disabled and experiencing stigma related to those identities. And these privileges and marginalized identities stack and intertwine—remember our discussion of Michelle Obama, who both perpetuated anti-fat bias with her "Let's Move" campaign and was the target of that bias, along with constant misogyny and anti-Black racism in terms of the public discourse about her body. Tabitha, a mom of two in Washington, D.C., had this realization the day her then five-year-old daughter, Emma, came out of the dress rehearsal for her dance recital and said, "Maddie saw me in my costume and asked me why I'm so fat." Emma is Black and at the time, was taller and bigger than many of her peers. Maddie is white and was one of the thinnest kids in their class. "For whatever reason, that day, Maddie noticed this difference in their bodies," says Tabitha, who is white and lives in a bigger body. "And I think the question could have been neutral. But the way Emma sort of recited it back to us, it felt like, 'Oh, yeah, there was some judgment in there.' Like, 'Why is your body like *that*?' It felt particularly crummy."

It's impossible to say if Maddie was responding only to Emma's size or also to her skin color. Research shows that white parents avoid discussions of race and racism, and when we do discuss it, it's often to tell our kids not to comment on darker skin tones. So, for a child who is noticing difference and, perhaps, also wanting to emphasize her superiority over the different child, a comment about body size may feel like fair game.

Tabitha says Emma seemed to brush off the comment. She and her wife, Susan, stammered out a response that they hoped sounded supportive: "We said something like, 'Oh, well, sometimes people notice differences between bodies, because bodies come in all shapes and sizes, and yours is healthy and strong,'" Tabitha told me. Emma didn't say much in response; she was quickly swept back up in the excitement of the recital and never mentioned Maddie's comment again. So, Tabitha hopes that Emma's real takeaway from the day was "Look how cool and strong your body is and look how you've learned to use it!" But: "It was this little downer moment in the midst of all of that," she says. And over the next few years, as Emma continued to be one of the biggest kids in her class, Tabitha wondered what other microaggressions—

those small-but-not moments of othering—Emma was experiencing as a Black girl in a bigger body.

Those microaggressions are as likely to come from the adults in Emma's life as they are from peers like Maddie. Researchers at Georgetown Law School's Center on Poverty and Inequality have found that adults tend to think that Black girls as young as five need less protection and nurturing than their white peers. As Black girls get older, adults also assume that they are more independent, less innocent, and know more about sex and other adult topics than white girls. Black girls are suspended from school more than five times as often as white peers, and they are 2.7 times more likely to be referred to the juvenile justice system. "To society, we're not innocent. And white girls are always innocent," one teenage Black girl told the researchers for their 2017 report on the experiences of Black girls aged five to fourteen.

The reality that Black and Latina girls, on average, weigh more, enter puberty earlier, and thus have less thin privilege than white girls also influences such racist assumptions about their behavior and maturity level. "We blame young Black girls for having larger bodies, for having larger breasts, for being 'too sexual,'" says Whitney Trotter, RD, a dietitian and nurse in Memphis, who provides nutritional counseling for adolescents and adults of color with eating disorders and complex trauma. When advocating for her patients, Trotter thinks a lot about how thin privilege informs who gets treatment for eating disorders—because doctors and treatment centers don't expect to see these issues in BIPOC kids or in kids in bigger bodies. And she also notices how her patients' experiences of their bodies as lacking thin privilege and white privilege contributes to their struggle. "One of my clients is one of just twelve Black girls in an all-white high school, and she's the biggest one," Trotter says.

The intersection of anti-fat bias and anti-Black racism is particularly important to spell out because in the United States, especially, our entire concept of "fat is bad" is so rooted in anti-Blackness, white supremacy, and the end of slavery. But other kids of color must also navigate unfair expectations of their bodies in ways that intersect with weight. "We never celebrate the fat Indians," writes Tenille K. Campbell, a Dene/Métis artist from English River First Nation in Saskatchewan, Canada. In a 2021 essay for CBC First Person, Campbell explored how both stereotypes and celebrations alike of Indigenous people privilege thin bodies over fat ones:

> When images of us go around, we see portraits of structured jawlines at dusk. We see chiselled cheekbones in ribbon skirts or regalia. We see skinny fingers drenched in turquoise rings. We see lithe and toned bodies on book covers advocating for decolonized diets—as if we never had fat people in our communities' pre-colonial times.
>
> We don't see double chins on a new lipstick ad for Indian Country. We don't see the thick arms of a fat woman wrapped in a star blanket. We don't see the round, fat bellies of an Indigenous woman in fashion articles.

This lack of visibility, of representation even within their own community, tells fat Indigenous kids over and over that they should take up less space. Asian writers have articulated a similar phenomenon in their communities, where bodies are measured simultaneously by their own and white standards of beauty—both of which prize thinness. "We are stereotyped as demure—and therefore, submissive," writes Rachel Kuo, PhD, a Taiwanese American scholar, writer, and educator in a 2015 piece for the blog *Everyday Feminism*. "Thus, our bodies must also be seen as easy to control, easy to dominate: Delicate and small." Kuo identifies as having thin privilege in the piece but notes:

> I *do* experience oppression based on a specific racialized expectation that normalizes *all Asian women's bodies as thin.* Racialized people cannot escape the "for/because" clause of their bodies. We are either seen as skinny *because* we are Asian women or as "too fat" *for* an Asian woman. [. . .] The "perfect" body for Asian women is an illusion. And yet, it creates a constant pressure to be seen as skinny, to try to be skinnier—and in turn, to be more Asian: *"Why can't I just be thin like 'the other Asian girls'?"*

What kids of all racial identities understand early on about thin privilege is that we expect anyone to be able to access it fully, through hard work and determination. This makes thin privilege distinct from every other kind of privilege except, perhaps, for socioeconomic status. Though a light-skinned person of color may benefit from white privilege through their physical proximity to whiteness, it's rare for anyone to be able to fully shed their socially constructed racial identity. And while gender identities and sexuality can be closeted for a genderqueer person to pass as cisgender or a gay person to pass as straight in situations where it's not safe to be out, a gay person cannot turn themselves straight and a trans person cannot convince themselves that they truly are the gender they were assigned at birth. (To be clear: This hasn't stopped conservative, homophobic, and transphobic communities from pushing the narrative that you can "pray the gay away" or from pursuing a terrifying legislative agenda designed to deny trans and nonbinary kids gender-affirming healthcare. These campaigns just don't reflect our scientific understanding of sexuality and gender.) But we're taught to believe that thinness, like wealth, is well within everyone's grasp—if only we are disciplined enough to obtain and maintain it.

This is toxic because it's wrong. Our bodies are not malleable like clay and our size is determined by our genetics, biology, and larger environment much more than our lifestyle choices. And the belief that "thin" is an achievable goal for all is also toxic because the thin ideal is also a white and heteronormative ideal. When we strive for thinness, we're reinforcing every other form of stigma at the same time. For people of color, "thin privilege gives you access to white privilege," says Trotter. For white people, maintaining thin privilege is about shoring up our white privilege, about further distancing ourselves from the bodies we view as "other" or "abnormal."

WHY THIN PRIVILEGE HURTS FAT KIDS

The most common and immediately destructive way that thin children learn to weaponize their privilege is by teasing peers in bigger bodies. In 1994, the US National Education Association reported that, "for fat students, the school experience is one of ongoing prejudice, unnoticed discrimination, and almost constant harassment. From nursery school through college, fat students experience ostracism, discouragement, and sometimes violence." Often the bullying comes from thin kids, but fat kids also bully other fat kids. A 2004 Canadian study of 5,749 kids aged eleven to sixteen found that older kids (that is, fifteen- and sixteen-year-olds) in larger bodies were more likely to be both victims and perpetrators of bullying. A more recent study from 2016 involving over ten thousand Chinese students confirmed those findings, noting that boys in larger bodies were slightly more likely to be bullies (while also being bullied themselves). One 2011 study, however, found that girls with BMI in the obese range were three times more likely than thinner peers to engage in "relational bullying" (excluding someone from a social group, giving them the silent treatment, or spreading rumors about them). This makes sense: If a fat kid has achieved some degree of acceptance from thinner peers, that proximity to thin privilege is powerful currency. Joining or even leading the fray against a kid who is fatter may feel like the only way to preserve that borrowed privilege. "We have a strong desire not to be grouped in with the wrong people," says Harrop. And that's true even if we recognize that anti-fat bias is wrong; we can disagree with it, and yet also be so terrified of it happening to us that we perpetuate it.

The discrimination fueled by thin privilege doesn't happen only between kids. Thin adults also use their privilege against fat kids, every day. One common example is when thin adults assume that children in bigger bodies must have terrible eating habits or get less physical activity than their thinner peers. In fact, some research suggests that kids in larger bodies don't necessarily eat more or eat less nutritiously than kids in smaller bodies. One small study on thirty-two randomly selected eleven-year-olds found that the children classified as "overweight" ate less over the course of a week, and ate fewer carbohydrate-based foods, than their thinner counterparts, though the researchers did not determine whether this was because of the children's innate appetites and preferences or because fat kids are pressured to restrict their food intake. But that finding feels surprising nonetheless, because we assume that thinness equals virtue and restraint and that fatness is evidence of a body untamed. What's more, we assume that thin people are doing something (or everything) right, which gives thin people a sense of entitlement over their bodies and lifestyle choices. The entire modern fitness industry rests on the premise that thin people who work out a lot know something you don't about health. Most of them are just genetically predisposed to thinness, or to building muscle in certain ways that give them an idealized body type. But we reward them for existing—and punish fat people when they do the same.

The assumption that fat kids are fat because they're doing something wrong leads adults to micromanage their eating and exercise habits and to frame every activity around how it will impact their weight. There is a critical difference in being encouraged to take swim lessons because you love the water and being encouraged to take swim lessons because it might help you shed a few pounds. When you're a fat kid, "your hobbies and personality and goals largely center around losing weight," says Jaclyn Siegel, PhD, a postdoctoral research scholar in the Body Image, Sexuality, and Health Lab at San Diego State University. "Your body is constantly on display. At school and other public events, your body becomes the center of attention in a way that other children's abilities and talents do." We also assign a whole list of negative traits to fat kids based purely on their failure to hold thin privilege. A 2012 study of 162 physical education teachers found that they had lower expectations of their students in bigger bodies, which affected their perceptions of those kids' physical abilities, academic performance, and social skills. Meanwhile, a 2013 analysis of data collected on kindergartners found that a student's weight had a bigger negative impact on a teacher's assessment of their academic ability than their test scores. Remember, it's not only thin people who hold these biases; it's anyone with proximity to thinness or who has internalized the belief that thin bodies are better. (So: pretty much everyone.) The National Education Association report concludes that fat students "are deprived of places on honor rolls, sports teams, and cheerleading squads and are denied letters of recommendation."

The adultification experienced most intensely by Black girls can also manifest in our treatment of fat kids of all races and genders. "Kids with thin privilege get to be kids in a way that fat kids don't," says Siegel. "And girls in fat bodies are either sexualized too soon or rendered invisible by their size." Given that choice—and especially if they've experienced the way, say, a school dress code seems to require more enforcing on their body than that of a thin peer—many fat kids choose invisibility. When Halloween costumes stop fitting, fat kids stop trick-or-treating. Aubrey Gordon recalls not fitting into the vest at her local laser tag place, which was where every kid wanted to have their birthday party. So she stopped going to the parties. "There is a social isolation that starts to set in," she says. "And it would never have occurred to me at the time, but boy, just a thimbleful of awareness from anybody's parents could have gone miles and miles." In other words, if your child has their heart set on a laser tag birthday party, you should ask them, "Do you think all your friends can do this activity with us? Will anyone feel uncomfortable?"

If you're the parent of a fat child, this conversation could be an opportunity to foster alliance between them and other fat kids in their peer group; to help them see that any teasing or singling out they have experienced because of their weight is not their fault but rather evidence of our larger, broken system. If you're the parent of a thin child, asking them to reflect on their friends' abilities and experiences in this way may feel awkward. But it is perhaps even more necessary because your child probably won't anticipate or even notice these issues on their own. And it's important that you aren't only talking about their friend's weight as a barrier to fun. "Theo can't fit in the laser tag vest, so we should do something else for your birthday" renders Theo a victim to be pitied, or a problem to be bullied, depending on how mad your kid is about not doing laser tag. To emphasize Theo's strengths and see him as a whole person, consider: "It's so unfair that the laser tag place doesn't offer vests in enough sizes. What if we do a trip to the zoo instead since you and Theo are both so into reptiles?" This puts the blame where it belongs (on the laser tag place that doesn't offer inclusive gear) and fosters connection by reminding your child why Theo is such a cool friend.

HOW THIN PRIVILEGE HARMS THIN KIDS

Asking your thin child to rethink a birthday party plan that would exclude their fat friend isn't just the right thing to do by Theo. It's also an important opportunity to help your child understand the innate unfairness of thin privilege and to start divesting their sense of themselves from their privilege, if only in that one small way. This is important because thin privilege doesn't just harm fat kids. It limits and defines thin children's experiences and understanding of themselves as well. Thin kids may be steered toward dance or certain sports because they have the "right" body for them—and then, as we'll explore in more detail in Chapter 11, the importance of that body will be emphasized alongside or even more than how hard they work. "For Olivia, thin privilege means that she can be standing directly next to a teammate of equal skill level, and she will usually get chosen to do a demonstration at a master class, or get singled out at a competition, because she has what they consider a 'dancer's body,'" says Rebecca, a stepmom in Tallahassee, Florida, of her twelve-year-old stepdaughter.

Rebecca realized that she needed to help Olivia understand her thin privilege when a classmate reported Olivia for body shaming her by making comments like "Oh, my waist is smaller than yours" while taking costume measurements. Rebecca thinks Olivia was just observing these differences, without much awareness of their potential to cause harm. But it's also possible that Olivia understands, on some level, the power she enjoys as a dancer with the "right" kind of body. "We've tried to be adamant that being thin is not something to aspire to, and to communicate that your body is doing so much more than presenting an image to the world," says Rebecca. "But I do worry this will become something she fixates on later." After all, not every thin kid grows up to be a thin adult.

When the adults in my life told me that I could eat as many treats as I wanted as a thin kid, while policing themselves, I learned that I was getting away with something. And there was a certain thrill to that—but it also gave those foods more power, which made me more obsessive about wanting to eat them. And when I did, say, eat an entire box of fudge in one afternoon, and didn't immediately gain weight, it reinforced my sense that my thinness was some kind of innate superpower; that I could eat whatever I wanted without gaining weight and was therefore superior to people who couldn't. Thinness gradually became wrapped up in my sense of myself as a talented and successful person. It felt deeply tied to my other achievements, like getting good grades and winning my high school's playwriting competition three years in a row, even though those were goals I worked for, and my childhood body size required no such effort. This made it that much more difficult to come to terms with my less-thin, and later, small fat adult body—because I wasn't just buying bigger clothing sizes. I was untangling my identity from thinness, even though the roles that make up my identity now—writer, mother, obsessive gardener—should not have a body type.

Harrop had a similar experience, growing up as a tall, thin kid who became a high school volleyball star. "In a weird way, I'm so glad I was socialized with thin privilege because there were so many sports I would not have tried otherwise," they say. "I could be good at a sport without being good at a sport, because I had that confidence, general athleticism, and body privilege." Harrop was the kid who would climb anything and jump off anything; they also played basketball and ran cross-country. "The narrative was, because I was a thin jock, I could do it." Their sister, who grew up in a bigger body, was much less active at least in part because she was told she couldn't do it. "There were an entirely different set of assumptions for her body," they say. But Harrop also had to wrestle with how much thinness felt essential to their identity. They were five when they first started choosing nonfat milk over 2 percent and exercising to avoid weight gain; their restrictive behaviors increased gradually over the years. By age thirteen, they were trying to eat fewer than 600 calories a day and purging whenever they ate more. But it took two more years—and even more intensive caloric restriction—to get a diagnosis because Harrop's obsessive exercise and health focus were praised as part of their athlete persona. "Thin privilege disguised my eating disorder for a long time," they say.

When they finally did lose enough weight to raise red flags, thin privilege also ensured they got treatment. They spent their late teens and early twenties in treatment for anorexia nervosa so severe that it led to kidney and heart failure before they achieved recovery—in a bigger body. Four years later, they relapsed. But this time, even though they lost 25 percent of their body weight, they were still heavier than they'd ever been during their earlier admissions. In Harrop's very first hospitalization at a lower weight, "I was carried on a golf cart from room to room because the doctors thought my heart was too unstable for me to walk safely," they recall. "When I was treated at my higher weight, I had the same heart condition—and I was encouraged to hit the gym a few times a week." During that inpatient stay, Harrop says, one therapist walked them into a room full of thinner patients and said, "They *need* to be here. Look at yourself. You're going to be fine." For Harrop, finding true recovery meant accepting that they now live in a larger body. It has also meant mourning their loss of thin privilege.

THE INTERSECTION OF PRIVILEGE AND PAIN

The anti-fat bias that Harrop experienced while seeking treatment for an eating disorder in a larger body is not at all rare. It's baked into the way eating disorders are diagnosed and managed—after all, the first diagnostic criterion of anorexia nervosa is that a patient is restricting their energy intake so much that they've reached "a significantly low body weight [. . .] that is less than minimally normal," according to the most recent edition of the *Diagnostic and Statistical Manual of Mental Disorders*. As a result, just 0.6 percent of Americans will be diagnosed with anorexia nervosa during their lifetime, according to the National Institute of Mental Health. But "atypical anorexia nervosa," which has the same diagnostic checklist as classic anorexia nervosa except for the low body weight requirement, may not be atypical at all: It may impact over three times as many people. It's not surprising that atypical anorexia would occur more often than its more famous sister diagnosis: There are more people in higher-weight bodies in general, so proportionately, they should also represent more cases of just about any disease. But because atypical anorexia is only a disorder subtype, it isn't receiving the same research dollars as anorexia nervosa and is often dismissed in treatment as a less serious condition.

This misconception—that only superthin people get serious eating disorders—also reinforces one of the biggest misconceptions about thin privilege: Somehow, thin privilege must not apply to you if you hate your body or are made dangerously ill by your thinness. "Thin privilege is how other people treat you, not how you feel about your body," says Gordon. "You can have profound body image struggles as a thin person, including body dysmorphia and eating disorders. But that doesn't change the fact that other people perceive you as thin and treat you accordingly." This can be hard to absorb, especially for kids in the vulnerable preteen and teenage years, when bodies change rapidly and almost nobody feels good in their skin. And it's also true that thin children, even while they are rewarded and validated for their bodies, can end up on the receiving end of harmful body scrutiny. This is where thin privilege differs again from most other privileges. As a white person, I might perpetuate racism against people of color, but I'll never have their lived experience of it because I cannot lose my whiteness. Similarly, a thin person who has never been fat cannot understand what it's like to be turned down for a job or receive subpar healthcare because of their weight. But in our culture, even a thin person can always be thinner. We all experience some level of fatphobia.

Hallie, a tall, thin, white dance instructor, and mom of two in New York City, has painful memories of growing up in a small body: "I got a lot of 'How can you eat so much and stay so skinny!' and 'You're so skinny, I hate you!'" she recalls. "I recognize that they feel like it's a compliment because they are struggling with the opposite, but I've never experienced them as compliments. I don't like having other women's jealousy directed at me so vocally. I was always mortified by my body and by having so much positive and negative attention."

Meeting her girlfriend, Soledad, has changed Hallie's understanding of the attention she received. Soledad is Dominican, has dark brown skin and an Afro, and lives in a larger body. "I can acknowledge now, for sure, that somebody receiving negative attention for being fat is worse than someone receiving negative attention for being skinny. And that even though it's hard for me to find clothes that accommodate my flat chest, that's nothing compared to what women in larger bodies go through to find attractive clothing that fits and that won't be questioned," Hallie says. "But it's still not a comfortable conversation. Why should either one of us have to spend hours figuring out the right number of calories or protein to eat to look like what everyone wants us to look like? I would obviously rather have to eat more than to starve myself on a diet. But neither is acceptable."

Hallie is right. Neither is acceptable. But what she's experiencing isn't oppression, at least, not against her. When people tell Hallie, "You're so skinny. I hate you!" they are expressing anti-fatness, not anti-thinness. Because these comments really mean, "I wish I had the same privilege as you." Says Harrop: "Jealousy is not the same experience as shame. Nobody likes ridicule, but if we had to choose, most of us would rather be ridiculed for having a 'perfect' body than for having a fat body."

Hallie's five-year-old daughter, Amalia, is not a huge fan of Soledad. Or her parents' recent divorce. Amalia's feelings have come out in lots of ways—mostly anti-Soledad ways. "She'll say things like 'She's not our family,'" says Hallie. One morning, Amalia spilled Soledad's coffee accidentally but then refused to apologize and had a meltdown instead. Later, trying to regroup, Hallie asked Amalia why she wouldn't say she was sorry. Her response was instant: "I don't apologize to fat people."

Hallie was shocked, not by her daughter's complicated feelings about her mom's new girlfriend but by that manifestation. Her first reaction was a harsh "It's not okay to talk about people like this!" But then, she tried to suss it out: "I said, where did you get this idea that fat is bad? And Amalia said, 'Nowhere, I got it from my own head,'" Hallie says. "Is it too much YouTube? Is it conversation she's hearing from relatives? Is it something we're doing? I have no idea." What Hallie does know is that it's time to have some deeper conversations with Amalia, about a whole bunch of things. And reckoning with Amalia's thin privilege and her own layers of privilege will be part of that work. It won't be easy, of course. This is work we all need to be doing as parents, and as people. But we don't see what we need to see until someone makes us look.

CHAPTER 5

Beyond the Scale

WHEN Beth Nathan, MD, was ten years old, her pediatrician grabbed her belly and said, "Okay! Time to switch to skim milk!"

Beth estimates that she weighed "maybe four pounds more" than her friends at school at that point. I'm interested but not surprised she can still estimate it so precisely. "But it was nothing where I really thought it was an issue," she says. Up until that point, Beth had never thought much about her body. But the doctor's comment hit its mark. Beth began thinking about her weight more and more and went on her first diet in high school. "From there, it's the typical story of lots of yo-yo dieting, and feeling like as a high-achieving professional, there's everything I can achieve, except this," Beth says.

As a kid and then a teenager, Beth never met the criteria for an eating disorder. But she also never shook the expectation that she should be thinner. She continued dieting off and on through college and then medical school. And then, Beth became a pediatrician herself. As Dr. Nathan, she now works in a busy private practice in New Rochelle, New York, which means she looks at growth charts and thinks about weight and BMI every single day. She's never grabbed a kid's belly, of course. "I think having some sensitivity to being gentle and nice is how most pediatricians roll," she says. But for many years, she advised parents to cut down on snacks between meals. "When talking to kids, my general line was always, 'This has nothing to do with how you look, you are beautiful, you are wonderful, I just want to make sure blah blah blah,'" she says. "But I knew it landed flat. Kids are clever." They knew she was prescribing weight loss because she was.

Beth was also still pursuing weight loss herself. In 2017, Beth joined an online coaching program called "Weight Loss for Busy Physicians," founded by Katrina Ubell, MD, a pediatrician–turned–life coach. Ubell declined my requests for an interview, so I relied on her website to explore her program. "Have you ever wondered why it's so hard to lose weight, when you're a doctor and you're supposed to be a health expert?" Ubell says in a video called "The Problem" on her website. "It's so frustrating when you know what you should be doing, and you just can't bring your-self to do it!" She goes on to paint a picture of "peace and freedom around food," while showing a decadent brownie followed by a sad woman in scrubs, gazing out a window. "Now, I want you to know, it's not your fault that you're an overweight doctor," Ubell says as another woman, wearing a surgical mask, gazes soberly around an operating room. "The culture of medicine [. . .] encourages us to basically ignore ourselves and our needs and focus all of our attention on other people."

Ubell notes that many healthcare workplaces fail to support doctors as they manage grueling workloads and complicated cases, and then, "con-stantly bring food around that totally doesn't serve you and is so hard to resist and avoid every day." She also blames diet culture, neatly detaching her own business from that paradigm: "I found myself so frustrated with the diet industry for not creating something that would work for a doc-tor like me." And she taps into the paradox that Beth had been wrestling with since childhood: "You might really be frustrated with yourself for not being more disciplined," Ubell says. "I often felt like it doesn't make sense that I can be so disciplined and so accountable to everybody else in my life, but when it comes to doing something for me—I'm probably not going to do it. [. . .] So many of my clients feel so disgusted with the body they've created; they're disgusted with themselves; there's an element of self-loathing and hatred toward themselves that they don't know how to shake."

Of course, Ubell has the solution to all those frustrations: Pay $7,000 for her six-month online coaching program, which she claims has helped "nearly 1,000 women physicians" lose weight and "keep it off permanently." (That's a bold claim for someone who only got in the weight loss business officially in 2016.) She promises to help clients stop eating for any reason other than fuel and preplanned pleasure, to stop "self-sabotage," and to navigate the impostor syndrome and perfectionism that she sees as rampant among the doctors she helps. Living this way won't just result in weight loss, Ubell claims; it also makes her clients happier, improves their relationships, and solves their work/life balance struggles. "I can even help you make more money," she says.

All of this is straight out of the diet industry playbook: Identify all the stresses and problems in your target customer's life and promise that they will be magically fixed once the weight comes off and real life can begin. Ubell comes across as smart and firm in her videos, but also warm and somehow relatable, especially, if you are also a smart, successful physician who likes to be firm but warm and great at taking care of everyone else. Beth absolutely connected. "There were a lot of amazing things about her program," she tells me. "Before I did it, I was like, I kind of wish I never went to medical school, and now I'm like, I have the best job in the world. I love being a pediatrician. Burnout mentality made it hard to see a way to show up wholeheartedly, and she made me work on figuring that out." Beth also loved that every person in her coaching group was also a woman doctor: "It was this little club where we just got each other." And she lost a significant amount of weight in just a few months. "I felt like the gold star student," she says.

But when it comes to food, it turns out that Ubell's plan is, very much, a diet: "The approach was all about intermittent fasting, plus meal planning and eating very low carb when you do eat," Beth says. She wasn't allowed to eat emotionally anymore because she was barely allowed to eat. "Every night, you plan out what you're going to eat the next day and then you just eat that because you're someone who is committed to honoring yourself," Beth explains. "So, if the pharma rep comes by with lunch, but you packed a salad, you eat the salad because you're in integrity with yourself."

After a few months of being in integrity with herself, Beth says, she stopped menstruating. Her hair began to fall out. She had no sex drive. She couldn't sleep. And she developed high cholesterol from so much fasting. Colleagues voiced concern: "They were like, 'I don't know what happened, but this is too much,'" Beth says. "Which, in retrospect, was very brave of them, to not just automatically congratulate skinniness." After a few months, Beth realized she couldn't sustain the restrictive eating style of Ubell's program. She found herself binge eating entire containers of nuts from CVS on her lunch break and feeling totally out of control. She found a therapist who helped her understand how this kind of eating was a response to fasting, and slowly, Beth began to work herself toward a less-fraught place with food. In the process, she regained most of the weight she had lost. "So here I am," says Beth. "Exactly where I started."

Ubell's program, which she has described as a multimillion-dollar business, is part of a cottage industry of doctors–turned–life coaches who sell weight loss (and life coaching) to other doctors. Over twelve thousand doctors participated in an online group called "Women Physicians Weigh In" in 2018, according to their website. They don't specify how many of those doctors pay only the $10 annual website membership and how many pony up $500 per month to participate in an online accountability group, where they complete workbook pages, post photos of what they ate, and report the results of their weekly weigh-ins. But I found around a dozen similar programs offered by doctors–turned–life coaches in one quick Google search. Diets for doctors is a smart business model because it turns out that an awful lot of physicians desperately want to lose weight.

Thirty-four percent of doctors classified themselves as "overweight" in a 2014 survey of over thirty-one thousand American physicians representing twenty-five medical specialties. Eight percent said they were "obese." Rates were highest among general surgeons, gastroenterologists, and family medicine doctors, where almost half of providers identified as overweight. A little over 20 percent of doctors in larger bodies said they were actively restricting calories, doing Paleo, or following another weight loss plan, but a nearly equal percentage of doctors in thinner bodies said they were following the same kinds of eating plans, which suggests that dieting is common across the medical profession, regardless of weight status. In a survey of 873 members of Women Physicians Weigh In conducted by Michigan University researchers, 72 percent said they did intermittent fasting, 46 percent were on a keto diet, and 26 percent were trying to eat low calorie and low carb. And they all said that they were likely to recommend the diets they were using to their patients.

Beth says that tracks with her anecdotal experience. She's remained friends with many of the women she met through Ubell's coaching program, but now they make her a little sad. "I found this core group of really wonderful, accomplished, intelligent, amazing physicians who are every day saying things like, 'Oh my God, I'm so bad, I ate this,'" she says. "I just want to say, 'What if you're just great the way you are? What if you just already have it all?' But I think they feel like they can't show up for their patients in that body and not be judged."

None of this is obvious to parents, let alone kids, when we show up for the annual well visit and a nurse pops our child on a scale. We may not be conscious of judging our pediatrician's body size—though we likely are—or of how they might be struggling with their own relationship to weight. But we do notice when a pediatrician seems to be judging our child's body size (or our own) as they discuss our child's BMI and growth trajectory. We may remember our own childhood experience with a belly-grabbing, skim-milk-prescribing doctor, or we watch our child absorb a stray comment like "Let's watch the beige foods" (advice I was given for one of my kids at her eighteen-month checkup), or "maybe less juice, Mom," and wonder how deeply it will embed in their sense of themselves. We may also feel like we must follow such advice because it's coming from a doctor we've otherwise learned to trust and respect, or because it's coming from a doctor, full stop. But before we do that, it's worth understanding the broader context doctors are operating in, and the way that anti-fat bias informs their thinking and medical practice. I say this not to discourage you from trusting your child's doctor, or doctors in general. But we can recognize that doctors exist in the same diet culture we do—and are perhaps even more vulnerable to its messaging.

DECONSTRUCTING PROVIDER BIAS

Andrea Westby, MD, practices full-spectrum family medicine at a University of Minnesota clinic in Minneapolis. Around three years ago, she stopped routinely weighing her adult patients. "It is pretty radical and I'm a little surprised, since I do work in a larger health system, how easy it was for me to ask my medical assistant not to weigh my patients, and she just doesn't," Westby says. She does check weight in a few specific circumstances, such as patients with heart failure, where fluid levels need to be monitored, or who are in eating disorder treatment. But for the most part, not weighing patients frees Westby up to have very different conversations with them. "Without a weight in front of me, I can focus entirely on health-promoting behaviors," she says. "It creates a more collaborative relationship with families, and we can talk about what's going well, or what might help them."

Westby is aware that her approach might make colleagues uncomfortable because a few years ago, it would have made her uncomfortable, too. Like Beth, Westby had a childhood doctor say that her weight was too high: "Even though I was in three sports, and we ate healthy foods at home," she notes, "I still got the message that there was something wrong that I needed to change." She says that experience led to a passion for health and nutrition that "was actually driven by disordered eating"; and like Beth, it wasn't until well after she became a doctor that she found a therapist who could help shift her thinking and begin critically evaluating the messages she had absorbed around weight and health. But it was difficult to heal her own relationship with food while still practicing medicine the way she'd been taught.

Doctors are steeped in diet culture, says Westby, and that impacts how they look at data, and the conclusions they draw. Indeed, every MD is taught in the same, weight-centric medical model. Research shows that future doctors come into medical school with plenty of built-in fatphobia. One 2019 survey of four thousand medical students found that nearly 75 percent displayed implicit bias (internalized beliefs we aren't aware we hold), and roughly two-thirds demonstrated explicit bias (beliefs we verbalize and use to make decisions). Thinner medical students and male medical students, as well as those working in specialties versus primary care, were more likely to show this bias. And the curriculum and conversations that happen within medical school can confirm and reinforce those biases: The researchers found that students' explicit bias increased, on average, during their time in medical school. One way this happens seems to be through a sheer lack of nuance: "From the very beginning of medical school, when we talk about risk factors [like obesity], we talk about them as if they are inherent and causative," says Westby.

Rebekah Fenton, MD, an adolescent medicine fellow and pediatrician in Chicago, agrees. "You hear all the time that correlation does not equal causation, except when you're learning about obesity research," she says. Then, the idea that high weight causes poor health is never questioned. For Fenton, a Black doctor in a larger body, who grew up with a pediatrician father and nursing professor mother who also live in larger bodies, that experience was particularly disorienting. "The assumption in every lecture on obesity seemed to be that they were talking to an audience who wasn't personally affected by this," she says, recalling presentations that featured photos of people in larger bodies eating fast food. "I've heard professors and colleagues make stigmatizing comments about large bodies, maybe thinking it doesn't apply to me. But it does, or it applies to someone in my family. I would leave those lectures and feel like, 'I have to go straight to the gym.'"

The bias nurtured in medical school is then continually reinforced for most providers as they enter the workforce because so many protocols and treatments revolve around weight management—and because our culture still treats doctors as the smartest and most important people in any healthcare context. "There is a power imbalance in the exam room, and that influences how much people are willing to talk about their concerns, what people are going to ask for, and whether or not they even expect to be understood," said Hilary Kinavey, MS, LPC, a therapist who specializes in the treatment of disordered eating, when I interviewed her for Health.com in 2021. Kinavey is a cofounder of the Center for Body Trust, a nonprofit organization in Portland, Oregon, which offers workshops, retreats, and e-courses for healthcare providers on trauma-informed and weight-inclusive care. She argues that this power imbalance means the onus must be on healthcare providers to recognize how their privilege limits their ability to help the person in front of them.

Instead, all too often, providers view patients in bigger bodies (as well as poor patients, disabled patients, and patients of color or non-conforming gender identities) as problems to fix. And when their weight loss prescriptions don't work, doctors view those same patients as noncompliant and uncooperative. One healthcare provider told me the story of a doctor colleague who was frustrated by how many of their pediatric patients had gained weight during the coronavirus pandemic. "How hard is it to just eat salad for lunch?" the doctor said, fuming. To the suggestion that making and eating salad every day might not feel accessible for busy working families on tight budgets, she replied, "There are ten places near my house where I can go pick up a salad!" And in this way, a patient's perceived failure serves to confirm provider bias, rather than sparking a much-needed examination of it.

CAUSING HARM

When Fenton began her pediatrics residency, she says that once again, weight bias was front and center in her training: "It was growth chart, growth chart, growth chart," she recalls. "Always look at it, always bring it up." Then one day, she brought up the growth chart to an eleven-year-old patient who was starting puberty and had gained a significant amount of weight since her last visit. "She started crying," Fenton says. "And it took me right back to crying myself when I saw my own doctor in college, after gaining some weight." Fenton's doctor was unnerved by her reaction and didn't say anything to reassure her that weight gain is normal in the late teenage years. Which it is; although the CDC's pediatric growth charts stop at age twenty, their curves are still trending upward rather than flattening out in these last years of childhood. "She just sat there awkwardly while I cried," Fenton recalls. "So then, fast-forward to this patient crying, and here I am, the perpetuator of that."

Fenton tried to emphasize to her patient all the great things her body could do, like play soccer, which the girl loved. But she didn't feel like she had the tools she needed to navigate the conversation without making everything worse. That's a sentiment I heard from almost every pediatric provider I interviewed, including the ones who treat my own kids.

Michelle Patrick is a pediatric nurse practitioner in private practice in Poughkeepsie, New York, and a provider I wrote about in my first book, the one who spotted my older daughter's dusky blue lips and fingernails at her one-month well visit. Patrick also noted that Violet had lost weight since her previous checkup and knew that we needed to be in an ambulance, on our way to emergency heart surgery. I share this to underscore how brilliant Patrick is at her job, and to acknowledge that clearly, there are times when a weight change is a symptom of an urgent problem. And yet, when I asked her recently how she discusses weight with kids past the newborn stage, she admitted it was a struggle. "I've always had a difficult time talking about a child's weight. Because I don't know how to do it without being harmful," Patrick says. "And I've heard a lot of kids, however many years later, saying they developed disordered eating because of something said at a well visit at our practice. And that is not freaking okay."

It's not just her practice. The American Academy of Pediatrics' 2016 clinical report previously discussed in Chapters 2 and 3 advises doctors to avoid discussing weight and weight loss with their adolescent patients because they might "misinterpret obesity prevention messages" and start dieting. But maybe kids and parents aren't misinterpreting what their doctors say, so much as directly absorbing their anti-fat bias. After analyzing audio recordings of 208 patient encounters by thirty-nine primary care physicians, researchers found that doctors established less emotional rapport with their higher-weight patients, according to a study published in a 2013 issue of the journal *Obesity*. That study and others like it were done in adult populations, but we are beginning to collect data on weight stigma in pediatric care, too: A 2016 survey of 308 nurses and support staff at an urban, pediatric hospital found that both groups expressed weight-based attitudes toward their patients in larger bodies, and that the support staff felt particularly negative about the experience of caring for those patients. They were also more likely to believe that body weight is controllable, a common misconception that then leads providers to blame patients who "fail" to control their weight.

Ironically, this kind of stigma appears to directly impact a patient's ability to even begin to follow guidance around nutrition, exercise, and weight loss. When University of Florida researchers conducted focus groups with forty-one teenagers in larger bodies, female participants, especially, reported feeling that they had to lose weight to meet medical standards set by healthcare providers. Their healthcare providers' combination of authoritarian behavior and hurtful language caused guilt and shame for all participants, and one kid noted, "I just do not even want to try." To be clear: Intentional weight loss rarely works and poses particular risks to the physical and mental health of children, as I've previously discussed. The failure here is not that kids don't want to diet or exercise more when they feel stigmatized by healthcare providers. The failure is that providers shame and stigmatize these kids, when they should be protecting them and promoting their health.

Medical encounters like these in childhood and adolescence can erode kids' ability to feel safe in healthcare, and to trust providers; recall Elena from Chapter 1, who simply stopped going to doctors' appointments in middle school, until she needed a physical for college. This is a common response. One 2014 study found that 21 percent of patients with overweight and obese BMIs felt that their doctor "judged them about their weight"—and as a result, they were significantly less likely to trust their doctor, which caused a breakdown in communication and reduced the quality of their care. This appears to happen regardless of a patient's socioeconomic status: In a 2006 study, only 68 percent of women in larger bodies scheduled Pap smears compared with 90 percent of women in straight-sized bodies—even though 90 percent of all participants had insurance. And skipping routine checkups and other preventive care means that when patients in larger bodies finally do seek treatment, they are sicker than they might otherwise have been, which could be another explanation for the often-cited correlation between higher weights and worse health outcomes. "It's not unusual for me to see a patient who hasn't been to the doctor in ten years and now I'm telling them they have diabetes or severe hypertension or sleep apnea for the first time," Kimberly Gudzune, MD, MPH, an associate professor at Johns Hopkins School of Medicine, where she directs the Healthful Eating, Activity and Weight Program, and lead author on the 2014 paper, told me when I interviewed her about this issue for *Scientific American* in 2019. "Who knows how many of those issues could have been prevented or at least better managed with earlier care?"

WHAT HELPS

As a family medicine provider, Westby treats children as well as adults. And while she feels good about her decision to stop weighing adults, figuring out a weight-inclusive approach to pediatric care has been a little more complicated, because knowing a kid's weight is often more relevant to their medical care. A dramatic weight loss in a newborn baby is often a sign of a larger problem, as we discovered with my daughter; her heart condition made the physical act of eating too exhausting and she wasn't able to take in enough calories to grow. In older children, it can be a common early symptom of an eating disorder or juvenile diabetes, as Lizzy's family learned in Chapter 2. And on a more mundane level, most children's medications—even the over-the-counter Tylenol we give for fevers—are dosed by weight. So, pediatricians need to know how much kids weigh, at least periodically. But that doesn't mean they need to talk about it in ways that cause harm.

Both Westby and Patrick told me they've stopped reviewing growth charts with parents at every visit, unless a parent asks what percentile their child is in. Patrick likes to use phrases like "They're growing well!" or "I have no reason to be worried about your weight," to move the conversation past that part of the visit. "I can see the relief in everyone's eyes," she says. Westby agrees: "I typically don't review growth charts in exam rooms or show them to parents because I don't think it's helpful in having the conversations I want to have with my families," she says. "If I do see a significant increase or decrease in a child's growth trajectory,

I'm not going to address losing or gaining weight." Instead, she looks at weight as a clue and gets curious about what any such change might represent. And in addition to physical health issues like diabetes or a heart condition, Westby thinks holistically: Has the family experienced some sort of big disruption, like a death or a move, since the last visit? Are they having trouble accessing food? Is the child struggling emotionally in some new way? If the answer to any of these questions is yes, then that's the problem she works with the family to solve.

Westby says that not talking about weight loss is only the first step: "I think it's important to talk about the cultural myths about weight and health and be intentional in preparing families for what they might hear outside my office about the 'risks' of weight," she explains. "I want to try to find a way to inoculate my patients from those harmful diet culture messages by letting them know explicitly what the science says and supporting them to listen to their bodies and come to me with questions or concerns."

This approach makes intuitive sense, but we don't yet have much hard data to back it up. "Right now, there is so much focus [in the research] on trying to prevent children from being large rather than accepting that some of them will be," says Lesley Williams, MD, a family medicine doctor who specializes in eating disorder treatment in Scottsdale, Arizona. She coauthored a review paper for the journal *Current Opinion in Pediatrics* in 2021, which drew on the small body of evidence that does exist to outline how to adapt the weight-inclusive healthcare model known as Health at Every Size, or HAES, to adolescent medicine. I want to note here that HAES is not a perfect model by any means. Disability rights advocates have challenged the inherent ableism of assuming everyone can or should pursue health at every size. And Black and Brown fat liberation activists including Marquisele Mercedes, Caleb Luna, and Da'Shaun Harrison, and others have rightfully critiqued HAES for centering the experiences and voices of white, thin people. But for our purpose of comparing the efficacy of a weight-inclusive approach to healthcare to that of the traditional weight management model, HAES is a useful starting point. Williams argues that weighing kids less often, or not discussing numbers when you do weigh kids, is just one part of shifting how we think about weight in healthcare settings. The bigger challenge is getting providers to identify and work on their own biases around weight, as well as gender, sexual orientation, race, socioeconomic status, and ability—since all these intersecting identities are more likely to face inequity in the healthcare system. "And one hurdle to that happening is the fact that there is no potential financial gain in body size acceptance," she says. Pharmaceutical companies can't sell drugs for it; diet companies can't sign us up for body size acceptance plans. "But convincing a parent you can prevent their child from becoming fat has financial promise."

Another big change that weight-inclusive providers want to see in pediatric and adolescent medicine is more regular screening for eating disorders among all patients, not just those that fit the "skinny white affluent girl" eating disorder stereotype. "I doubt most doctors would say that kids in larger bodies don't get eating disorders, but I also think they're not stopping to think about that risk when they're treating kids in larger bodies," says Patrick. And this leads to a huge disconnect where doctors who treat adolescents are aware that anyone with a diagnosed eating disorder needs to do a blind weigh-in and avoid discussions of pounds and calories, but they also do the exact opposite with their other patients. "Why on earth do we take such a sensitive approach to one group of patients but give everyone else the regular treatment even though we know these are the details that can take someone from one end of the spectrum to the other?" says Fenton.

Fenton and Williams both advocate for obtaining consent from kids before any discussion of weight; with adolescents, providers should also ask if they want weight discussed in front of their parent or only in private. "I ask patients, 'Would you like to talk about your weight?' And if they say no, I just move on," says Fenton. "If they say yes, I talk about the problems with BMI and why I don't care about numbers." She also explains that shifting to healthier lifestyle behaviors can sometimes impact weight, but often doesn't, and that to her, that's not the point. "For some people, you can implement changes in activity and nutrition and weight doesn't change," she says. "And that's fine." Fenton also talks about eating habits and exercise with every family:

"Why wouldn't I talk to all patients about this?" she says. "It's both a disservice to people at lower weights to assume they're fine and stigmatizing to assume that anyone at a higher weight needs to make these changes."

Of course, the risk of talking about healthy habits—even if you're doing it with every kid, and without a weight loss focus—is that too often, the advice doctors give is generic, prescriptive, and unrealistic or too difficult for kids and their families to follow. Fenton likes to brainstorm with kids and parents to come up with one or two small goals that feel doable to them, whether that's eating breakfast every day or trying a new sport. "Then we discuss barriers because spoiler alert, people generally know how to care for themselves," she wrote in a popular Twitter thread. "Doctors spend so much time learning and 'educating' patients who know what to do, but may not have the time, resources, or privilege to do it. Education is most likely not the problem." Instead, she tries to figure out suggestions that feel doable, like family-friendly YouTube workouts for kids who don't have backyards to run around in. Williams also encourages providers to think in terms of health-promoting behaviors kids can add to their lives if time and resources allow—eating a serving of vegetables at lunch and dinner alongside their usual meal or reading a book in addition to their current screen time—rather than cutting things out, since the latter leads to restriction and fixation.

MAKING CHANGE

All the providers I interviewed for this chapter encouraged parents to advocate for less weight talk, even if you are working with doctors who haven't begun to evolve their thinking around weight. You can write a short note explaining that you don't want to discuss weight or BMI in front of your child (but are happy to answer the provider's questions in a private conversation), and either email it through your clinic's Patient Portal or ask the receptionist to pass it to the doctor when you check in for the appointment. You may also need to ask for a blind weigh-in (or decline to have your child weighed altogether) when a nurse or medical assistant takes your child's vitals. "I can't say for sure that every provider will respect these requests, sadly," says Patrick. But if they don't, at least your child will see you advocating for them rather than accepting a doctor's assessment of them without question. I've found myself borrowing Patrick's phrasing in such moments and saying, "We trust her body and know she's growing well," or "I have no reason to worry about her weight."

What both parents and providers eager for less weight talk have in our corner is the substantial pile of evidence that prescribing weight loss is bad for kids' health, along with a more slowly accumulating body of research demonstrating that a weight-inclusive model of healthcare can be good for it. As of this writing I could find no published studies on pediatric populations. But a 2020 analysis that assessed evidence from ten randomized control studies found that weight-neutral, HAES-informed protocols led to small improvements in adult patients' blood pressure, cholesterol, blood glucose, and hemoglobin A1c levels that mirrored what patients following a weight loss protocol experienced, though presumably without the potential for dieting's negative side effects. Other research suggests that patients treated according to HAES principles tend to exercise more consistently and eat more fruits and vegetables than patients assigned to control groups. But the measure of success where the weight-inclusive model shines—not surprisingly but importantly—is in how it improves patients' relationship with food and reduces disordered eating behaviors. "The benefits of HAES interventions on eating behavior and psychological well-being more broadly outweigh the potential risks of weight-focused care," Williams wrote in the paper she coauthored in 2021.

The power of this kind of weight-inclusive healthcare to reduce disordered eating is what should make it so appealing—but also makes it such a tough sell—to so many doctors still caught in the weight-centric medical model, as well as their own personal body struggles. Katrina Ubell is right to call out the culture of medicine for training physicians to stop taking care of themselves, to ignore their bodies' signals to eat, sleep, and pee while working long shifts. The problem is that she stops there, and sells weight loss as the solution, instead of recognizing that medicine screws up how physicians relate to their bodies because of the same set of racist, sexist, anti-fat biases that train doctors to equate weight with health in the first place.

We know that prescribing weight loss fails to improve the health of most people who try it. It shouldn't be a big leap to also realize that making stressed-out doctors temporarily thinner will not, in the long term, reduce their professional burnout caused by institutions that don't see them as fully human. Westby hopes that more change will come as healthcare institutions are, increasingly, recognizing the importance of anti-bias training to reduce healthcare disparities around race and gender identity. "I see more and more providers fully embracing the need for race and gender stigma reduction, while weight is still this sticking point," she says. "But the whole process is like this house of cards. Once you pull one out, the whole house falls; there is just no ability to fence-straddle once you realize the harm that every kind of stigma causes."

For Dr. Beth Nathan, the shift toward a more weight-inclusive model of pediatric care has been "an ever-evolving process." She still takes weights, but her nurse faces every patient away from the scale. For a while, she asked for permission to discuss weight with patients, and always respected it when they said no. But when we speak again in the summer of 2022, she reports that she's stopped bringing it up at all because she's so convinced it has the potential to do harm. "In the past two years, have I seen any kids develop type 2 diabetes or hypertension? No," she says. "But I have seen a lot of kids hospitalized for eating disorders and they often tell me a conversation with a pediatrician planted seeds."

Beth does talk with every kid about the importance of finding ways to move their body for pleasure, but she emphasizes that weight loss is not the goal. Which it isn't for her anymore, either. She schedules our Zoom session around her new passion, a weekly pickleball match, and then hops on the call sweaty and gleeful about how much fun it is to move her body without tracking how many calories she burns or calculating how much she can eat in response. "I play with this group of women in their fifties, sixties, and seventies and they're just, like, so fun," she tells me. And she loves telling patients about it. "I'll say, I was really into yoga for six months and then I got bored and now I love pickleball," Beth says. "I just want them to understand that there are infinite ways to move our bodies and none of us are going to be professionals at it, so you just need to find a way to move that feels joyful in your body."

Beth says the kids she works with seem to appreciate that weight talk is off the table in her office. "Sometimes, the parents still want to know their child's weight, and I'm trying to navigate that," she notes. But more often, like Patrick, she sees the whole family's relief. For parents who have spent years on the defensive about their child's body size, finding a doctor who doesn't automatically jump in with judgment and prescription is enormously reassuring. "I'm still deconditioning myself to think, *Yes, I still did a good physical even if we didn't talk about their weight*," says Beth. "It still feels slightly illicit. Am I allowed to just totally flip this paradigm, after thirty years of life and ten years of medical training? Can I do that and still be a good doctor?"

She won't be the same doctor. But she might be a much better one.

PART 2

. . .

"ARE YOU SURE
YOU WANT TO
EAT THAT?"

CHAPTER 6

What We Teach at the Dinner Table

GROWING up in Saskatoon, Saskatchewan, Canada, as one of four kids in her family, Kirsten spent a lot of long nights at the dinner table, refusing to clean her plate. "We were a 'sit at the table till it's done or get sent to bed early because you didn't finish' kind of family," she says. "And I was a picky kid who could absolutely taste it when my mom tried to hide vegetables in the pasta sauce." Kirsten also resented that her parents made her drink a glass of water before she could have a glass of juice: "I wished it was the other way around because the juice left a residue in my mouth I wanted to rinse out," she says. And she hated that she was only allowed to eat dessert if she finished her dinner.

When I meet her, Kirsten is thirty-six, an archivist and a mother of a four-and-a-half-year-old named Sophie. She sympathizes with the pressure her parents were under to feed four kids, often on only one income. "I'm sure it was super tricky to feed everyone in a way that would make everyone happy, and I don't blame my parents for that, or for not wanting to waste food," she says. And there are good food memories, too: "My mom is a great and prolific baker, so we always had delicious baked goods available outside of mealtimes." But her parents and grandparents were often critical of Kirsten's aversions to mixed-texture meals like lasagna and beef Stroganoff, and Kirsten knew it. "I tried hard to be a 'good kid,' and a big part of that was forcing myself to eat foods I didn't really like," she explains. "There were some I could never bring myself to eat. But I was forever trying not to be 'difficult' around food."

When it came time to introduce Sophie to food, Kirsten says she didn't know how, exactly, she wanted to go about it—but she knew what she didn't want to do. "I remember how awful and unfair it felt to see meals where I didn't like any of the parts, and then feel forced to eat them anyway, or be hungry," Kirsten says. "I just really wanted to make sure that I didn't do what I experienced."

Friends who already had kids old enough to be eating solid food told Kirsten to check out Ellyn Satter's Division of Responsibility in Feeding model. Satter, a registered dietitian and family therapist, developed this approach (more commonly known as DOR) in the mid-1980s, very much in response to the "clean plate club" school of parenting that Kirsten grew up with, and that continues to underpin a large part of how we interact with kids around food. That ethos didn't develop in a void; the importance of cleaning your plate is a message often hammered hardest in homes where there isn't a lot of extra food to waste, or where food scarcity has long been a part of the family story. My own grandmother, who turned thirteen the day World War II was declared in England and survived the next fourteen years of food rationing, was then understandably horrified when my mother, a postwar picky child, refused to eat cake or finish her Sunday dinner, and even more unimpressed when I eschewed a homemade shepherd's pie in favor of peanut butter and jelly on crustless white bread during my 1980s childhood.

But the belief that children should eat any food put in front of them, without complaint, doesn't allow for much individuality of preference. And worse, it frames eating as a moral and a behavioral issue. Kids are labeled early as either "good" or "bad" eaters. And those labels are hard to shake. When the goal of family dinner is clean plates, then a child's refusal to eat certain foods is perceived as rude, disrespectful, wasteful, or rebellious. No matter what motivation drives it, demanding clean plates is, at its core, a lesson in control. It's a parent saying to their child, *I know what's best for your body. You need to put this in your body even though you don't want to—because I said you should.* And this is where the "clean plate club" can become dangerous. Because we're also communicating, on some level, that kids shouldn't trust their bodies. We want them to ignore their desire to stop eating and put more of the food we've made in their mouths; to chew, swallow, feel it slide down their throats. There is a straight line for many people from these kinds of high-pressure dinner tables to allowing diet culture to control how and what they eat. And this is especially true when "clean your plate" is mixed together with "but don't get fat." When we take control of how much our children eat, we may inadvertently be setting them up for a lifetime of not feeling in control of their bodies.

Most parents aren't consciously deriving some sort of sadistic pleasure from forcing their child to finish their broccoli. In fact, every parent I've ever interviewed about force feeding has ranked it as one of the most unpleasant acts of parenting. Staying in control of what and how much your kids eat just feels like the right thing to do. But we now have scientific evidence to confirm what so many parents understand anecdotally after a few hundred family dinners spent trying to persuade a child to eat: Pressuring kids to eat doesn't work, by just about any measure. It doesn't make them eat more. It doesn't transform them into healthier, happier, or more eclectic eaters. And neither does restricting their access to the foods we want them to eat less.

The best evidence for the twin failures of pressure and restriction is the developmental psychologist Leann Birch's landmark 2006 study, which showed that when kids were told they had to eat their soup to earn dessert, they ate less soup overall and liked it less than kids who were allowed to decide for themselves how much of each food to eat. Other research has found that many children need to see a new food ten to twenty times before they will even consider eating it, let alone like it. That's "see" without any requirement to eat it. And even that range is just an estimate: I've shown my younger daughter pasta with red sauce at least once a week for the five years she's been alive, and she still wants her noodles plain. We don't really know how long it takes to learn to like a food—and that probably shouldn't even be the goal, at least not for every child with every food.

Most of us don't grow up to love the vegetables we were forced to eat as children. But while, for many kids, the pressure to eat broccoli as a child eventually fades into an unpleasant memory, for others, these experiences can factor into lifelong struggles around food. And even when the pressure-to-eat experience itself doesn't register as profoundly damaging, we may still absorb an insidious message about how much we're allowed to control our own bodies. Without ever intending it, we're normalizing the idea that it's okay for somebody else to dominate your body, to decide what you put inside it—if they love you.

Kirsten was relieved to discover that Satter argues for an entirely different approach, and instead tries to understand a child's eating preferences from a developmental perspective. "Trust your child to eat," Satter counsels on her website. "Your child wants to eat, and they want to grow up to eat the food you eat. [. . .] Sooner or later (maybe even months or years later) they will eat almost everything you eat."

The key is to remove the power struggle. Instead of counting bites or negotiating over which foods on the table get consumed and how much, Satter encourages parents to divvy up mealtime responsibilities with their child, according to the child's developmental readiness. Young children are naturally curious and want to explore the world, but also need constant reassurance that we're keeping them safe. This push-pull of independence and attachment encapsulates the entire experience of childhood—so parents who force kids to eat new foods, or certain quantities of any food, are setting themselves up for a losing battle. Instead, Satter puts parents in charge of choosing what foods get served at each meal and tells us to decide where and when eating happens. She casts an eye toward nutritional balance, by encouraging parents to serve treats with a glass of milk, and to put individual servings of cookies or other dessert items on the table alongside the rest of the meal. But children are entirely responsible for how much they eat at every meal and snack— including which foods they eat, from what you've offered. "It was super helpful to have someone say, 'They actually don't have to eat it,'" says Kirsten. "That resonated immediately, and still resonates quite hard."

It resonated for me, too. As I wrote in my first book, the ethos of body autonomy that informs Satter's model helped us to support my older daughter when she had to learn to eat again after undergoing medical trauma as an infant with complex congenital heart disease. For Violet, eating only felt safe when she could do it on her own terms. When we came at her, however gently, with bottles and spoons, it felt too much like the well-intentioned but suffocating onslaught of tubes and other medical interventions she experienced regularly throughout her first years of life. It was only when we turned our attention away from whether she ate, and instead made family meals something that happened around her, that she was able to begin to explore food in a pressure-free way. Understanding that it wasn't my responsibility to make her eat liberated me. I still find it valuable to revisit DOR whenever we hit a rocky stretch of grouchy family dinners; to remember that my jobs are to offer food and provide the overall feeding structure—and that those jobs are hard enough on their own, without me heaping on expectations and pressure around what and how much to eat. For several years after our success with a DOR-inspired approach, I championed Satter's work in articles for the *New York Times*, *Parents* magazine, and other outlets.

But not everyone has the same kind of epiphany when they try DOR. It's worth noting that for a child struggling with a restrictive eating disorder, DOR can't and doesn't work, because the eating disorder brain can't decide "how much" to eat. But even in families where it could be useful, the approach can feel both too permissive and too rigid, depending on your own relationship with food and bodies. To a "clean plate club" parent, the idea of letting kids eat three helpings of pasta while requiring none of broccoli may feel wanton. To a parent like Stella, from Chapters 2 and 3, who has a kid like Phoebe, sneaking food regularly, Satter's advice that parents declare "the kitchen is closed!" in between meals and snacks (in order to ensure that kids come to the table hungry) feels counterproductive. "It's a useful idea, to say kids should sit down to a satisfying meal or snack and not just graze, but I feel like something changes when it becomes a rule," Stella says.

Phoebe was eight when Stella tried to implement DOR structure; old enough to know why her parents were anxious about her seemingly insatiable drive to eat. The pressure to eat differently was there, in the air around them, even when Stella didn't say a word. "I think Satter is the best method we have, and I feel Satter did not work for our family," Stella says. "I think any model that tells parents not to say anything—because if you say anything, your kid will get the message that they're doing something wrong—is a model that ultimately won't work. Because it's asking parents to be perfect, all the time."

Kirsten also felt the pressure to be perfect all the time. And that meant that assuming the full responsibility for which foods her daughter would be offered at each meal became wildly anxiety-provoking. "I really wanted my kid to have a good relationship with food and her body and to make sure she was getting everything she needed in terms of nutrition," Kirsten says. "It felt like the stakes were just so high." If Kirsten's partner, Scott, served toast for breakfast, she would worry that she had planned to make sandwiches for lunch, and that Sophie wouldn't be getting enough variety if she ate bread at two meals in a row. And she worked hard to cultivate a facade of not caring when Sophie rejected many of the foods she offered, but inwardly she would panic and obsess. "I was constantly thinking about what we needed to eat and grocery shopping and how to make sure she was getting all of the nutrients she needed in a day," Kirsten says. "I started to wonder, *Is this how people feel when they have an eating disorder?*"

When I run these scenarios by Ellyn Satter herself, she's not surprised. Now eighty, Satter has worked with thousands of families and seen the full gamut of ways that parents and kids can chafe at the DOR model. And when this happens, she thinks parental mindset is most often to blame: "Parents really have to be following the Division of Responsibility correctly," she tells me. "They cannot secretly, in their heart of hearts, be wanting their child to eat less. They have to really, really trust their child to eat what and how much they need."

Satter knows that this is a leap of faith for most of us; that it requires steady nerves to watch our children inhale Oreos and only Oreos or ask for thirds and fourths of pasta while ignoring their chicken and vegetables. But she wants parents to stay the course. "If the parents are giving and taking away, or not quite putting on enough cookies to let the child get filled up, or saying cookies only on Sundays, or saying you can have ice cream but first eat your vegetables," she explains. "I mean, there are all kinds of ways of putting the hook in." I agree with Satter that all these subtle cues can undermine a kid's trust that we'll let them eat as much as they want. And I agree with Stella that a model that only works when parents can completely divest themselves of a diet mentality won't work for many families. And Satter blaming parents for not doing DOR "correctly" feels a little (maybe a lot) like the way diets blame dieters for not trying hard enough to be good.

Kirsten, who identifies as small fat, says she never viewed DOR as a tool to control Sophie's weight. "I have no fear about my kid being fat someday," she says. "It's always been about me trying to give her what she needs." But this nutrition perfectionism is difficult to untangle from our ideas about kids' body size. The reason the "clean plate club" parent worries about the three servings of pasta is because we've been taught that eating too many carbohydrates is unhealthy because it leads to fatness. The reason that Phoebe interpreted a "kitchen's closed" rule as restriction and responded by sneaking food is because she had already internalized the idea that her body size was a problem in need of management. Fatphobia can be an overt driver of a parent's feeding practices, leading parents to resort to high-pressure or restrictive tactics. But it can also show up in far subtler ways, even for parents who are sure they have the opposite goal. So we can't start to envision a better way to feed our kids until we understand how our anti-fat bias has been showing up, night after night, at the family dinner table.

FATPHOBIA. IT'S WHAT'S FOR DINNER.

One way we know that anti-fat bias informs our expectations for family dinner is because the cultural value of family dinner is so often defined through its ability to prevent kids from getting fat. "Lower rates of obesity," along with more coded phrases like "healthier eating patterns" and "prevention of overeating" show up on every list of family dinner benefits from organizations like Stanford Children's Hospital and the Family Dinner Project, a nonprofit initiative from Massachusetts General Hospital, both of which are frequently cited in morning show segments, on parenting blogs, and by other media. And studies about the link between family dinners and "obesity prevention" are always guaranteed a flurry of media buzz. One 2011 evidence review found that eating at least three family meals together per week was associated with a 12 percent reduction in "the odds of overweight." A more significant finding from the paper was that family meals reduced a child's risk for disordered eating by a full 35 percent—but the researchers' own press release led with "family meals promote healthier weights," and the media coverage followed suit: "More Time at Family Dinners Might Curb Obesity in Kids," reported MedicineNet.com.

But the research linking family dinners to lower body weight does not establish a causal relationship. And even if it did, this framing ignores how family dinners can be nightmare scenarios for kids in bigger bodies. In 2014, when researchers at the University of Minnesota asked families of 120 children to record eight days' worth of meals, and then studied the way families interacted at the table, they found that kids with higher BMI were more likely than their thinner counterparts to experience meals filled with what the researchers described as negative experiences like hostility, indulgent or permissive parenting, inconsistent discipline, and food-related lecturing. Parents of bigger kids were more likely to talk constantly about food, to use pressure or issue threats to get their child to eat certain foods (and eat less of others), and to inconsistently discipline their kids around food. Meanwhile, the family meals of thin kids tended to be warmer, more communicative, and enjoyable for both parents and child.

The study only documented correlations not causations; researchers found no evidence that kids' bodies caused parents to be more negative. And they also didn't show that parental mealtime hostility was making kids fatter, as opposed to responding to the bodies kids already had. But *Time* magazine staff writer Alice Park summarized the study's findings by noting, "The current data suggests that simply sitting down at the same table at the same time isn't enough to influence obesity," as if parents should be motivated to speak with more kindness to their children to make them thinner—rather than to avoid hostile meals, which are in and of themselves objectively stressful for any child to experience. And as if any savvy kid wouldn't already know if weight loss is an unspoken goal of their family mealtimes.

What the University of Minnesota study teaches us is why making "obesity prevention" the mission of family meals only makes family meals miserable for all involved—and, potentially, quite traumatic for kids whose weight is already subject to this kind of parental scrutiny. What would happen if we removed "obesity prevention" as a goal for family meals? This could mean that more kids would experience meals like the thin kids in the study: warm, supportive, and full of positive reinforcement. When researchers analyze the potential of family dinners to provide a kind of refuge for kids, they document all sorts of positive associations: better vocabularies and early literacy skills for younger kids, lower risk for developing depression, less substance abuse, and less harmful emotional consequences for teenagers who experience cyberbullying.

But we can't overlook the role of privilege in this. It's unlikely that eating together is in and of itself so powerful that it can prevent teen depression, and far more likely that the families who have the time and resources to make family meals a priority also have other privileges that enable them to enrich their kids' lives and support them through rough times. In other words: If you're able to worry a lot about getting family dinner "right," you are likely operating from a place where your kids are already at less risk for the kinds of struggles that family dinner evangelizers claim it can solve.

And yet getting family dinner "right" often feels like one of our most important parenting priorities. Our discourse around family dinner, especially on social media, worships its potential without acknowledging how difficult, if not impossible, it can be to execute for many families. Work schedules (especially for parents who do shift work), daycare pickups, and after-school activities may have everyone arriving home late, cranky, and hungry, if they're home in the evening at all. Parents are supposed to somehow put together a home-cooked meal—a project that requires advance planning and shopping before you even get to food preparation and factoring in what your picky eater is or isn't eating this week—while also balancing kids' needs for attention or homework help. Everyone (in my house, at least) reliably wants a snack fifteen minutes before the meal is served. And someone has to do the dishes afterward.

Of course, family dinner could be way less of a project. Eating take-out or fast food or bowls of cereal together, with at least some members of your immediate family, is still a family dinner. Skipping the ordeal of coordinating everyone's schedules for six p.m. on weeknights in favor of a Saturday morning diner breakfast is still a family meal. But a big part of the labor of family dinner is the work it takes to make it nutritious. And mastering family meals that meet our increasingly impossible standards for good nutrition is hard in large part because "nutrition," especially for kids, has come to mean "obesity prevention." That means we think of food as something we should be consuming less of, when in fact: "The most important nutritional need children (and adults) have is getting *enough* food," says Katherine Zavodni, MPH, RDN, a registered dietitian and nutrition therapist who specializes in disordered eating in Salt Lake City, Utah.

For families dealing with food insecurity, or a child with a restrictive eating disorder, the reality may well be that kids aren't getting enough food and are at risk for nutritional deficiencies that impact their growth and health. But when kids are getting enough to eat, nutrition tends to work itself out. "If your kids are growing consistently and have energy, there is no reason to suspect their nutrition is inadequate," Zavodni explains. You may need to look closely and work to put your biases aside to assess whether that's true: Remember Erin Harrop in Chapter 4, for whom eating disorder symptoms like fatigue were disguised by their obsessive athleticism, and everyone's assumptions that a thin, sporty kid was automatically healthy. But in the broader sense, Zavodni's advice is a line I think most of us should write down and paste to the fridge. Because it's true even if you think they don't get enough protein. Even if you can't remember the last time they ate a green vegetable. Even if they fill up on afternoon snacks and eat two bites of dinner. Even if they consistently measure at the very low or the very high end of your pediatrician's growth chart.

Zavodni often has to reassure the families she works with of these facts. "A child's higher-order nutritional needs for a variety of macro- and micronutrients are met much more easily than we are conditioned to believe," she says. "They don't need to be eating a cornucopia of vegetables every day. They can get what they need from a few favorite fruits." She encourages parents to think about nutrition as a need that can be met over time rather than a test to pass or fail at every eating opportunity. "The nutritional stakes of any one meal are relatively low," she notes. "But even if they were higher, we cannot accurately gauge the nutritional needs of a child's body in any given moment because they fluctuate a great deal during different developmental stages and even at different times of day."

This is not to say that parents should pay no attention to how or what their kids eat. Kids do need to be fed because they won't be developmentally ready to assume full responsibility for feeding themselves until sometime in the teenage years or later. And sharing family meals gives you a chance to check in and see how eating is going for your kids: Is your six-year-old still struggling to use a fork? Is your thirteen-year-old dropping food groups in the name of "healthy" eating? "Taking the focus off nutrition is not neglecting your responsibility to nourish your kids," says Zavodni. "It's quite the opposite. It means you're honoring and prioritizing the nourishment of your kids as an important aspect of life and well-being, which goes far beyond the nutrient profile of what's on the plate."

This kind of big-picture approach to nourishment may explain why family dinners can play a role in eating disorder prevention—which, to me anyway, is one of their strongest selling points. Kids who ate family dinners most days were less likely to purge, binge eat, or diet, according to a prospective study of over thirteen thousand kids. And parents also benefit: Mothers, especially, were less likely to diet or binge eat when families shared meals in a 2012 study of nearly thirty-five hundred economically and racially diverse parents. Again, we don't know that there was anything particularly magical about dinner per se that offered this protection; families who eat dinner together are likely connected to their kids in other health-promoting ways. It's easier, however, to envision a direct mechanism here. If you're in charge of what kids eat, serving foods that everybody likes without policing how much they eat of any one thing, and sharing that experience with them, your own eating may also benefit from that mix of structure and permission. And your kids may be less likely to experiment with disordered eating—plus, you'll be more likely to notice, and intervene, if they do. But none of that can happen when parents, consciously or not, use family dinner as a weight management tool.

WHEN DOR BECOMES A DIET

Savannah was shamed for her weight growing up and began dieting as a teenager, but says she started to struggle with disordered eating and obsessive exercise in college after an experience of sexual assault. "It was me not being able to say no," she says. "It was like, 'I'm a fat girl, I have to do this.'"

When it became clear that Savannah's oldest child, Ariel, who is now twelve, would also live in a larger body, Savannah, who now describes herself as "midfat," found herself deeply triggered by the fear of history repeating itself. "I did not want her to have the same relationship with food and body that I did," says Savannah, who is now a Health at Every Size dietitian in Matthews, North Carolina. She didn't want Ariel to be bullied or hurt in the ways she had been. She didn't want Ariel to be as vulnerable as Savannah had long felt. "I would lose sleep most nights thinking about her body." She began to try to control her daughter's access to food and to push exercise, signing Ariel up for soccer and swimming and suggesting a "family walk" anytime they needed an activity. "I was overspending and underfeeding, and not listening to what my child needed," Savannah says. Not surprisingly, Ariel, then age five, began to sneak food.

After beginning treatment for her own eating disorder, Savannah learned about Division of Responsibility and resolved to implement it with her family to break through the cycle of anxious restriction and food sneaking. Like Kirsten, she appreciated how it took pressure off Ariel and her two younger siblings. But for Savannah, DOR was terrifying because it advised more permission around food than she knew how to handle. "The idea that I'm supposed to bring doughnuts into my house—what?" she says. "I'd spent years trying to be a good fatty. To even think about doing that activates my inner child that was hand-smacked for eating doughnuts." Meanwhile she found herself getting obsessive about DOR rules—like needing to always serve cookies and other treats with milk and fruit to make the snack "balanced"—in ways that felt just like a diet. Like Stella, Savannah discovered that, for a parent who has lived with anti-fat bias, DOR can be just as restrictive as the "clean plate club" approach it's supposed to counter. "This system was developed to help parents with feeding, but it doesn't help us process our own trauma," says Savannah. "The hardest thing about DOR is being fat and doing it."

We see this tension play out most vividly in the version of DOR that circulates on Instagram. Accounts with six- and seven-figure follower counts like @SolidStarts, @Kids.Eat.In.Color, and @Weelicious are all influenced by the DOR ethos, if not full-on ambassadors for the cause. These brands pair the principle of "parents decide what to serve!" with aspirational rainbows of produce arranged on pristine white backgrounds, and, in doing so, dramatically narrow the definition of what parents should serve. When treat foods are featured, it's only in tiny, perfectly photogenic portions: one adorable mini muffin with rainbow sprinkles, or three M&M's added as garnish to a lunch featuring three kinds of fruit. Satter is exasperated by this reworking of her message. "They're not content with letting the Division of Responsibility stand," she says. "They load it up with instructions about what and how much to eat of particular foods. And of course, that spoils the utility of the model." But it's also true that Satter encourages some similar limits around treat foods: "Put one serving of dessert at each person's place when you set the table," she wrote on her blog. "Eat it before, during, or after the meal. Don't have seconds."

When I ask Satter about her approach to dessert, she readily admits that this rule "violates" DOR but says it's necessary because "children will push themselves to learn and grow with food acceptance, but they'll also take the easy way out—and dessert is the easy way out." At the same time, Satter argues that kids should be given "frequent" opportunities to also eat as much as they want of treat foods at snack times—when a tray of cookies is fresh out of the oven, say, and the aroma won't overpower your dinnertime broccoli. "The problem with the dessert guideline [at dinner] is that it creates scarcity, and with that, you get sneaking around," she says. "You have to neutralize the scarcity." But many influencers and dietitians ignore this part of her advice. Instead, they rave about the power of that single-serve "child-size portion" to give kids "strategic exposure" to treats, glossing over how much covert restriction is wrapped into such presentations. For many kids, the strategic exposure of just one cookie will feel just as restrictive as not getting the cookie at all—and maybe even more manipulative and confusing.

The "clean food" version of DOR popularized on Instagram is both a distortion of Satter's work and an unveiling of some anti-fat bias that was there all along. Satter's 1987 book *How to Get Your Kid to Eat . . . But Not Too Much* included a chapter titled "Helping All You Can to Keep Your Child from Being Fat." If kids balk at the one-portion rule, Satter and other DOR proponents advise "playing the scarcity card," where you tell kids "we only have this many cookies to share among everyone," regardless of how many cookies are in your kitchen. "This is implicit fatphobia," says Naureen Hunani, a pediatric and family nutritionist and registered dietitian in Montreal who specializes in neurodivergent children with feeding challenges, and often works with kids in bigger bodies. "We don't play the scarcity card with other foods. It's just with dessert where we think we can't trust kids to eat the 'right' amount for their bodies."

Satter's own perspective and the work of her institute have evolved over the years. As we saw in Chapter 1, she was a vocal critic of Michelle Obama's initiative to fight childhood obesity. Her more recent writings encourage a matter-of-fact, non-shaming response if your child asks, "Am I fat?" But it's unclear if Satter has ever fully acknowledged or reckoned with the anti-fat bias woven through her earlier work. "I made most of the mistakes and I learned from my errors and changed my ways," she tells me. But later she adds, "That's not to say all weight is good weight. Because if a child's weight is accelerating, that's something that needs to be evaluated." She doesn't think the solution should ever be weight loss. But I can see why fat parents like Savannah feel triggered by Satter's desire to classify weight in this way.

Kirsten is reluctant to blame Satter or the social media influencers she followed for her own rigidity around DOR. "In the beginning, I didn't have a compass and following their content helped me sort of find out where I stood on things," she says. But she also acknowledges that posts about "variety" and "balance" did feed into her perpetual sense that she wasn't "doing DOR right," especially when her partner, Scott, tried to be involved. "He knew I was doing a lot of the feeding stuff, and he wanted to take some of it on, but then, you know, he'd do it 'wrong,'" she says. If Scott made a dinner without a fruit or a vegetable in it, Kirsten would panic about the lack of balance. If he served the same fruit two days in a row, she worried about the lack of variety. "I'd think, 'We can't just eat apples all week!'" she says.

Part of the trouble is social media's universal tendency to reduce any nuanced concept into something bullet-pointed, buzzy, and quotable. But it's also an inherent failing of modern nutrition to be so reductive. The nutrition guidelines that come out of the American Heart Association, the American Academy of Pediatrics, and other major health organizations paint a picture of ideal nutrition—make half your grains whole, no added sugars under age two, and so on—that Instagram influencers then translate into aspirational lifestyle content. "I get that what they're showing is 'best practices,' but I also think that's where the disconnect comes in," says Kirsten, because influencers also want to be authentic and relatable—their success depends on the parasocial relationships they build with a loyal following. "I feel like the distinction is not always made clear between what's best practices and what's real life," Kirsten notes. "And we go there for that aspiration."

The Instagram version of DOR promises solutions to the perpetual frustrations of family dinner and feeding kids. But these solutions only work if you can organize your life and your family's eating by their rules. This ethos comes straight from Satter's model, which presents a clear right and wrong way to feed kids and, in that way, bumps up uncomfortably close to diet culture, where there are always right and wrong ways to eat. And it assumes that every family starts from the same baseline in terms of resources and abilities. This makes DOR "a fundamentally ableist framework," says Hunani. "It promises to help parents raise 'competent' eaters—but that can be deeply triggering for kids who are labeled 'incompetent' in so many areas of their lives." Hunani also worries that DOR is not trauma-informed enough for the families she works with. "These kids have experienced trauma around food and will continue to experience trauma because the world doesn't work for the way their brains are wired," she says.

Trauma around food shows up especially around questions of access to food. Like Phoebe, many of the kids Hunani works with respond with panic to being told the kitchen is closed. "That's their warning that anytime they can eat, they must overeat, because they won't have access later," she says. Others, especially kids with avoidant restrictive food intake disorder (ARFID), who tend to eat small amounts at meals because of sensory challenges or discomfort with the sensation of satiety, will be hungry again quickly and need more frequent eating opportunities than the typical schedule of three meals and three snacks. "Kids are interpreting all of our rules around food to figure out if they are safe or not," Hunani says. "And what's fine for one child will be anxiety-provoking for another." Hunani also points out that plenty of adults with functional relationships to food will grab a handful of chips right before dinner or want a cookie an hour after eating. "We can trust kids to know their hunger as well."

But it's also true that adults grabbing some chips before dinner often do so apologetically, with a self-deprecating comment about how much we're eating—even when it's an appetizer served at a party for the express purpose of feeding people before a main meal. We apologize for eating the cheese plate someone put out for us because we've been conditioned to associate any form of pleasure-based eating with fatness and shame. To what extent is that same association there when we tell our kids they can't have a snack ten minutes before dinner? Maybe not exclusively. It's also just annoying to get that question when you're working hard to make a family dinner happen. But what if we gave family meals a little less power? What if dinnertime felt less like this daily pass/fail test of our parenting success and of our ability to raise healthy, happy kids? And what if we didn't so closely tie our definition of a "healthy and happy" kid to vegetable consumption and thinness? How would we understand our kids' eating habits and our own role in shaping them then?

"HOME IS THE SAFE SPACE"

Well, for starters, our kids might, someday at least, talk about family dinners the way Amelia, seventeen, describes hers: "We always say that dinner at our house is a treat to witness, but you have to be ready for it!" she tells me. Amelia, who lives with her family in Alexandria, Virginia, eats most nights with her mom, Eliza; her dad, Todd; and her younger sister, Hazel, who is thirteen. Eliza, a former professional baker, cooks, unless Todd grills. Favorite family meals include pasta with bacon and brussels sprouts, coconut curry shrimp with rice and sugar snap peas, and pulled pork sandwiches served with cabbage salad. The conversation centers on what Amelia and Hazel have going on in their lives; a running joke is whether anyone can beat Eliza to asking them, "How was your day?" Lately family dinner is when Amelia and Eliza strategize about her college applications; Amelia plans to study musical theater, so there are auditions to coordinate, as well as essays to write. "We get to celebrate what went well with the day, but it's almost never about the food that's on the table," Amelia says.

When Amelia and Hazel eat at friends' houses, they're used to hearing parents pressure kids to finish their plates, but that pressure never appears at their house. "I go with it at other people's houses because I can't be rude, but that's always interesting," Amelia says. When I ask Amelia what's for dinner on the night we're talking, she laughs. "Oh, it's chicken, which is probably my least favorite," she says. "I'll just have to figure it out." I'm amazed she's not stressed out by the prospect of a family dinner featuring a food she dislikes. "Normally, if we don't like the main dish, we just eat the other stuff on the table," she says.

It's a skill she's honed over the years because there are a fair number of foods that Amelia doesn't like, including tomatoes, polenta, and most kinds of meat. "I struggle with texture stuff," she says. But to Amelia, being a self-described picky eater can coexist happily with being a food lover; she doesn't see her limited palate as a weakness or a source of shame. "I love to travel because I get to try different types of food," she tells me. "It's comforting to know even if I don't like one thing out there, there are so many other things I can try."

Eliza used the basic principles of Division of Responsibility with her kids from the start, even though when Amelia learned to eat seventeen years ago, almost nobody around her was feeding kids in this way. "I could have very easily gone the other way," she acknowledges now. Eliza is a registered dietitian and has a master of public health. This gives her a level of expertise around family meals that the rest of us may find daunting—and it's also worth noting that Eliza and her whole family benefit from thin privilege—but she says she also had a lot of unlearning to do from her initial training. "So much of what we learned in grad school was grounded in diet culture and fatphobia." Her previous career as a baker helped: "I think sweets bring us incredible joy," she says. "So, whenever we had to do projects where we made treats low-fat or low-sugar, I would just think, 'But why would we do this?'" And when Eliza discovered Satter's work after grad school, during her own initial work as a dietitian, she felt things click into place. "I knew I didn't want to layer in the health-ism and the pressure that I was raised with and that I saw other families doing," she says. But she also didn't buy into the hype that DOR would be a "solution" to her kids' cautious palates. "We've just never focused on 'picky' as something negative that we needed to fix," she says.

The result was a DOR-informed approach to family meals—and yes, a commitment to having family dinners as often as work and kids' extracurricular schedules allowed—but without the rigidity or focus on balance and variety that confounded Kirsten, Savannah, and so many others. "I just personally tend to not do anything especially rigidly," Eliza says. She deconstructed soups and salads to serve components separately if it made it easier for her kids to eat, or added bread and milk to the table to round out a meal that they weren't excited about. If her kids said they were hungry at a non-mealtime, Eliza would feed them if it felt practical to do so, regardless of how they had eaten at the last meal or would eat at the next one. "If you're in the car or on the way out the door, then the answer is 'No, you have to wait,'" she notes. She never bothered to plate the single portion of dessert with dinner because her kids were happier helping themselves to something sweet right after the meal. "Putting dessert with dinner, to me, is a tool to reassure kids who are overly fixated on sweets," she says. "My kids were used to getting Teddy Grahams or some other kind of cookie at lunch and a treat after dinner, so they weren't anxious about sweets."

Eliza's approach, which is similar to Hunani's philosophy, layers what they and other child-feeding experts now call "responsive feeding" onto the foundation of Satter's work. Leann Birch and other researchers began to discuss responsive feeding in the mid-1990s, but it didn't fully solidify as a concept until the International Nutrition Council sponsored a symposium on the issue in 2011. Researchers studying the importance of "responsive parenting" (when we receive and respond to our children's attempts to communicate with us) argued that feeding children with a focus on meeting their emotional needs would support their ability to self-regulate their energy intake. More recently, responsive feeding practitioners have defined their approach as:

> Responsive feeding is an approach to feeding children that facilitates autonomous eating in the context of a warm, attuned relationship, and appropriate structure. This is with a view to supporting the development of a positive relationship with food, characterised by effective self-regulation of energy intake, and optimised competence and eating enjoyment.

To the uninitiated, that might sound very similar to Satter's Division of Responsibility, and the terms are often used interchangeably in pediatric feeding literature. Many practitioners view DOR as the "best practices" method to implementing the responsive feeding philosophy. But Hunani and others argue that responsive feeding needs to go farther—to avoid the potential for rigidity baked into DOR, to empower families to make more contextual decisions and even to ditch labels altogether, and to never let perfection be the enemy of just getting people fed. Hunani also wants responsive feeding practitioners to work on accepting feeding differences rather than marching every family toward the same goal of "kids who eat everything." In practice, responsive feeding might mean adjusting the meal and snack schedule to accommodate the fact that your preschooler is always hangry at four thirty p.m., even though dinner is served at five p.m. It might mean getting up from the table to add some cheese sticks or strawberries when your child requests them—and thinking of that not as a failure that they aren't eating what you've offered, but instead, as their contribution to the menu.

A responsive approach to family meals also means accepting kids for the eaters they are rather than working ceaselessly to mold them into the sophisticated, eclectic, "healthy" eaters we want them to be. "Normalizing eating differences from the beginning is so important," says Hunani. "It's okay to say you don't like it. It's okay to say you prefer crunchy textures to sticky ones. It's okay if you only eat twenty foods; not everyone enjoys the same level of variety." Empowering kids to own their relationship with food, without apology, may pave the way to more adventurous eating in the future. Or it may just give them the confidence to enjoy food in their own way. Both are important.

Eliza's approach to family dinners hasn't inoculated Amelia against the pressures of having a body as a teenage girl in America. Amelia does benefit from thin privilege, but as a future musical theater major who has taken dance classes since childhood, she's also been exposed to higher-than-average levels of diet culture. "I'm basically going to be a college athlete. My body is what's getting me roles and scholarships, so I have to protect it," she tells me. "There are always times where I worry I'm not going to nurture it the right way, where I think, am I eating enough, or am I eating too much." Amelia attended performing arts school for two years and dreaded her eight thirty a.m. ballet classes. "It was three hours of staring at myself in skintight clothing next to people with active eating disorders," she says. "And hearing things like 'Suck in your stomach' or 'Your food is showing.'" Amelia worried about her friends who skipped meals: "They would say they forgot to eat breakfast, but that didn't always feel like the full truth," she says. "I was the friend with a breakfast bin in my room, right by the door, so people could grab an extra granola bar or an applesauce or whatever."

But when Amelia came back home, she found herself struggling, too, especially during the months of pandemic lockdown in 2020. Bored and isolated, she started following Chloe Ting, a YouTube fitness personality based in Singapore, and tried her Two-Week Shred Challenge. "It was like, oh my God, I'm starting to have abs, I should do this forever!" Amelia says. "But it also took up most of my day. And it started to feel like my day wasn't good or complete if I didn't do my workout." Once lockdown was over and Amelia started to get back to her normal routine, finding the time to work out got harder. Eliza intervened when Amelia started exercising at eight or nine p.m. "She would say, 'You're getting nothing out of this, you're just making yourself fixate,'" Amelia says.

Amelia eased up on her workout routine but says she still struggles with the pressure to make sure her body is "good enough." She says, "There's just a lot of noise coming at me right now." But she's aware that, while her friends' parents play into that pressure, limiting doughnuts or tracking workouts, her house has a different code. "For me, home is the safe space," says Amelia.

Amelia also appreciates that Eliza finds ways to say "Your body is not your value" as often as possible. "We point out the lack of body diversity and weight discrimination when we see it, and honestly, both of my kids now tend to point it out before we have to, which is great," Eliza says. "But I'm sure we could do a better job of saying clearly and out loud that her body isn't a measure of her worth as a human." Or maybe that's the message she's been giving Amelia all along, at so many family dinners, every time she respected Amelia's right to say no to a food she didn't want—and, in the process, taught Amelia that her body belongs to her, and her alone.

CHAPTER 7

Snack Monsters and Sugar Addicts

IN the spring of 2020, Dana and Harry of Grand Rapids, Michigan, responded to the onset of the COVID-19 pandemic, as most Americans did, by stocking up on their most important household supplies. They bought toilet paper, sure. But also Oreos, candy bars, and ice cream. "We are a family that believes in dessert after lunch and dinner" is how Dana puts it to me when we first begin to talk in the early summer of 2021. Her husband, Harry, is a foodie and a dedicated home chef; the kind of dad who serves homemade bread bowls for dinner on a random Wednesday. Both thirteen-year-old Ella and nine-year-old Ava brag to me about what a great cook their dad is; they especially love his pizza and noodle stir-fries. "We sit down to family dinner together 97 percent of the time because we're a very food-centric household," Dana says. "We're not hikers or athletes or musicians or whatever else. We are cookers, bakers, and eaters, so this is our thing, as a family."

There was a lot that Harry and Dana couldn't control about lockdown life: Getting the kids through remote school. Keeping their own busy careers afloat; Harry is an engineer and project manager for a software development company; Dana works in marketing and communications. Navigating the many debates around how to respond to the pandemic that circulated in their community. But they knew they could eat well. They never expected food to become the problem.

Then one day, Dana noticed that four cartons of ice cream were missing from the freezer.

She knew that she and Harry had only eaten a couple of bowls. Ava, too. Although dessert is served at both lunch and dinner at their house, the girls are only allowed to have it if they eat their main meal first. "You don't have to finish anything. But if you have room for dessert, you have room to finish your meal" is how Dana explains it. "Sometimes we compromise and say they have to finish their fruit or veggie, but we don't make them finish starches like their hamburger bun." Ava accepts the rule but also refuses to eat foods she doesn't like, so she tends to eat less dessert than anyone else in the house. "I'm okay with her approach," Dana says. "And we've always patted ourselves on the back that Ella, on the other hand, always finishes her meal because she will do anything for sugar."

Anything, including hiding candy in her room, layered between clothes in her drawers, under the mattress, or behind books, à la Claudia Kishi in *The Baby-Sitters Club*. Sneaking sodas out of the fridge after bedtime. And surreptitiously eating the better part of four cartons of ice cream over a few days, without anyone spotting her.

"The non-parent in me kind of had to admire it," says Dana. But as a parent, she was horrified, and so was Harry. It confirmed their perception of Ella as a "sweets maniac," and they worried they were at the top of some sort of slippery slope of preteen rebellious behavior. "If there is sugar, Ella will eat it," says Harry. "And it's just like, where does that stop?" He and Dana decided it would stop with them. They began locking the freezer and spent $60 on a combination lockbox that now lives in their bedroom and houses the family's stash of Oreos, candy, and other treats. The girls are still allowed to eat dessert if they finish their lunch and dinner, but now one of their parents takes them upstairs to unlock the box of treats and supervise their choice.

When I ask Ella and Ava why their parents locked up the candy, they both reply, almost automatically: "Because it's not healthy." This is the family line: Harry and Dana don't want Ella eating unlimited amounts of sugar because they're worried about her health. "Anecdotally, people who eat a lot of sugar or simple starches just don't seem to be as healthy as people who don't," says Harry. He admits, though, that he hasn't looked into the science on this. "If I were really worried about it, I guess I would do the research and know, like, if this percentage of your diet is sugar, these are the potential health risks." And the more we talk, the clearer it becomes that "healthy" is synonymous with "thin" in this family. "Right now, I'm carrying an extra fifteen pounds I don't need," Harry says. He ties his weight gain directly to the way he eats sweets, which is to say, even more compulsively than Ella: "Oh, for sure, sugar is my drug," he tells me. "Whether you want to call it my addiction or my vice, sugar is my thing. If I need a pick-me-up, I'm going to have a piece of candy." And it's never just one piece. "If there are only four Oreos in the box, I can be happy with that," he says. "But because there are fifty, I will take twelve."

Harry isn't worried about Ella's weight, though he notes she's less physically active than he was at her age. But for Dana, sugar, health, and body size are even more intertwined: "Ella has put on weight in the last few years," Dana says. Ella weighed ten pounds, ten ounces at birth and has maintained her curve in the upper 90th percentiles for height and weight throughout childhood. "She hit puberty in sixth grade, and she's now the size of an adult woman," Dana says. "I was shocked by her weight at the last checkup; it's close to mine." To be clear, Ella and her sister, Ava, both benefit from thin privilege. Dana also tells me, "I would have killed to have had Ella's legs at that age!" But the way Ella's body has changed makes Dana worry that it could become a problem down the road. "I'm agonizing over how to be less controlling with snacks and sweets, while, at the same time, not enabling her desires for sugar and more sugar," she explains. "Because I know she's already worried about her weight and that her eating habits are likely to increase her size, which will increase her worries." This is a classic example of blaming a child's weight—rather than their experiences of anti-fat bias—for their body struggles. Dana thinks that keeping Ella thin will protect her. But the level of restriction that requires will cause its own harm.

This blurry entanglement of health, weight, and body image is at the core of most parental anxieties about dessert and snacks. "When you drill down into this sugar thing, it always ends up being about fear of fatness," says Lisa Du Breuil, LICSW, a clinical social worker in Salem, Massachusetts, who specializes in the treatment of eating disorders and substance use disorders. "You don't hear parents saying, 'She ate five cupcakes, I'm so worried about her teeth!' It's, 'I don't want them addicted to sugar' because sugar makes you fat." It can be hard to face the anti-fat bias that underpins our fears about kids and sugar. It requires unlearning a lot of what we thought we knew about these foods—and letting go of some control of our kids' appetites and bodies. No wonder parents are terrified.

But the alternative, as Dana and Harry know, isn't working. "I feel like we are being insane," says Dana. "Other kids walk around the neighborhood with Popsicles and slushies at all hours of the day, and we're locking our freezer." Harry agrees. He spends his life as an engineer collecting data and solving problems and is baffled that he can't figure out a better way through this family system malfunction. "It's just crazy banana pants," he tells me. "I guarantee this is not the optimal choice for how to parent Ella." But by the time I talk to the family, the lockbox system has been in place for the better part of a year. "There's a kind of inertia to what we're doing now," Harry explains. "It's going to take a lot of emotional and cognitive energy to figure out how to do it differently." And in the meantime, Ella is continuing to sneak food. One day when I talk to Dana, she sounds particularly exhausted. "Ella had a huge meltdown last night," she tells me. She'd gone into Ella's room and found empty bowls, a mug that had gone moldy after she'd made cocoa, candy wrappers, and stray Goldfish crackers.

"It's like we're putting our finger in the dike," Dana says. "But we're not changing the overall, fundamental model."

OUR SUGAR STORIES

To understand how two smart, rational, and deeply loving and involved parents found themselves with a safe full of Oreos—and indeed, to understand how any of us have internalized our culture's fear of sugar to the extent that we have—we must first look back, to understand how Harry's and Dana's own relationships with food developed. Harry's earliest food memory is being three years old and pulling out the lower kitchen drawers to use as a ladder so he could climb up and find something to eat in an upper cabinet. He would carefully grab down a jar of peanut butter or a half-empty box of cereal and that would be what he and his older sister would have to eat that day. He doesn't have many other memories of his early childhood, though he knows his mom was struggling with addiction and that life was generally chaotic. One day when Harry was four years old, his mom dropped Harry and his sister off at their grandparents' house in Bellaire, Michigan, to be babysat for the day. She didn't come back for eleven years. "It was good for me, in the long run," he says now. "My grandparents were poor as dirt, but they both worked super hard and gave us a stable home."

Harry's grandparents' poverty meant that food was still often scarce, however, and when they did have enough to eat, it was plain and bland. The family relied on government cheese and other surplus foods. Harry's grandmother often made a big pot of what she called "boiled dinner": a hambone cooked in a stockpot with some cabbage, carrots, and potatoes until it all turned into a big mush. One of Harry's favorite meals was fried snapping turtle. "People in town would call us if they saw one on the side of the road," he remembers. "My grandma would grab it and put it in the back of the station wagon, and then my grandpa would come home and put a bullet in its head." Store-bought treats were in much shorter supply. One of Harry's first culinary experiments was something he calls "guvment candy." "You take peanut butter, honey, powdered milk, and Rice Krispies and mix it together in the right proportions," he says. "That was something I could make with stuff that my grandma didn't care if I wasted because we always got these giant jugs of honey and gallon cans of peanut butter, and we never used the powdered milk for anything."

Real candy only showed up at Halloween, or when Harry could recycle enough soda cans to buy some. "In Michigan, you get ten cents for every can you recycle, so I'd ride my bike around looking for cans on the side of the road and then take them to the grocery store," he says. "Then I'd have twenty cents, so I could go pick out twenty pieces of penny candy." Harry didn't eat it all in one sitting the way he does today; he'd make whatever candy he got last as long as he possibly could. "I'd break it down and eat the individual pieces, then eat them together, smell them, assess them," he says. "That's the engineer in me, I guess." But it was also part of the same scarcity mindset that today makes it hard to leave any Oreos in the box.

Dana also grew up craving food she didn't have, but for different reasons. She was born in South Korea and adopted at six months old by a deeply religious, working-class "very, very, very white" family in a farming community in Iowa. Her parents had also adopted Dana's older sister, Lauren, from South Korea. But while Dana had been well cared for in a foster home, Lauren came from an orphanage and was undernourished and frail. She struggled with various health issues her whole life and died young, in 2020. "She was the underweight, fragile one and I was the robust, overweight, healthy one," Dana recalls. "They were constantly worried that Lauren wasn't eating enough and that I was eating too much. I'm also the loudest person in my family, by far. So, my whole life has been lived in contrast to my quiet, underweight sister."

Dana stood out for being smart and loud at school, too—but also because she was the only Asian kid, and one of the only fat kids in her grade. She wasn't teased particularly; she says she identified as white as a kid because she didn't have any other way to identify. Her parents never traveled, spoke only English, and didn't try to keep either of their daughters connected to their Korean heritage. "Their attitude was, 'You're American now!' I still jokingly refer to myself as Fake Asian," Dana says. But she did know she was different. "I've always felt like, I'm too loud, I'm too large, I'm too talkative."

And she was always aware of the adults in her life monitoring her food intake. "They were very much about, 'Two strips of bacon and no more,'" she says. Dana's family ate three large meals a day, but snacking between meals wasn't permitted. This was partly about her weight, but even more part of the family's religious frugality: "My dad is a Baptist minister, and I definitely have this puritanical fear of excess," she says. Dana began dieting as a teenager and later lost a significant amount of weight using Weight Watchers in her early thirties. And she is among the small fraction of dieters who succeed and sustain; she has maintained most of that loss for the better part of fifteen years. She credits some of that success with the tummy tuck she had in 2016, but she also exercises almost daily and eats carefully. The same candy bar that Harry would finish in one sitting, Dana will eat a few bites of, and then let sit in the cabinet for months. Some of that is because Harry does make delicious food so often: "I'll look at a restaurant menu and think, *Eh, pretty much everything on here is something I could have Harry make anytime,*" she says. "Going out to eat no longer feels like, This is my one opportunity for amazing food."

Dana is now an adult who has learned how to take up space. She uses her intelligence and big personality to her advantage at work. She's the kind of smart, passionate friend who is always sending around thought-provoking articles and asking deep questions on the group chat. After sharing a few of my pieces with friends, she writes me long, detailed emails dissecting their different responses. But that childhood fear of excess, fear of being too much, still plagues her, especially when it comes to food. "I never eat the whole candy bar because that feels like too much," Dana says. "When Harry eats two candy bars, it's hard for me not to yell at him. I feel the same way I would about someone getting drunk or watching TV for fourteen hours straight."

Dana and Harry identify as a family of food lovers. But they are also a family where poverty, religion, and fears of fatness and excess have all intersected and informed the ways in which they, and their children, are allowed to love food. And so, Harry finds himself eating the candy that he's locked up from his kids. And Dana finds herself micromanaging both how much and how often her kids want to eat. "I have said, 'That is disgusting. That is too much!' when I see them eat more than one candy bar," she admits. Even with the lockbox, she'll find herself policing further: "We let them pick out whatever they want, and then they'll say, 'Is this okay?'" she says. "Like it's understood that they can only take one cookie, but if they're small, I'll say, 'Okay, you can have two.'"

SUGARPHOBIA MEETS FATPHOBIA

The way our kids can joyfully engage with sugar and snack foods, eating them with apparent abandon, feels, for many parents, counterintuitive to everything we've learned about "healthy eating." It can be deeply uncomfortable to watch, whether our kids are eating these foods in the same way we do, or in the way we never allow ourselves to do. And when we see kids eating sugar and then behaving badly, we attribute this to their alleged "sugar high," because we're so sure that pleasure-based eating must have a dark side. But the theory that sugar can induce hyperactivity or any other kind of high isn't supported by the research. The notion that sugar intake could lead to what was then called "the neurotic child" was first proposed in the medical literature in 1922, and later gained popularity during the 1970s, when researchers were first studying attention deficit hyperactivity disorder. But these early studies failed to control for many other factors that we know now can play a role in a child's ADHD management, including their sleep schedule, parents' stress levels, and genetics. Food routines also matter, not in terms of how much sugar kids consume but the larger context of how often and how much they eat, says Sumner Brooks, MPH, RDN, an eating disorder dietitian in Portland, Oregon, who is also the co-author of *How to Raise an Intuitive Eater*.

In 1994, researchers at Vanderbilt University conducted a double-blind, placebo-controlled trial with forty-eight kids aged three to ten, about half of whom were described by their parents as "sensitive to sugar." The kids were assigned to follow diets containing different amounts of sugar (sucrose) and the artificial sweeteners aspartame and saccharin; they and their families stayed on each diet for a three-week cycle, while having their behavior and cognitive function tested weekly. A major drawback of most nutritional research is that it relies on subjects' self-reported data, which is notoriously unreliable; we forget what we ate, or we guess or overstate how it made us feel. In this study, researchers provided families with everything they were allowed to eat, and even went so far as to remove all the other food from their homes. Then they removed packaging and other clues from the food they provided, so nobody eating it would be able to tell if it had been sweetened with sugar or an artificial sweetener. The families weren't told which diet they were trying for each three-week cycle, so parents had no idea how much sugar their kids were or weren't consuming on any given day.

The result: None of the kids, even the "sugar-sensitive" ones, showed any meaningful differences after following each diet. "Even when the intake exceeds typical dietary levels, neither dietary sucrose nor aspartame affects children's behavior or cognitive function," the researchers concluded. The "sugar high" had been officially debunked.

The 1994 results have been replicated in several subsequent studies and yet—I've never attended a child's birthday party where someone didn't invoke the specter of the sugar high as soon as the cake is cut. Katja Rowell, MD, a family physician and childhood feeding specialist, recalled how her own daughter's preschool had a "no treats in the classroom" policy, except when they celebrated "Sugar Day" once a year, when I spoke with her for a *New York Times* story in 2020: "There was so much conversation from all the adults to the kids of, 'You're going to be crazy! It's crazy sugar day!' And the kids were kind of bonkers," she said. "But there was so much anticipation of their behavior problems, it was almost like we gave them permission." Sugar doesn't make kids crazy. But constantly narrating our own anxieties about sugar is a great way to pass them along to our kids. Harry and Dana's ice cream–sneaking daughter, Ella, has certainly internalized this fear of sugar, too. One day as we were chatting, Ella mentioned she was tired because she'd spent the day working as a theater camp counselor, supervising a group of high-energy nine-year-olds. "Their parents are packing them, like, two cupcakes for lunch, and they'll have a cinnamon roll for snack," she told me. "But I guess they don't have to deal with it."

This parental fear of the sugar high in little kids rolls seamlessly into our larger cultural anxiety about the compulsivity with which many of us sometimes eat sugar. They aren't alone in this fear. The concept of food as addictive—and sugar addiction, in particular—has been wildly popu-larized by diet culture. Best-selling books like *Hooked* by Michael Moss, *The Case Against Sugar* by Gary Taubes, and *Animal, Vegetable, Junk* by Mark Bittman argue that our modern reliance on what researchers call "highly palatable" or "ultra-processed" foods is the result of predatory food marketing. They also blame food manufacturers who tinker with the sugar (and salt and fat) content of their products to make them as appealing as possible—so delicious, in fact, that we become powerless zombies in the face of these foods, mindlessly turning into the Dunkin' drive-through, or serving our kids Uncrustables and Go-Gurt so often that they become overly dependent on sweet foods and fail to develop an appreciation for the more subtle sweetness of a blueberry or a tomato.

Celebrities and influencers ranging from author Gretchen Rubin to Gwyneth Paltrow, as well as diet brands like Whole30, have taken these arguments and run with them to the point that, in many parenting circles, but especially those with relative affluence and other forms of privilege, it has become the norm to assume that good parenting means depriving your kids of sugar at every possible opportunity. We make self-deprecating "bad mom" jokes to other parents when we show up at the playground with Chips Ahoy! and fruit snacks instead of bento boxes full of produce. We tell our kids that they must eat "something real" after a day of "too much junk." We feel guilty if fast weekday break-fasts are Eggo waffles or Cinnamon Toast Crunch instead of eggs and overnight oats. A cottage industry of supplements, lozenges, and dis-solvable strips with names like "Sugarbreak" and "Sweet Defeat" prom-ise to make us, and our kids, crave sugar less. And we use our kids' sugar consumption to grade parental performance—sometimes literally.

Looking back, Abby, a lactation consultant in the San Francisco Bay Area, says she shouldn't have been surprised when her ex-husband began to use her eating habits against her in the custody dispute over their now fourteen-year-old daughter, Lucy. A year before they sepa-rated in 2015, she remembers posting on Instagram about indulging in some favorite comfort foods after a tough day at work: a Coke, Cheez-Its, and Reese's Peanut Butter Cups. "That's fucking disgusting," her then husband wrote on the post. "Fucking disgusting" is also how he described things like ranch dressing and the boxed Annie's Macaroni and Cheese that Lucy continues to adore to this day. And for many years, Abby went along with it.

"We read *Diet for a New America* back when we first got together, and it felt revolutionary," Abby says. Together they got into the legendary San Francisco foodie scene; her ex worked in a café known for its artisanal green juice and when he cut out gluten in a quest to cure his migraines, Abby agreed that it seemed to help. She also agreed to stop eating dairy while breastfeeding Lucy because they were told it would help the baby sleep. Later, when Lucy began having meltdowns in preschool, Abby dropped gluten from the family's diet. "In hindsight, I feel like it was all a placebo effect," Abby says. But focusing on her then four-year-old's diet meant Abby didn't have to look so closely at the larger issues driving Lucy's behavior: her own anxieties, a difficult marriage, and a chaotic household. "It's not a surprise she was having these huge tantrums," she says. "I wasn't able to parent in a way that was stable for her."

Money was also a huge source of stress, especially around food. "He went Paleo and would buy these super expensive cuts of meat we couldn't afford," Abby recalls. "But I'm vegetarian, so I'd be looking in the cupboard at a can of lentils and an onion, thinking, *Can I make something sort of good out of this?*" Both Abby and her ex lost a lot of weight in those years, though Abby couldn't see it at the time. "I'm aghast when I see old photos; I truly thought I was fatter than everyone," she says. She ties that body loathing directly to her anxieties around her marriage and food, and the feeling that she was perpetually failing at both.

When the couple split up three years later, Abby was initially granted 70 percent custody of then seven-year-old Lucy and says, "We had a food rumspringa." They ditched the expensive meat, the quinoa, and the gluten-free rules. Abby bought all the "fucking disgusting" foods and gloried in being able to eat peanut butter cups and put ranch dressing on everything. It was part liberation and part depression—Abby was also drowning under the pressures of a new job in tech, and the emotional fallout of her divorce. She fed Lucy and herself lots and lots of Annie's Macaroni and Cheese. "And on the weekends, we wouldn't go anywhere, we'd just stay in, watch *Gilmore Girls*, and be lazy together," Abby says. "Because I could not cope."

In 2016, her ex filed for fifty-fifty custody and, in making his case, focused intensely on Abby's lack of physical activity and how she fed Lucy. A letter of support that his new girlfriend submitted to the court notes that at Abby's house, Lucy ate "mostly boxed carbohydrates" because "nutritious foods are not often provided for her." In contrast, Abby's ex emphasized how hard he worked to teach Lucy about fruits, vegetables, and protein, and how much time they spent riding bikes together. Their judge granted him fifty-fifty custody.

Abby isn't sure how much the food critique played into the decision, but she still worries about how she'll be perceived before every court appearance. Abby began to gain weight during her post-separation "food rumspringa" and now identifies as "small fat." Lucy has reported that her dad makes jokes about Abby's weight. "So do I wear Spanx or do something else to try to alter my appearance?" Abby says. "Honestly, maybe yes. Because I don't need more things to other me in the eyes of the judge." But she won't diet again. She's fought too hard to find that freedom, for herself and for Lucy, and she wants their house to be full of foods they both want to eat.

THE TRUTH ABOUT FOOD ADDICTION

When Abby's ex labeled her favorite foods "fucking disgusting," he meant that her pleasure in those foods was disgusting—as well as what he perceived as her eagerness to eat them with wild abandon. It's not that delicious food has no impact on our brains—but it doesn't induce this total lack of control in the way that most people think. "Eating pleasurable foods does induce a dopamine response," says Brooks. Dopamine is also known as the "feel good" hormone. It surges in our brains whenever we experience pleasure, and defenders of the sugar addiction model cite this as evidence because the sugar-dopamine response can look like the response seen in the brains of people using narcotics. But we also get dopamine responses from purely benign activities like seeing a puppy, hugging a loved one, or feeding our babies. And people who feel addicted to sugar interact with it quite differently than people who struggle with alcohol or drug dependency. So-called food addicts don't endanger their children or lose their life savings to obtain their highs.

Of course, some of that might be related to how much more afford-able and accessible sugar is than, say, illegal street drugs. But it's also a function of how we engage with the substance itself. We don't tend to crave straight sugar, eaten from the bag with a spoon; we are more often drawn to foods that provide a combination of sugar, fat, and salt because they offer us a certain blend of taste, texture, and mouthfeel. "These foods feel rewarding and can induce strong cravings for many reasons, the most common of which is deprivation," says Brooks. That depriva-tion can be physical; because our bodies require glucose for survival, we will crave carbohydrates when we aren't getting enough of them. But this isn't addiction, at least, not any more than craving water when you are thirsty makes you a hydration addict. Sugar deprivation can also be psychological: "People who have been restricted, [have] dieted, or [have been] food insecure in the past may experience a constant looming emotional threat of deprivation, which makes their drive to eat sugar even more intense," Brooks explains.

This threat of deprivation may linger long after someone has begun eating enough and it's often a big part of what drives binge eating. Even if you haven't experienced significant caloric restriction due to dieting or poverty, it's virtually impossible for most of us to separate our restric-tive cultural beliefs about sugar and processed foods from our experi-ence of consuming those foods. And the studies cited by Moss, Taubes, and others as evidence for sugar's addictive properties fail to account for this nuance of the human condition. "Many studies on food addic-tion don't report controlling for whether subjects have a history of diet-ing," notes Brooks. "And yet we know the vast majority of people who struggle with food addiction are recurrent dieters." When researchers study sugar addiction in rats—creatures without diet culture—they can only show rats engaging in addictive behaviors (eating huge quan-tities, or compulsively and repeatedly pressing a lever to make more food appear) with sugar if they first inflict a diet upon them. Restriction breeds fixation.

Now that Lucy divides her time evenly between Abby and her father, Abby sees this pattern firsthand. At Lucy's dad's house, access to food is tightly controlled by adults. At fourteen, Lucy still isn't allowed to pack her own lunch even though she's done so at Abby's house since the fourth grade. Her father and stepmom seem annoyed by Lucy's choice to be vegetarian, so regularly make meat-heavy meals that she can only pick at. "She'll often tell me that she's going to bed hungry there," Abby says. Now that Lucy has two toddler-age half-siblings, her dad's stance on "boxed carbohydrates" has relaxed a bit; they, too, make Annie's Macaroni and Cheese for easy kid lunches. But her stepmom will expect one box to feed all three kids. "At my house, we make a box for each of us," Abby says. "Lucy is fourteen, not three." But Lucy is also in a bigger body, a fact that her father and stepmom seem determined to address. Their focus on teaching Lucy "healthy eating habits" leads her to regularly buying forbidden snacks from the corner store after school that she hides in her backpack to eat after they go to bed. And when she gets back to her mom's house, "she eats so much, all the time," Abby says. "It feels like this very prolonged restrict/binge cycle. And I do really wonder, if she were not deprived of food half the time, if her eating would level out."

Indeed, some research suggests that living in a perpetual state of deprivation might change how our brains respond to sugar and other highly palatable foods. When neuropsychologists placed a lemon lollipop on people's tongues and measured their brain activity, they found that the people whose brains light up the most were volunteers from the National Weight Control Registry, a long-running study of over ten thousand people who, like Dana, have lost at least thirty pounds and kept it off for at least three years. There are many theories around the secret of this group's "success," but what's clear from this and other studies is that these people can live on diets long-term in a way that most of us can't and shouldn't. In the lollipop study, these chronic dieters had the strongest neurological response to the lollipop, indicating that their brains anticipated the reward of eating it more intensely than the brains of other subjects. But they also followed up with the strongest inhibitory processing response, meaning they stopped themselves from eating the lollipop.

One interpretation of this study is that these "successful maintainers" have more self-control than the rest of us. Another is that they're constantly subjecting their brains to a kind of torture, by denying these cravings that seem to become stronger the longer they restrict. The non-dieters, on the other hand, who presumably felt like they had permission to eat the lollipop if they wanted it, craved it much less. Other research has found that chronic dieters pay more attention to food cues in advertising and product labels than non-dieters and will often eat more in response.

Non-dieters can still crave sweet foods, of course. We might associate them with certain memories or emotions; Abby and Lucy love Annie's Macaroni and Cheese in part because they ate it while watching *Gilmore Girls* during those early months of rebuilding their life together after the divorce. I love Cheez-Its and Krispy Kreme doughnuts because I grew up eating both with my Grandma Betty, and I loved when we would sit at her kitchen table with our snacks and Diet Cokes (and her cigarettes) and discuss the world. Craving foods that we learned to associate with comfort, safety, or joy is a feature of our pro-social tendencies, not a moral failing. "Sharing meals is probably our best way to bond and connect other than sex," Du Breuil told me when I interviewed her for my first book in 2017, and it's a line that has run through my head at least once a week ever since. "It doesn't make you an addict to miss that. It makes you human."

We can also use food to deal with, or escape from, negative emotions. "If someone has a drive or need to numb, dissociate, procrastinate, or avoid, sugar can be a way to do that," explains Brooks. "And that can certainly look and feel like addiction, but it's actually a coping strategy." We use all kinds of coping strategies to survive periods of stress or anxiety. Some of them, like journaling or yoga, are revered in our culture. Others are less celebrated. But it's our fear of fatness that causes us to demonize emotional eating as a coping strategy. "Fatphobia adds another layer of shame and judgment that, say, watching TV for emotional avoidance doesn't come with," says Brooks. "We don't have a national war on TV watching."

And when we zero in on food as the problem, we often ignore the underlying emotional struggle that necessitated eating as a coping strategy in the first place. I saw this one afternoon when my own three-year-old threw a tantrum because we were out of Goldfish. No other snack would do, and to the untrained eye, sure, she looked like a cracker addict. But then I looked in her lunch box and realized she hadn't finished either her lunch or her snack at camp that day. She wasn't addicted; she was hungry. And tired. And probably a thousand other emotions that are hard for anyone to articulate. If I stopped buying Goldfish because she yelled about them, I wouldn't be doing anything to help her learn to manage her feelings—and I'd very likely create even more of a fixation on orange snack crackers.

I think about that Goldfish tantrum a lot when I talk to Ella, even though she is ten years older than my child; still a kid, yes, but old enough to be taking care of other kids, to be navigating the world on her own in so many ways. When we aren't talking about food, Ella is chatty, funny, and warm. She loves musical theater and she's quick to tell me that she has recently come out as pansexual. "I'm also playing around with my gender identity," she says. "Right now, I identify as a demi-girl. Which is like, a girl, but just not fully, I guess." A few months later, Ella says she resonates more with "gender fluid." She's comfortable and confident here, fluent in the language of gender identity in a way that an elder millennial like me could not have fathomed back in middle school.

But she has much less to say when we talk about food. Sneaking food, she says, is mostly just something she used to do. "My sister and I used to take pieces of candy to eat later at bedtime. It was our way of revenge. Because there's not a lot of things you can do to get back at your parents when you're ten." She doesn't acknowledge that it's still happening, and she doesn't bring up the lockbox until I ask about it in our third conversation. Then she tries to brush it off: "I mean, I was mad at first, but it doesn't really have that big an effect on me," she says. "If I want something, they just go and get it for me. There's not a lot of good stuff in there anyway." Ella also often gives answers that sound more like what she thinks her parents want to hear: "I think it's pretty fair," she tells me when I ask how the lockbox policy strikes her. When I tell her that I'm not so sure it is, she doesn't blink. "I haven't thought that much about it," she replies coolly. It's clear that we are no longer on safe ground.

But Ella does talk about her body anxieties; she doesn't like what she calls her "bubble chin" or her "hip dips." "I make random mean comments about myself but laugh it off as a joke," she says. "A lot of girls my age do it. It's like we're bringing our friends up by putting ourselves down." And she acknowledges that her parents are much stricter about food than most of her friends' parents. Another of Harry and Dana's food rules is that after-school snacks must be fruits and vegetables, and nothing after four p.m. They want the kids to be hungry for dinner, but Ella comes home from school already starving and envies her friends who get to snack on other foods. "Quite a few of my friends get Popsicles every week, and they have a lot of chips and stuff lying around," she says. "There's just a lot more junk food than we would ever have in our house." And yet, she sounds a bit amazed that her friends seem like they can take or leave the food in their cupboards. "It's definitely just normal to them," she says. Then she returns to the safer subjects of gender identity and theater. "I'm always putting on all these fancy clothes and piling on the makeup for theater, right?" she says. "I know a lot of girls who do their full face of makeup even when they're not going anywhere. But to me, I already use it a lot, so I want to use it less. It's just there."

"Kind of like the food at your friends' house?" I ask. She nods.

"I guess I don't understand their logic," she says, and I know we're talking about her parents again. Harry's fear with Ella's sugar consumption is "Where does it stop?" But if she was allowed to eat as much as she wanted—if it was "just there" the way her makeup collection is, instead of locked up—maybe she would want it less. It's an experiment they've never even attempted, because they're so sure that taking treats away is the only way to ensure their kids don't eat too much.

WHEN RESTRICTION WORKS

But here's the thing: For nine-year-old Ava, the lockbox has had exactly that effect. And that's even scarier than Ella's understandable need to chafe against her parents' rules. "I don't really mind it," Ava tells me when I ask how she feels about the lockbox. "I like it, because it feels a lot less tempting to go grab something if it's all put away."

Ava is much more introverted than her older sister. Her passions are Cub Scouts and her ball python snake named Junior. She's happiest wearing T-shirts and baggy shorts and has never seemed to care much about her appearance. But for a while now she has been trying to stop herself from grabbing too many treats. She tells me that she began wondering, "Am I too fat?" when she was seven years old. One day she was playing tetherball at recess with her best friend, and another kid came up and said, "Wow, I'm surprised you're able to play that because you're so fat. I'm surprised you aren't lazy." Ava told one of the recess aides, but she didn't tell her family what happened or talk about it again for a long time. Instead, she started putting more salad and less of other foods on her plate at meals. "I've tried to eat just a salad for lunch, and it worked for a while, but then it stopped filling me up," she says.

Midway through the pandemic, Ava announced to her mother, "I'm only eating one dessert a day because too much sugar isn't good for you." To Dana, the comment came out of the blue, but this is the kid, after all, who said she hated school pictures because "you just sit there, wasting your time, when you could be getting an education." So Dana chalked it up to Ava's quirky but deeply pragmatic personality. "Ava is very matter-of-fact and engineer-like and is also very good at self-regulating," Dana tells me. Compared to Ella's hidden candy stashes, Ava's one-a-day rule seemed downright sensible.

But Dana didn't know that Ava had also begun weighing herself before and after every meal whenever she could. The family's only scale is in Harry and Dana's bathroom, so she had to find ways to sneak in without their noticing. Sometimes she said she needed a Band-Aid or an ibuprofen. If her weight went up after she ate, which happened most meals, Ava worried and tried to eat less at the next meal. A few weeks after I first began reporting on the family, I got a panicked email from Dana. "Ava has never said anything about her size, so imagine my shock on Saturday when she asked to talk to me privately and started to cry and told me she was worried she was fat and that she was scared of being 'Fat and lazy,'" she writes.

Ava told her parents that she had googled "average weight for a nine-year-old," and she knew her weight was fifteen pounds heavier. Harry explained that "average" meant that 50 percent of people would be bigger, and 50 percent of people would be smaller, which Ava seemed to find reassuring. But Dana focused more on the "fat and lazy" connection. "I told her the important thing is to make sure her body can do what she wants it to do and that this has nothing to do with size," Dana says.

Ava tells me that talking to her parents helped, but she's still worried about eating too much. Having the candy in the lockbox reassures her that she won't. In their effort to manage sweets for their older daughter, Harry and Dana have inadvertently jump-started their younger daughter's first diet. I want to be clear that when they made their rules for family meals and snacks, the couple never intended to teach their daughters not to trust their bodies. Harry and Dana thought they were setting their kids up to develop healthy eating habits and a love of food and family togetherness. "All of this comes from a loving, protective place," says Du Breuil of this common parental tendency. Even Dana's fears about Ella's weight gain come from a place of love and empathy. "We see how the world treats fat people, and we want to spare our kids that experience, especially if that's what we experienced," says Du Breuil. And kids do benefit from structure around feeding: As Harry knows, no three-year-old should be fending for themselves for meals. He prepares beautiful food for his family now as a way of giving his daughters what he didn't have himself as a child. But too much control also backfires. "This is so counter to how we approach our children's other bodily needs," notes Du Breuil. "Imagine telling your child that she can't possibly need to pee again, or that he shouldn't be tired again tonight because he napped earlier. We don't police these other appetites, so why is it different around food?"

When we try to control both *when* kids eat and *how much* they eat, we're telling our kids to trust us more than they trust their own hunger. When we make dessert conditional—something that must be earned by eating vegetables or through good behavior, something that can and is taken away, often arbitrarily—we give those foods too much power. And when we thread through all this our belief that a thin body is the goal, we reinforce our kids' fear that their own body, their own hunger, is too much. "What parents really need to be asking themselves," says Du Breuil, "is, 'What price am I willing to have my child pay in order to be thin?'"

In January 2022, I get another email from Dana: "The food safe is no more!" she writes. "We're taking a much more relaxed approach to food and snacks, and parenting in general." They made the shift a few months after my first round of interviews with the family, in response to Ava's revelation about her secret weigh-ins and Ella's increasingly fraught mental health, and with the support of the therapists they enlisted to help both kids. The girls ride their bikes to Target or Walgreens and spend their allowances on candy and other treats. "I don't feel the need to police that," Dana tells me. She has also stashed her scale in the back of her closet and says, "I think Ava, for the most part, is past the worry about her weight."

Things remain more complicated with Ella, perhaps because she's older and already more immersed in the world of body expectations. And because she's gained more weight; at her high school orientation in August, a group of boys called her a "fat whale." A few days later, Ella asked her mother to help her lose weight. When Dana hesitated, Ella added, "If you don't help me, I'm going to do it anyway, but I'd rather do it with your help." Dana has been where Ella is. In some ways, she's still there: "I'm really torn because I've gained some weight in the last two years and I'd like to lose a few pounds just so I don't have to buy new clothes," she says. "So I have a lot of sympathy for how she stated this." And she has even more when Ella calls home from school crying that another boy called her fat. "I don't want her to feel like she has to lose weight," says Dana. "But I know she would be happier if she did because of how fat-biased our society is."

But Dana refuses to enable the bias anymore. She doesn't put Ella on a diet. She doesn't buy another food safe or start making rules around treats. She asks Ella what she would do if she lost the weight and people still made comments about her body. "Because that is very likely to happen," Dana says. "So do you lose more weight? Where's the end point?" She thinks that resonated. At least, she hopes Ella isn't googling diets behind her back the way she once hid candy bars. But she knows they aren't done figuring this out.

CHAPTER 8

The "Nervy Mothers" Myth

WHEN Sarah's sons were growing up, she loved cooking family dinners most nights. Unlike a lot of her friends, she didn't have to worry about picky eaters rejecting what she made. David, now twenty-one, and Finn, now eighteen, were big kids who grew up to be "huggable linebackers," as Sarah puts it. They are both, like her husband, Chris, over six feet tall. And they were always hungry. Extended family members and friends offer a kind of benign amusement bordering on pride when it comes to the boys' size and their "manly" appetites. A favorite family story is the time a friend suggested Sarah use a frozen bagel to soothe baby David's sore gums—and at not even one year old, he ate the entire thing. They are both foodies, especially Finn, who spent the summer before eleventh grade at cooking camp in New York City, learning from chefs and eating out at cool restaurants. More recently during COVID, he was the family member who bought a sous vide machine and got super into baking sourdough bread.

But for her own part, Sarah spent much of David and Finn's childhood quietly panicking about how much and what they ate.

"I would always hesitate if I was making something I knew they really loved," says Sarah, now fifty-two and a longtime attorney on the East Coast. She recalls measuring out pasta and planning not to have leftovers. "I would think, well they like this so much, maybe I shouldn't make too much of it," she explains. "I'd try to make 'just enough.' Whatever that means." Sarah had other strategies, too, all designed to subtly enforce a degree of portion control on her ravenous children: Potato chips were only allowed once a week. Hamburgers and fries were okay to order in a restaurant but not the kind of food they ever had at home. When the boys clamored for ice cream, Sarah bought a box of little Popsicles instead of the pints of Ben & Jerry's they craved. "Most of it was about: 'No junk food, no sugar. If you're hungry, have an apple and a piece of cheese,'" she says. "I always said, 'No way am I bringing that junk in the house because either I'll eat all of it or they will.'" These rules were familiar to Sarah. And so was her boys' frustration with them. "Growing up, there was a clear difference between my house and my friends' houses in terms of the kind of food available," she says. "I hated it. And then, I made it exactly the same for my kids."

Sarah's parents were lifelong dieters, perpetually starting and restarting Weight Watchers, and theirs was a house of cut-up vegetables and no desserts. Home was where Sarah learned that bananas were too fattening, and the so-called right amount of peanut butter to put on a sandwich. She describes her mother as "more of a vanity dieter"; a size 12 to 16 who was forever striving for what she considered true thinness. But her father lived in a larger body his whole life, reaching four hundred pounds at one point. "Family members still talk about the time he ate an entire cheesecake in one sitting," Sarah says. It's a painful memory. As is her own memory of being eight years old and reveling in eating an entire plate of French fries in a restaurant—only to be reprimanded by both of her parents. "Shortly after that, I wanted a toy at the store and my mom offered to buy it for me if I lost five pounds," she says. Sarah responded to their restriction by sneaking food at night; she remembers eating slice after slice of Pepperidge Farm white bread while watching TV.

But Sarah was also acutely aware that she was "the fat kid" in her grade, and she turned to her mom frequently for advice on losing weight. At sixteen she, too, joined Weight Watchers and lost a significant amount of weight, only to regain it a few years later in college, when her mom died unexpectedly. "My dad really fell apart after that,"

Sarah says. Still grieving, she found herself in a caregiving role until her dad died as well, just a few years later. Throughout that strange, sad time, Sarah beat herself up for failing at diets. "Now when I think about all the stress eating I did as a college student or law student, I realize, 'Oh, there was a lot of emotional stuff going on.'"

But when Sarah had her sons, she was still dieting, and still blaming herself when a diet didn't work. She knew enough to know she wanted better for her boys. "I wanted to fix it for them," she says. "I wanted to teach them some magical set of skills so they would not be fat. I wanted it to just be eating for them. But I had no idea how to do that." And so, history began to repeat itself. When the kids were little, Sarah periodically caught them sneaking food. Once, when David was twelve, and Sarah had allowed a bag of Oreos into the house, she saw him taking four in the middle of the day and was horrified. "He was like, 'I'm hungry, and we have Oreos! Why is this bad?'" Sarah didn't know how to articulate it to him. A few years later, when Finn was fourteen, he asked Sarah if he, too, could go on Weight Watchers. "I said sure!" she says. "And then I saw him so clearly frustrated with the whole thing."

At first, Sarah was frustrated by his frustration. "He'd say something like, 'I've been good all week, I can have fries,' and I don't think there was a lot of shame, which sort of stunned me," Sarah says. Her version of dieting didn't allow this concept of "cheat days" for balance. After all, her version of dieting didn't include balance. "I think my reaction was, 'Really? You don't feel bad about those fries?' Could we have a little bit of perfectionism about this?" Finn withdrew. Food and weight became giant no-fly zones in their family life. And Sarah started to wonder about what, exactly, she was passing on to him. She knew her compulsion to monitor and comment on her sons' eating habits and bodies was putting distance between her and them.

Precious few of us show up to parenthood with a glowing relationship with our bodies. And moms and other parents and caregivers socialized female are uniquely vulnerable to these struggles. A 2020 study by British researchers found that 15.3 percent of women will have had an eating disorder by the time they get pregnant. In a previous study of 739 mothers-to-be, the same researchers found that while only

7.5 percent of the women met criteria for a current eating disorder, nearly one in four reported high levels of concern about their weight and body shape. And while some (though not all) women experience pregnancy as a reprieve from weight anxiety, we are often then whip-lashed into an even more fraught place with it after giving birth. Non-biological mothers and stepmothers struggle, too, because parenthood can so completely superimpose itself on our previous identities and lifestyles—all of which shows up on our bodies.

And here's the thing: We're not just unhappy with our bodies or our relationship with food—we're unhappy that we're unhappy. We're sure our angst means that we're destined to pass these same anxieties on to our children. We worry that we'll teach them by example to fear their bodies in the same way we do, or to believe that a woman's value is her body.

We arrive at this fear honestly. As we saw in Chapter 1, mothers have always been blamed for our children's bodies. We are blamed when they eat the wrong way, as Abby experienced in Chapter 7. We are blamed when they are too big, as we have seen repeatedly through the moral panic of the "childhood obesity epidemic." And we are blamed when children themselves start to fear fatness. The early scientific literature on anorexia is littered with references to "abnormal mothers," who cause their children's eating disorders through "dominant and intru-sive" or "scolding and overbearing" parenting styles. Such determina-tions were not evidence-based. In a 1978 review article titled "Current Approaches to the Etiology and Treatment of Anorexia Nervosa," a psychology researcher named Kelly Bemis described these conclusions as "impressionistic and speculative" due to "the virtual absence of con-trolled studies." But the lack of empirical data on the role of mothers did not stop researchers (including Bemis) from continuing to speculate that children with anorexia, particularly boys, must suffer from "patho-logical mothering."

That phrase comes from a 1980 case study published in the *Journal of Nervous and Mental Disease* by David Rampling, then a psychiatrist at Hillcrest Hospital in Adelaide, Australia. Rampling's paper analyzes the anorexia of "Peter B.," a twenty-eight-year-old music student, pri-marily through Peter's relationship with his "nervy" mother. Rampling blames Peter's mother for her grown son's condition because when he interviews her, she does not remember having written a letter sent to Peter's doctor about his feeding struggles as a toddler twenty-five years earlier. That letter is included in the case study and explains that during Peter's early childhood, his mother was raising three children, all of whom had complicated health concerns, while also caring for an elderly father almost single-handedly. "I was ordered constant rest myself by a doctor some months ago, but afraid with the three children, my husband and now my father to do for, I don't get time for rest," she wrote in 1950, though it's a sentence too many mothers today will relate to profoundly. But Rampling seizes on inconsistencies between the 1950 letter and his interview with her in the late 1970s, when she recalls Peter's sister having more feeding troubles than he did. Rampling concludes these lapses in memory demonstrate her "denial" and unreliability as a parent. Rather than, I don't know, more than two decades of sheer exhaustion? Rampling doesn't interview Peter's father, and I would bet both of my children's college funds that he would have remembered even less about Peter's childhood eating habits. But in the 1970s and all too often today, we don't pathologize fathers for being unreliable narrators. We expect it.

Rampling also zeroes in on a note from another psychiatrist in Peter's file that his mother "did not want this child during her pregnancy":

It may be that the dyadic bonding for predestined anorexics is specifically characterized by its dependence on ambivalent maternal attitudes, of which preoccupation with feeding as a reaction formation to infanticidal wishes is a necessary, if not sufficient, component. In this station, the child's eventual enactment of these wishes through starvation would seem a predictable component of the identification process and one likely to engender intolerable maternal anxiety.

Translation: Peter starved himself because his mother didn't love him enough. Of course, we never hear evidence of this from Peter or his mother. We don't even know if her initial ambivalence about her pregnancy persisted during the entire pregnancy—and is there a mother alive who doesn't have at least one moment of ambivalence during those nine months of gestation?—let alone whether it continued after his birth. For his part, Peter asserts that he's much closer to his mother than his father, who he describes as "insensitive and unemotional." But Rampling never bothers to ponder the impact of that relationship on Peter's feelings about food and his body.

Indeed, early eating disorder research either ignores the existence of fathers altogether or views them as passive and uninvolved. "The prevailing belief, which stems from Freud's theory of psychosexual personality development, was that any psychological illness was the fault of the mother," says Jennifer Harriger, PhD, a professor of psychology at Pepperdine University who studies body image and eating disorders. "But the early research doesn't provide any empirical support for this." Nevertheless, mother blame became the foundation of early anorexia treatment, with patients regularly cut off from their families in ways we know now to be deeply traumatic. This didn't begin to shift until the late 1990s, when a psychology researcher named Kevin Thompson developed what's known as the Tripartite Influence Model, which explains disordered eating and body dissatisfaction as the result of intersecting influences from parents, peers, and the media. Parents (all parents!) play a role—but it is the combined and cumulative impact of each of these forces, along with a child's genetic predispositions, that determine whether they will develop an eating disorder. Or simply struggle sometimes, in that subclinical, garden-variety way that we all struggle to have a body in this world.

But if there is a downside to this more recent shift, it's that we still haven't found a way to talk about the fact that mothers do influence our children on food and weight without blaming and stigmatizing us for that influence. The early researchers who analyzed Peter's mother and other mothers of the first generations of people diagnosed with our modern definition of anorexia completely ignored the ways in which those mothers were victims of the same pressures they were accused of inflicting on their children. Peter's mother parented young children during the 1940s and 1950s, a time when her own mental health was nobody's priority, when her body was barely her own, and when her entire identity would have been wrapped up in her motherhood. Eighty years later, women's roles in society have transformed and yet maternal mental health remains one of our lowest priorities. We still chafe against the expectation that our personal identities should be subsumed by motherhood. And our cultural definition of motherhood has become even more rigid, in some ways, as our other freedoms have increased. Mothers today are much more likely to work outside the home, and yet in 2019, we spent an average of 1.43 hours per day caring for our children, up from just 54 minutes per day in 1965. In comparison, fathers in 2017 invested an average of 59 minutes per day on such tasks—up from just 16 minutes in 1965 but still a long way from equal.

Mothers also continue to perform the majority of our households' "mental load," or cognitive labor; all the behind-the-scenes work of writing grocery lists, buying snow boots, choosing pediatricians, making appointments, and signing kids up for soccer teams and dance classes. These efforts are both essential and yet so invisible that many researchers studying parental time use don't even include the mental load in their tallies. In a 2019 Pew Research Center survey, for example, we learn that 71 percent of mothers do all the grocery shopping and food preparation for family meals, but the researchers didn't ask about specific mental load tasks like planning menus, making grocery lists, and keeping track of kid food preferences and eating abilities. We can only assume that it's folded into the physical labor. I found just one study, a 2013 survey of over three thousand American adults over the age of 20 who had a spouse or partner, which asked about meal planning directly. These researchers found that 40 percent of women reported taking the main responsibility for meal planning and preparing, compared with just 6 percent of men. And women were much less likely than men to say they personally took no role in meal planning. This makes sense. It's harder, and far less common, for women to opt out of meal planning because we are socially conditioned to do that task and held to higher societal expectations about what "good meal planning" looks like. I should note that 60 percent of women and 54 percent of men did say they viewed meal planning as a "shared job." But the researchers didn't clarify whether we're all using the same definition of "shared job." I suspect at least some of these men were giving themselves participation trophies for answering with a noun when their wife asked, "What do you want for dinner tonight?" Occasionally volunteering "pizza!" does not a meal planner make.

And women do all of this while navigating complicated cultural messages about how we and our children should eat and look. Meal planning means assuming responsibility for your family's nutrition, and that almost always means some level of participation in diet culture. A search for #MealPlanning on Instagram brings up over 1.5 million posts, the vast majority of which are about dieting: Meal plans that are dairy-free, grain-free, low-carb, raw, or keto. Meal plans with stringent calorie counts. Meal plans that make you start each day with a glass of warm lemon water. Meal plans that use egg whites in every meal. Meal plans that are just smoothie recipes because you're apparently planning to stop chewing. I even found a meal plan based around "pickle bites" where you use pickles the way another person might use bread. This is all before we even get into #WhatIEatInADay TikTok, which is pretty much all before and after weight loss photos and diet rules.

So many of these posts come from women. Women getting their beach bodies, or their pre-baby body back. Women sticking to their diet by packing salads to take to the office every day. Women planning to eat the rainbow and feed it to their family, too. Social media has convinced us of the utility of meal planning, and it has also taught us to crave the meal planning aesthetic—adorable printable calendars, fridges full of produce organized by color in clear acrylic bins. Meal planning offers a whitewashed vision of domestic life, sponsored by the Container Store, and inextricably linked to the thin ideal.

So yes, we do impact, and, in some sense, even create our children's body image and their foundational relationship with food. And that power means we can cause harm: Studies show that mothers who model dieting or encourage weight loss are more likely to have kids who engage in binge eating and restriction. We also pass on our own internalized body ideas and weight biases to kids as early as preschool. But rather than staying stuck in shame or denial, we need to now reckon with all the expectations we've absorbed—and figure out how to begin the process of letting them go.

THE MATERNAL PERFORMANCE OF HEALTH

One reason it's so hard to let go of these expectations is because of how tangled our ideas around weight and family meals are with our definition of "health." As we've seen, the relationship between a child's body weight and their current or future health is not as linear as we've been led to believe. And defining concepts like "healthy eating" and "nutrition" purely in terms of how they relate to weight management does not help us raise healthy kids. But "health" itself remains perhaps the hardest parenting ideal to let go of—not because we are all so pure in our love for our kids but because "health" is one of our most powerful forms of cultural capital.

The term "cultural capital" was coined by the French sociologist Pierre Bourdieu in 1986 to describe any noneconomic resource that we use to signal our power and value in society. The more cultural capital you have, the more resources and social connections you can access. So, it's both understandable and practical for parents to raise our kids in ways that both shore up our own cultural capital and transmit that capital to them. In 2015, Stefanie Mollborn, PhD, a sociologist at the University of Colorado in Boulder, set out with two colleagues to study how families transmit health as cultural capital. In their paper, "Healthier Than Just Healthy," published in a 2021 issue of the journal *Social Problems*, Mollborn, Bethany Rigles, and Jennifer A. Pace explain that parents focus on health in part because our kids' physical bodies are "important repositories of cultural capital through classed signals, such as clothing, teeth, height, hair, and mannerisms." Lunch boxes are another kind of cultural capital. So are our kids' extracurricular schedules, and how many days a week they spend doing swim team, ballet, or another time-intensive, expensive physical activity. "They were sporty at various times," recalls Sarah. "And I remember being so delighted at how that resulted in their leanness." A thin, athletic child's body is perhaps our most sought-after proof of "health," and our highest-value cultural capital.

Savannah, who we met in Chapter 6, says she invested heavily in her own quest for the cultural capital of her children's health. "Some of my kids' friends, I'd see pictures online of them looking so happy, but their hair wasn't perfectly done," she says. Savannah was too afraid of being the "Sloppy Fatty" for that. "My kids were always in certain outfits. They could not be dirty." By the time I start interviewing Savannah, she has relaxed on this front tremendously: When I meet her twelve-year-old daughter, Ariel, over Zoom in the fall of 2021, she's wearing sweatpants and has a messy short haircut. But it's clear she carries the memories of the (still quite recent) years that her mom spent trying to control her body.

We chat a bit about Ariel's decision to quit softball a year earlier, which they both mark as a huge turning point in their relationship. "I always pushed Ariel into sports, because my thought was, 'As long as we're athletes, we can be in larger bodies,'" Savannah explains. They started with soccer at age three, and Ariel cried through every practice. They switched to swimming, which she liked better, and then softball, which she hated. During one game, Savannah looked at her daughter, then age ten, on the pitcher's mound and realized: Ariel was terrified. "She had been telling us all day that her stomach hurt and now here she was, eyes really big, shaking, just frozen," Savannah says. "We had always had an agreement that if you start a season on a team, you finish it. But I saw her and thought, 'I have to check my stuff at the door.'"

Ariel, for her part, doesn't want to label herself as scared of softball. "It wasn't interesting," she tells me. "It just felt like I was going there for absolutely no reason, and I didn't like it." But she appreciates that her parents let her quit, both because she wanted out of softball and because it happened as Savannah began reevaluating so many of her decisions around food and bodies. "We always used to only have the whole grain bread with the seeds in it, for PB&J," Ariel tells me. "I hated that sandwich. Sometimes I would just throw that sandwich away as soon as I got to school."

Sociologists refer to the kinds of choices that Savannah and Sarah made around food and activities as "intensive parenting." Mollborn writes: "Intensive parenting is a strategy expected of parents—but particularly mothers who experience more pressure—to build cultural capital and generate educational advantages for their children. [. . .] Parenting intensively demands considerable time, money, and energy for managing children's lives." Intensive parenting also goes hand in hand with what Mollborn calls "the medicalization of motherhood," where parents (again, mostly moms) feel compelled "to manage children's health behaviors in order to correctly perform social advantage."

A mother named Hannah in Mollborn's study talks about trying to get her kids to pack their own lunches "to be independent" and then taking back that responsibility when the lunches they packed (relying heavily on snack bars and other processed foods) didn't measure up to her goals for their lunchtime performance of health. "I was just like, 'Forget it. I am taking over the lunch packing. I will slice the fruit and put it in the little BPA-free containers,'" Hannah says. "I think of it as [. . . my] upper-middle-class privilege of knowing nutrition."

Many heterosexual mothers find themselves in a similar place when a male partner attempts to take over lunch box packing or other food preparation but "does it wrong," as we saw with Kirsten and Scott in Chapter 6. That phenomenon is often labeled "maternal gatekeeping," a blame-laden term that ignores what Mollborn frames as the "additional pressures on mothers to ultimately be responsible for their children's health." Men do less parenting and less health-related parenting especially, because they are judged less intensively for the outcomes of their labor. But the answer isn't for women to lower their standards and "let" their partners take over. The answer is to explode the standards themselves.

"THE FAT SHEEP OF THE FAMILY"

Both Savannah and Sarah say they felt the need to perform intensive parenting as a form of protection for their children and themselves against the anti-fat bias they encounter daily, for Savannah as a fat parent and for Sarah as a formerly fat person. "I was doing what I thought I needed to do to feel safe," says Savannah. "But just because it's what I did to feel safe doesn't mean that I always needed to do it." Or that it didn't take its own toll on her kids, especially Ariel, who, like Savannah, lives in a larger body. Our interview takes place just two weeks after Halloween, and Savannah is excited to report that, for the first time, she did not attempt to police her kids' candy intake. She even allowed Ariel, as the oldest, to keep her candy in her bedroom instead of in the kitchen with the rest of the family's food. "This is a real big shift that I felt as a parent," Savannah says. And the even bigger victory: She did not get angry or anxious when Ariel came downstairs and told her that she'd finished all her candy in one day. "We had a great conversation about what tasted good to her and what she would want us to have more of in the house," says Savannah when the three of us get on Zoom.

But in our conversation, Ariel still seems a little defensive about how fast she ate the candy. "I only ate it all like that because it had been a long time since I had candy," she says. "Also, I barely had any candy. We got way less than last year." I ask her how she felt when her mom first started to ease up on all the rules, about sports, about clothes, about food. Did Ariel trust it? "I don't know," she says. "It kind of felt like, this is a mousetrap. And she's under the box. Like, I want it, but if I get it, will I have it taken away again?"

On hearing this, Savannah looks back at me with her own huge, scared eyes. "There are some parts of this that are going to take a long time to repair," she says.

On the surface, what Ariel and Savannah are working through is a reorganization of their family's rules around food. They are both stepping tentatively, learning their way through, and writing a new playbook for how their family interacts around these topics as they go. And that's hard enough. As we've seen, the line between structure and freedom around food will look different for every family. Sometimes, it looks different depending on the day within a family. But underneath these sorts of logistical challenges is a deeper fear that Ariel voices when she wonders if her mom is setting a trap. That this is not just about the candy; it's also about Ariel learning to trust her mother again. It's about Ariel's body, and whether Savannah can trust and accept it. Because, for years, she didn't. And on some level, Ariel knew. "I love my daughter so deeply," says Savannah. But as Ariel got older, and it became clear she would not be thin, Savannah found herself recoiling from Ariel's body with what she describes as "a learned disgust." Now, she says, "I cry just thinking about the day I figured out that what I was feeling was disgust for my own child."

These are hard words for any parent to say out loud. They fly in the face of every expectation we have of ourselves as mothers, especially, because we are supposed to be our children's providers of unconditional love. It feels impossible to hold with both hands our love for our kids and this kind of disgust. But when we remember how universally conditioned we are to feel repulsion at fatness, and how easily we feel that same repulsion for any perceived fatness on our own bodies, what's more surprising is that we do so rarely voice this silent part. We may feel ashamed for thinking about our child's body in such a negative way because that doesn't square with our vision of motherhood. But maybe even more, we feel shame because of how our child's body size and shape reflect on our mothering. That sense of disgust is also a recognition that we have failed by this crucial measure of maternal success that society has set for us.

This can be true even if we've made a conscious decision to parent differently from the way we were parented. Melissa, a stay-at-home mother of three in Kitchener, Ontario, says she was determined to embrace her kids' bodies in a wholehearted way she never experienced as a kid. "I grew up in a house where I was the fat sheep of the family," she says. "Even though I'm straight-sized. But everyone else was so thin that 'fat' was, and still is, my identity in the family. And I remember so clearly every little comment my mom ever made." When Melissa started having her own kids, she braced herself for what her parents might say to them. "I thought a lot about when they might start to make comments like, 'Maybe you don't need two cookies?'" she says. "I was sure I'd be all over it. It was such a surprise that, at the end of the day, this came from me."

Melissa's oldest son, Simon, now seven, started gaining weight, as so many kids did, during the COVID-19 pandemic. "I guess it happened gradually, but it felt like he grew overnight," Melissa says. "One day he took his shirt off, and I zoomed in on his belly. And I couldn't stop myself from being horrified." She didn't say anything, but she felt the energy shift with Simon, in how he noticed his mother noticing his body. "I don't think I did a good job of hiding it," she says. "I did recognize that this is not where I want to be. But I'm still working on how to move past it." This is a universal challenge of dismantling our own fatphobia: How do you start to reprogram your brain to notice fat bodies differently? "Intellectually, I can say, 'I like bigger bodies,'" Melissa says. "But my family has such an ingrained dislike of fat bodies, and I can't get over it. When I see a fat person walking down the street, my eyes zoom in on whatever is jiggly."

Because this aversion feels so visceral, it can lead us to confuse it with some primal, biologically driven instinct: Did we evolve to love thinness, as humans but also as mothers, for some Darwinian, "survival of the fittest" reason? It's a logical question, but as we saw in Chapter 1, our feelings of repulsion around fat bodies are conditioned, not innate, and driven by the need for those in power to preserve the social hierarchies that support them.

And for mothers, this repulsion ties directly to that other conditioned desire, to ensure our children's health not for their own well-being but as a form of cultural capital. Melissa says that her initial disgust over Simon's stomach immediately triggered a kind of chain reaction of worries: "I went straight to, 'Well, he's not a very active kid. He's a gamer, a thinker, a dreamer. We have to get him moving!'" she says, noting that it is true that Simon moved less and ate for comfort more during the pandemic, which made it even easier to think of his newfound chubbiness as a problem to fix. The temptation was also there, she says, to start cleaning out the kitchen cupboards, to ban processed foods and sugar. But Melissa also acknowledges that all those reactions would have more to do with her status as a mom than genuine concern for her son's well-being. "When he was a skinny kid, it was to my credit—I did it, I raised a thin kid," Melissa says. "But now that he's not, that means this is also my fault. It's hard not to feel like I'm to blame."

It's easy to hear Melissa and Savannah talk about feeling disgusted by their children's bodies and think, *Well, maybe those early anorexia researchers had it right. Maybe mothers do cause eating disorders, maybe these mothers will cause eating disorders, and maybe I will, too.* But to begin and end the conversation there, with blame, doesn't allow any space for mothers to change. It acknowledges the potential for harming our kids but doesn't look at how we have also been harmed or continue to harm ourselves. In putting words to their disgust, both Melissa and Savannah opened the possibility of releasing it. They realize their kids deserved better; that Ariel and Simon do not deserve to be blamed or shamed for their bodies. And maybe, that means Savannah and Melissa deserve better, too.

WANTING TO FIX IT

Changing these deeply embedded narratives about good and bad bodies, and good and bad mothers, can feel impossible. But we are starting to see research suggesting that the kind of surface-level changes that Savannah made with Ariel do matter. They may even start to heal the deeper wounds. "The research tells us that what you say matters more than what you do," says Kendrin Sonneville, ScD, RD, the assistant professor of nutritional sciences at the University of Michigan School of Public Health, who we also heard from in Chapter 3. This is an important distinction because we cannot will ourselves to stop hating our bodies by magic if we've spent decades learning to do that in a dieting-obsessed, fatphobic culture. We may also not be ready to stop dieting or pursuing thinness for ourselves. But if we can recognize how harmful these activities can be for our kids, we may be able to insulate them from our own struggles by making a concerted effort to have a different conversation.

For a 2018 study, Yale School of Medicine researchers surveyed 581 parents of children ages nine to fifteen about the different kinds of "fat talk" they used around their kids, and then collected data about their children's weight and relationship with food. They found that 76 percent of parents denigrated their own bodies in front of their children, and 51.5 percent talked more generally about the "dangers of obesity." But 43.6 percent talked directly about their kids' bodies, taking note of weight gain or commenting on "flabby bellies." And it was this last group that was the most likely to have kids who engaged in binge eating, secretive eating, or other disordered behavior. "At the very least, don't comment on your child's body in a disparaging way," Sonneville said when I interviewed her about this research for the *New York Times* in 2019.

That might sound obvious. But think of Savannah's and Melissa's moments of recoil, and of Sarah's persistent involuntary monitoring of her sons' eating habits and weight. Think, too, of Dana in Chapter 7, worrying that if Ella ate too much sugar, she would gain weight and worry about her body even more. When our child's appetite makes us anxious, or their body starts to resemble a body we've been taught to dread, we often can't help but display our concern in negative ways. This becomes especially true if their body starts to resemble the body we also have or had as a child. If we can just get control of the situation—by which we mean, if we can just control their eating, just control their unruly body— maybe we can save them. "I wanted to fix it for them," as Sarah says. We want, so badly, to fix it for them.

But what if we reframed these moments of panic and disgust as opportunities to model and teach resilience? What if we stopped trying to fix our kids and started naming diet culture and anti-fat bias as the problems that need fixing, for ourselves and for them? "We don't want our kids to learn to change themselves anytime they're teased or feel like they don't fit in," Rachel Millner, PsyD, an eating disorder therapist in private practice in Newtown, Pennsylvania, told me for a *New York Times* article in 2020. "We want them to stand up to that kind of stigma." Then disgust at your child's round body becomes disgust at a culture that teaches you to hate your child's body, and your own.

This isn't the easy choice. It may require rejecting some amount of cultural capital, because we will not conform our kids' eating habits or bodies to our modern health ideals of thinness, and soccer, and eating the rainbow. But it may pay some dividends immediately, as Melissa found when she resolved to change how she thought about Simon's body, by deliberately embracing the parts of him that had triggered her disgust. "I thought, how can I possibly teach him to love himself and his body when I can barely touch him?" Melissa says. "So that's where I started, just putting my hands on his body in a loving, playful way, especially on the very spots that caused such disgust in my fucked-up brain." She and Simon started to have biggest belly competitions in the mirror. They talk about their big butts. They do a lot of tickling and hugging. As it turned out, the physical part was easy; it felt good to be affectionate, to reconnect physically with her kid. It's harder to be playful about her own body, but she tries. "I think a big part of this is showing him that I can accept my body the way it is," Melissa says. "That's hard. But I can honestly say, when I look at his body now, I don't feel anything but love."

For other families, where the damage has run deeper, the road will be longer. "I think if I could tell another parent one thing, it would be that this is going to take a long time," says Savannah. "To earn back Ariel's trust, for her to see that I mean this, that the candy isn't going away? I think it may take years."

Sarah wonders if repair is even possible. She declined my request to interview her sons because even bringing up this topic with Finn and David feels fraught. On the one hand, she thinks that they got off lucky: "What's funny about my kids, and maybe this is just being white and male in America, but they just shake stuff off," she tells me. "If someone tells them to do something that turns out to be too hard, they just shrug, like, 'Yeah, that didn't happen!'" But she also worries about the potential for damage she can't see. In between bouts of sourdough baking and other culinary experiments, Finn will announce he's counting macros, for example. Sarah isn't sure how to talk about that, either; after years of policing her kids for eating too much, it feels hypocritical and awkward to express concern in the other direction. And both Finn and David will also lean into their big appetites, talking about how many tacos they ate on a Saturday night, with a pride that borders on rebellion. "The way some college students talk about alcohol or weed, they talk about food," Sarah says. "I think it's at least partly a reaction to that message of 'But do you really need seconds?' that they were always getting from me."

A few years ago, as Sarah started to wrestle with her own years of obsessive dieting, she began working with a dietitian who specialized in intuitive eating, to explore a less restrictive way of engaging with food. Around the same time, David came home from his freshman year of college having gained what to Sarah felt like a significant amount of weight.

"I recognized that I could not bring it up with him at all, in any way, without causing harm," Sarah says. And yet, she still found herself bringing it up. "I knew I needed to stop; on some level I had known that since forever. But I had to keep reminding myself and recommit to say less."

Then David started his summer job as a camp counselor, a job that involved running around outside all day with a pack of nine-year-old boys. He was exhausted—but his watch reported that he was getting in thirty thousand steps per day. "He told me this with great pride," Sarah says. The weight started to come off, and David was happy. But Sarah was happier—and that bothered her. "I just noticed how much I cared," she says. One weekend she found herself wondering whether David might "ruin it" by going out with friends for pizza and ice cream—and decided she had lost the plot. "I wanted to get to a place where my kids don't feel like they have to lose weight to earn my love."

Sarah's dietitian suggested that she bring David in for a session where Sarah gave what she describes as "a mediated apology." She doesn't recall exactly what she said, only the awkward sensation of stumbling through a conversation neither of them was fully prepared to have. When they walked out, David's only comment was, "Mom, that was weird. Why did we do that?"

Sarah still doesn't quite know how to answer that. She knows one apology doesn't undo her years of obsessing over her kids' bodies and eating habits. And her boys are now adults; she can't go back in time and let them keep their Halloween candy and eat all the Oreos. But I get enough messages from adults still fielding fatphobic comments from their parents to know: Sarah doing this work still matters. Releasing ourselves from the blame and the expectations on our mothering and on our bodies always matters. For our kids. But even more, for ourselves.

CHAPTER 9

(Straight, White) Dads on Diets

WHEN his daughter Francine first started losing weight in the fall of 2018, Kenneth, forty-three, says he "kind of thought it was good." Francine has always been artistic—she paints pet portraits and sells them in her own Etsy shop—but never particularly athletic, which puzzled Kenneth, who is a runner with dozens of half marathons and even one ultramarathon under his belt. When she started to express an interest in exercising and joining Kenneth's wife, Tracy, for workouts, they both thought it was a positive sign.

Kenneth runs a company that specializes in business and life coaching from the family's organic farm near the Appalachian Trail in Central Pennsylvania. Tracy is a former civil engineer who stays home with their kids and works part-time at a pottery studio. They are both thin and active and embracing healthy habits has long been the family ethos; something they've always tried to do for Francine, who is now eighteen, and her three younger siblings. So when Francine announced she was now vegan, they rolled with it. "We knew she thought she was a little bit 'heavy,' and we did think she should be active, so we thought, 'Well, it's good, right?'" Kenneth says now.

Then Francine's hair started to fall out.

"I thought we just didn't understand veganism and what proteins she needed," Kenneth says. He asked a friend who is a vegan weight lifter to give Francine some tips, and after Francine described what she was eating, the friend responded, "Girl, you've got to eat! You can't live on salad!" "That's when the first alarm bells went off," Kenneth says. But it took over a year of trying different therapists, while Francine got progressively worse, for Kenneth and Tracy to grasp just how sick their daughter was. The date that sticks in Kenneth's mind is February 9, 2020, an otherwise ordinary Sunday. Kenneth walked into his family room and saw Francine, then sixteen, standing in profile next to her fourteen-year-old sister. He was stunned. "My fourteen-year-old was just beautiful and full in every way—face full, energy full, happiness full, body full," he says. "And Francine was gray. She was working out twice a day, not eating, hearing voices. We couldn't leave her alone. The life had just gone out of her."

Kenneth started to add up exactly what his daughter was eating in a day and realized it wasn't nearly enough calories. He also realized that some of Francine's new eating habits—like replacing breakfast with bullet coffee—she had learned from watching him. During that same late summer of 2018 as Francine's eating disorder began, Kenneth was following an intense diet of his own, in a quest to improve his running time. A chiropractor friend offered a "metabolic reset program" that Kenneth signed up for—and when Francine asked, he explained what he was doing and why. "I think I was probably malnourished myself, and in that place where you can't help obsess about food and talk about it constantly," he says. "It's that shared misery thing. I had to talk about what a good boy I am, to be eating this way." Kenneth thought that he was being healthy and modeling healthy eating and exercise habits to his daughter. "I just had no idea that the stuff she was asking me was really her disease asking," he says. And that's because he couldn't see how much his own choices were driven by his own biases around weight, health, and the kind of man he thought a father should be.

"WE DON'T HAVE A SCRIPT FOR THIS"

For decades, when researchers who study eating disorders wanted to understand the role of a child's family, they looked almost exclusively to mothers. "The literature on fathers' child feeding practices is scant," concluded the authors of a scientific review paper on the topic published in a 2014 issue of the journal *Appetite*. They could find only twenty studies that included fathers in a meaningful way, and if that sounds like a lot, consider that when I searched the scientific literature for "mothers and eating disorders" while researching the last chapter, I found over three hundred papers published in the past fifty years. "The research that has included fathers has focused on fathers who are part of a family in which the mother has an eating disorder, rather than examining fathers' unique contributions," wrote two Yale researchers in their analysis for a 2016 study published in the *Journal of Psychosomatic Research*. The idea that a father might also struggle with anti-fat bias, dieting, disordered eating, or a full-blown eating disorder—and that these struggles might impact his children—has long been ignored. Men aren't supposed to care about their weight in our culture. Men, especially the straight, cisgender, white, mostly thin men I'm focusing on in this chapter, aren't defined by their appearance in the same way women and other marginalized people tend to be. They hold all the cards, after all.

And yet, we've all seen a dad on a diet.

He almost certainly won't call it that, of course. Instead, like Kenneth, dieting dads might get super into long-distance running. Or CrossFit, or body building, or Ironman training. They may become passionate about vegetable gardening; Kenneth says his passion for organic farming also led him to preach about "good" and "bad" foods. "I'd go to a church party and then post on Facebook about how I can't believe these people are feeding my kids nothing but Doritos and hot dogs," he says. "It was part of marketing our farm, I guess, but I was also a pretty self-righteous bastard about the whole thing."

All these pursuits, on their surface, are about health and wellness—even science, the environment, social justice!—not weight. But they are rooted in fatphobia. "I used to do a lot of banter about, 'Look at that person, she's fat,'" Kenneth says. "Or I'd say to the kids, 'Hey, don't eat that pizza or don't eat too many desserts, that will make you fat.'" He's not alone: One 2018 study by Yale University researchers of 658 parents found that while nearly everyone (93 percent) demonstrated some sort of weight bias, fathers were more likely than mothers to agree with negative stereotypes like "severely obese children are unusually untidy" and to associate "fat children" with words like "bad" and "stupid." Thinner fathers, as well as fathers with more education and a higher family income, were the most likely to endorse fat stereotypes. In other words, the men with the most privilege to lose were the most likely to reinforce the kind of bias that upholds their privilege. And kids absorb this stigma: Adolescents were more likely to diet and binge eat if their parents talked about weight, according to a 2013 survey of 2,793 kids published in *JAMA Pediatrics*.

But even while they experience the benefits of white male privilege, many men also chafe against their conditioning and the way our culture normalizes behavior that can quickly become destructive. The National Institute of Mental Health reports that roughly one million men live with eating disorders, a figure that many experts say is likely an underestimate, because men don't tend to disclose their disordered eating behaviors and healthcare providers don't think to screen them for symptoms. "Men tell me they don't have a script for how to talk about diet culture," Jaclyn Siegel, PhD, the social psychologist in the Body Image, Sexuality, and Health Lab at San Diego State University, told me when I interviewed her about gender and eating disorders for *Elemental* in 2020. "But there's also no script for men to express their own concerns, or to seek help, because it isn't seen as normative for men to develop eating disorders or body image dissatisfaction."

What happens instead is a normalization and even glamorization of anything men are doing with food and exercise, no matter how disordered. This rests on our misconception that men not only don't get eating disorders, they don't get emotional about food or bodies, period. We don't question that premise and the unquestioned authority we give men, especially dads, around food and bodies impacts their kids: Girls whose fathers reported binge eating were 3.38 times more likely to report binge eating themselves, according to a study of over twenty-seven hundred kids published in 2014. Other studies have shown that the more fathers report dissatisfaction with their own bodies, the more likely they are to monitor and restrict their children's eating habits, especially sons. If they don't actively engage and model disordered eating habits, they may withdraw from family meals altogether, something men can often do more easily than women due to our societal gender norms around food labor. But kids notice their dads' lack of engagement, too. "Everybody has a relationship with food and with their body," explains Kyle Ganson, PhD, a clinical social worker, and assistant professor at the Factor-Inwentash Faculty of Social Work at the University of Toronto, who studies eating disorders in boys and men. "Even if it's a totally disconnected relationship, that is still a relationship. And that still drives how you engage with the world."

THE PERFORMANCE OF MALE DIETING

Peter Attia, MD, has long been a well-known proponent of intermittent fasting (IF), the diet trend also known as time-restricted eating, where dieters only allow themselves to eat during certain hours of the day, or on certain days of the week. Attia measures his blood glucose, lactate, and ketone levels fastidiously on three or four different devices during his monthly three-day fasts. Then he shares pictures of these results with his more than 350,000 Instagram followers. His blog tagline is "Learn how to live longer, be healthier, and optimize your performance." In between fasting posts, he details his intensive workout regimen and analyzes his sleep.

Some IF disciples indulge in food free-for-alls during their permitted eating times; others continue to adhere to strict rules about which foods they're allowed to eat. Both models involve white knuckling through a fair amount of deprivation, which makes these diets easy to market to men, who are taught to equate their gender with endurance, control, and strength from an early age. IF has also long had the reputation of being a science-based approach to eating. It was developed by researchers studying longevity by starving mice and later themselves. And the stack of scientific papers supporting IF, as well as the number of doctors, like Attia, who promote it, has also given it a gravitas befitting a man's diet.

But starting in 2020, a series of randomized trials published in *JAMA* and the *New England Journal of Medicine* concluded that intermittent fasting offered no benefit over regular old caloric restriction—a finding that has rocked many of the diet's advocates. "I was a devotee," Ethan Weiss, MD, one of the *JAMA* study's co-authors and a diet researcher at the University of California, San Francisco, told the *New York Times*. "This was a hard thing to accept." And while Weiss admitted that he'd started eating breakfast again, as of this writing, Attia has not accepted it. In a YouTube video responding to Weiss's research published in February 2022, Attia doubles down on the importance of fasting long enough, noting that if you "only" fast for sixteen hours a day, you'll also need to significantly restrict your caloric intake and eat only certain foods to "get lean and healthy."

Attia is also a father of three, a role he loves but also seems to perceive as a threat to his perfectionist definition of health. "It's like I can't stop finishing my kids' food, even 'good' food like steel-cut oatmeal," he wrote in January 2020 for an Instagram post I reported on for *Elemental* later that year. "The logic is, 'Hey, I'm fasting so often, I can eat whatever I want when I'm not fasting . . .' which of course is not true." He went on to explain how he approaches feeding his family: "I wish I would tell you we have zero junk food in our house, but that's simply not the case. We work hard to restrict it, but it's there. Chex Mix, Goldfish, those damn 'veggie' chips. I'm susceptible to all this stuff, especially when it's laying around in a half-eaten bowl. So, I'm thinking that I need more accountability. [. . .] Anyone else game to join me?" Attia began posting photos of chocolate chip muffins, homemade mac and cheese, and other carb-heavy foods that he encounters in his house because his kids eat them, with the hashtags #Denied and #Avoided, to hold himself accountable for being susceptible to what he calls their "potential blindside[s]." The series garnered thousands of likes and comments, many from other parents, announcing that they were also dieting, also tempted by their kids' "junk food," and therefore, very game to participate in the sort of food-shaming ritual that would raise all kinds of red flags were Attia not white, male, and a doctor.

Attia does not speak for or to all men, though his brand of data-obsessed gym bro clearly resonates with many, and perhaps especially with other fit, affluent fathers—the group that the Yale University researchers found most likely to display explicit weight bias. Trends like intermittent fasting, as well as Paleo, keto, and macro counting have become mainstays of male diet culture because of how they promote weight loss under the guise of optimizing your performance. And when male influencers like Attia talk so authoritatively about nutrition or fitness, we are conditioned to listen; we assume men are doing their research and considering this question of how we eat empirically, and unemotionally. We see this, too, in the book sales of, and awards conferred on, male health journalists like Michael Pollan, Gary Taubes, and Michael Moss. And it's also what happened when Kenneth unwittingly taught Francine how to skip breakfast. He trusted a (male) doctor who told him eating less would improve his running game; in turn, his role as Francine's male authority figure let him impart the same "wisdom."

To Attia, to Kenneth's doctor friend, even to Kenneth before Francine got sick, food is fuel; something to analyze and optimize, but not to have feelings about. Eating your kids' leftover Goldfish is a sign of weakness. It couldn't possibly be that Attia is hungry or feeling deprived when he encounters these snacks because he has already determined just how hungry he's allowed to be and what foods he's allowed to eat to satisfy this hunger. There is no space for a deep discussion of emotional eating and self-worth. This is not Oprah mining her childhood traumas to understand why she can't lose the weight. This is Jack Dorsey, the billionaire and former CEO of Twitter, saying he only eats one meal a day because it helps him "focus" on building his empire. When Dorsey first talked about his regime, it was framed in our larger cultural discourse as extreme, but in a way that only underscored what we understand as his brilliance and success. We didn't immediately recognize it as an eating disorder symptom, the way we do when Kim Kardashian or another famous woman shares a similarly extreme diet hack. We didn't worry about Dorsey's mental health. And I'm not here to argue that billionaire tech bros need our empathy—but when we revere this kind of restriction without examining the toll it takes, we make it that much harder for any ordinary guy to talk about his struggles. "Male diet culture is all about how can we optimize our performance; how can we hack eating to be this much more efficient at work, this much more successful," explained Aaron Flores, RDN, a dietitian in Calabasas, California, when I interviewed him for *Elemental* in 2020. "This is men needing to say, 'I'm in charge, I'm in control, I'm going to see results.' It's an exertion of power through the system for guys who, on some level, feel like they don't measure up."

When men exert that power publicly, whether by posting on social media about their diet success, or by telling their friends and family members how to eat, they're engaging in what Siegel calls "the performance of male dieting." This need to perform masculinity appears to cut across differing definitions of masculinity. Kenneth the organic farmer personifies a gentler version of masculinity than Attia's jacked gym bro vibe or Dorsey's eccentric billionaire persona—but I see his professional Facebook still littered with running selfies and photos from hunting weekends with buddies. And this fits with how precarious our cultural definition of manhood is: "The status of manhood is elusive, hard won and easily lost, and it needs to be consistently proven through public demonstrations of your masculinity," Siegel explains. "In this context, diets like intermittent fasting make a lot of sense. They're all about pushing your body to its limits. And men can put it on display by talking about it."

The first thing Cody, thirty-seven, wants to talk to me about is not his diet but his height—because he's only five foot six, a fact that intersected with his understanding of his own manhood for a long time. "I've never been the athlete," he says next. "I was labeled the short and stocky kid, the one built like a proverbial brick shithouse. And I always thought, 'Okay, I'm never going to be skinny. I'm never going to be the "attractive all-star" type.'" This was sort of fine. Growing up in rural Montana, Cody didn't want "skinny," exactly. But he did want to be ripped, like the male models he saw on the covers of muscle magazines in the grocery store. "I grew up thinking, 'That's what I want to be.'" If he couldn't be tall, he thought, he should at least be built.

Cody joined the wrestling team, but quickly came up against the fact that other guys his height tended to be fifteen pounds lighter. To make weight before meets, Cody and his teammates chewed tobacco. "If you consistently spit, you can lose two or three pounds of water weight in a day," he explains. "All the teachers understood, it was, 'Oh, you have a meet after school? Go sit in the corner.' And we'd sit there and spit." Cody liked the ritual of that, but eventually he decided that football and hockey were better sports for him, in part because they didn't require weight loss. That's around when he shifted to drinking beer every morning before school. "Sometimes I'd wonder why I was gaining weight, but nobody said, 'Maybe it's the twelve-pack you're drinking every day,'" he says. Cody didn't think too much about what he was putting in his body; it wasn't something he saw the men around him focusing on. In a town where most kids got up at five a.m. to do farm chores, fatness was equated with laziness, but food was also there to be eaten, not dissected for its health benefits. This is another flavor of the ways that men get a free pass around food; since they aren't expected to feed families or be responsible for everyone's health the way women are, they don't have to eat perfectly. They are allowed to have appetites if those appetites aide in their performance of masculinity.

But a few years ago, Cody started to think a lot more about how he ate. He now lives outside of Boise, Idaho, with his wife, Carolina, his seventeen-year-old stepdaughter, Zoe, and their five-year-old daughter, Avery. He works as a procurement manager for a company that supplies pharmaceuticals to vets, dairies, and animal feedlots, a desk job that he says contributed to gaining more weight than he wanted in his early thirties. Around the time Carolina got pregnant with Avery, Cody saw his doctor, who cut to the chase: "He's very old-school, and just said, 'Yeah, you're fat, go do something about it,'" Cody recalls. Cody's cholesterol level was above the recommended 160, and he started to worry that maybe he should make some changes. "This was when we had the new baby on the way, and I thought, 'I need to ensure that I'm here for both my daughters as long as possible,'" he says. "That set me on the path of getting healthier."

To do that, Cody turned back to the body builders he had admired in muscle magazines as a kid. He picked up a book called *Bigger Leaner Stronger: The Simple Science of Building the Ultimate Male Body* by Michael Matthews, a weight lifter and diet coach with his own supplement line and a moderate social media following (around a hundred thousand followers each on Instagram, Facebook, and YouTube). Cody followed the book's guidance and started meal prepping and working out for sixty to ninety minutes seven days a week, tracking his calories burned and other metrics on his Apple Watch. Cody doesn't do intermittent fasting, but he tries to control his output and his appetite in much the same way that Attia teaches his followers to manage theirs. He has lost weight—about fifty pounds in five years—and credits the lifestyle shift with helping him manage his depression and stress. But Cody also knows that he's walking a fine line between pursuing health and chasing this performance of the body he always thought guys like him don't get to have. He doesn't make plans unless he knows he can fit his workouts in around them. He gives himself weekend cheat days but religiously sticks to his meal preps Monday through Friday. "If it's nine p.m., and I still have two hundred more calories to burn for the day, I'm going for a run. It doesn't matter what time it is; I need to complete that. I worry that if I miss one day, I'll miss two days, and then I'll spiral out of control," Cody explains. "It's a healthy obsession, but it is an obsession."

VALIDATION THROUGH THINNESS

Matt, thirty-four, a new dad who works in the public sector in Washington, D.C., doesn't identify much with gym bro culture or life hacking; they both seem like clubs he never felt cool enough to join, as a kid growing up in a bigger body. His dad called him "Piggy," and kids at school teased him, too. And Matt had a hard time laughing it off the way he knew he was expected to. "It's all teasing and ribbing and 'Hey, man, you're looking doughy,'" Aaron Flores, the dietitian, notes of the way men talk to one another about bodies starting in childhood. "You're not supposed to take it seriously, because there is some cultural acceptance for men to have larger bodies."

Indeed, white, straight, cisgender men can access a much more flexible definition of fitness and beauty than women and anyone else more marginalized. If a man jokes about his "dad bod" and revels in pizza and beer, we assume it is a privilege of his manhood not to have to care about health, nutrition, or thinness. After all, his value will never be tied to his appearance in the same way it is for women. This is the stereotypical sitcom dad paired with a nagging, much-thinner wife who wants him to eat salad, and yet she is still somehow the butt of the joke. "We allow men to engage in food and exercise in quite different ways than we allow women to engage with these things," says Ganson, the University of Toronto researcher. But men in bigger, or otherwise nonnormative, bodies still regularly encounter anti-fat bias. "Lots of men struggle with not having the bodies we see in sports and superhero movies. There's a shame around how that lessens their value as men," says Flores, who also hosts a podcast called *Men Unscripted*, about men's relationships with their bodies. "Internally, there is no acceptance."

Matt felt like he also couldn't be as aggressive as he was expected to be—another way he failed to measure up to that superhero ideal. "I can be performatively aggressive because it's expected of me, but I'm not. I don't like loud cars. I don't like yelling. I've always had difficulty connecting with men and felt sort of intimidated by them," he says. "Most of my close friends have been women."

Matt went out for sports in high school, not so much because he cared about running or football for their own sake, but because it felt expected of him. And then, he started to lose weight. "My whole life changed," he says now. "I was suddenly cool. And I started gaining a lot of validation through women wanting to sleep with me." Matt liked being attractive to women in a way he'd never been aware of before—but even more, he liked how his status as a thin athlete "made me more acceptable to men." The bullying stopped at home and at school. Matt kept working out and, by the time he was twenty-five, had developed what he now describes as an eating disorder rooted in restriction and compulsive exercising. "My weight got low enough that I did have a friend or two point it out," he says. But their concerns were drowned out by the larger reinforcement Matt got going to Washington, D.C., bars with his friends, meeting women and sleeping around. "I would get shit-faced and sleep with someone and regret it in the morning," he says. "Throughout high school, college, and my early twenties, I thought that kind of validation from women was the most important thing in the world." And that validation from women led to validation from other men.

Just like women have been conditioned to want a body that will be sexually attractive to men, body standards for men (including gay men) also demand being sexually attractive to gain approval from men—which means they are also about appealing to an oppressor. The key difference is men perpetuate their own oppression. "It's especially hard for white, cisgender males in average bodies to connect to the harm that diet culture causes because they don't experience marginalization in any other way," Flores says. "We don't have the resources to be resilient through it or call it out as marginalization, so we just internalize it and isolate."

By 2015, Matt had internalized, isolated, and overexercised himself into several chronic injuries and began therapy for anxiety and depression, which ultimately helped him understand that he had an eating disorder as well. "I don't think I'm in recovery," he tells me when we talk in the spring of 2021, as he is wrapping up a fifteen-week paternity leave after the birth of his first child. "I intellectually understand that we don't have a healthy way for people to permanently lose weight. But I haven't internalized it yet. I do a lot of comparing myself to other people." Matt compares himself to his wife, even though he's six foot one and she's five foot two. "There are some days I'll eat less than her and still feel like I'm eating too much," he says. And he especially compares himself to other men, like his friend down the street. "He has a baby the same age as my son, and he's much smaller than I am," Matt says.

Matt says he doesn't talk about his eating disorder or recovery struggles with any of his male friends. "My best friend is an infectious disease doctor who once asked me why a bunch of my wife's friends are obese," he says. "He thinks that humans are just little robots, and weight is all inputs and outputs." This, too, is a narrative reinforced by male diet culture; think Peter Attia with his glucose monitor, telling his followers to post #Avoided on every bagel they meet, as is the narrative that men can't or shouldn't be emotionally vulnerable with each other. "Sometimes women friends will tell me their husbands are going through the same thing," notes Matt. "But I haven't talked to them about it." Tapping into the emotional side of their struggles was hard for every man I interviewed for this chapter. Kenneth could talk matter-of-factly about their journey through Francine's treatment and explain which therapists had helped or hurt. But he would drop more loaded statements like "for about a year I thought my daughter hated me" quickly, and then dart to his next point before I could ask a follow-up.

"The assumption is, because we're white men, we don't need anything," one male eating disorder patient told Siegel when she interviewed him for her master's thesis about eating disorders in the workplace. Siegel says she had to sit with that idea. "As someone who studies sexism, it was such a learning moment for me," she says. "As a feminist, I had such a visceral reaction to a man saying, essentially, 'You don't understand my man problems!'" Same. I admit to occasionally thinking, "But you're a guy!" when one of the dads interviewed for this chapter told me about feeling like their body wasn't good enough. But that reaction is itself complicit with male diet culture—because all "But you're a guy!" does is reinforce our narrow ideas about who a guy should be. "People assume men can't suffer, but they do, and they are," says Siegel. "And by not recognizing it, we're perpetrating the harm."

"THIS ISN'T REALLY MY TERRITORY"

We're also leaving space, often unwittingly, for men to perpetrate this harm on their kids, when they bring their diet culture mindset to the family dinner table. Cody says he can't quite figure out how to mesh his "healthy obsession" with the needs of his family. He took over the cooking so he could oversee his meal preps, which Caroline mostly appreciates. But his kids don't want to eat "a whole bunch of chicken," as Zoe puts it. "I do like his cooking. If he makes chili or spaghetti, I'll eat it." But when Cody is deep into meal prep mode, he often ends up cooking three different dinners because the rest of the family doesn't want to eat all his vegetables. Cody doesn't love that Zoe would rather live on Hot Cheetos and liters of Coke, but he worries more about the weeks when she decides she hates her body and won't eat at all. "I've struggled with feeling overweight basically my entire life," Zoe tells me. "I don't want to say I've had an eating disorder, but I go through a lot of moments where I just don't eat whatsoever. And then I binge eat a whole lot and gain everything back. It's a whole cycle."

When we talk in early 2021, Zoe has pale skin and hair dyed a mix of purple and black and wears comfy sweats when she Zooms with me from her bedroom. She isn't paying much attention to the kind of fitness magazines that influenced Cody's understanding of body ideals during his teenage years. But fitness Instagram is a different story: "Being skinny is not even important to me," she says. "But social media makes me feel like I have to be, like if I'm not the ideal body type, then I'm not going to be pretty or good enough. I think all the time, like, why can't I just look how I look?" It isn't just social media; Zoe has also been bullied in school to the point where she withdrew from her public high school as a sophomore. "They saw a whole bunch of Zoe struggling, like from sixth grade on, and decided to bash me for it," she says. She switched briefly to online school but is now getting her GED instead of finishing her senior year, in the hopes of going on to beauty school and becoming a makeup artist. Zoe's passion is wildly elaborate costume makeup; transforming a woman into a dragon or an alien. Her Instagram is a portfolio of the looks she's given herself and her mom, which aren't so much about replicating normative beauty standards as they are about turning human faces and bodies into ethereal, otherworldly creatures. But in real life, Zoe sounds overwhelmed even just articulating that larger goal of beauty school to me; day to day, she struggles with chronic depression that often renders her unable to get out of bed, let alone create fantasy worlds or dream about her future.

"We've been on suicide watch with Zoe multiple times," Cody tells me. He's been in Zoe's life since she was a toddler, and they've always been close; his Facebook is filled with old photos of Zoe as a little kid, snuggled up with him and their dogs. But he's responded to her swirling depression, body hatred, and disordered eating the same way he responded to his own: by making a workout plan. "Sometimes I go to him crying and he gives me, like, a full-on eating schedule and says, 'Well, this is what you need to do to lose weight,'" Zoe says. "Well, I don't want to do that. That's not helping." Cody admits he focuses on how Zoe is eating or encourages her to be more active because he doesn't know a better way: "I don't want to say I push, but I do try to inform my wife and my seventeen-year-old of the daily choices they make, like around how they eat and how that makes them feel," he says. "I want her to be as happy as she can in who she is, but if she's not, well, here are some things that will help drive that change."

The little research we have on how dads influence their kids' relationship with food and body suggests that Cody's approach is a common one. Dads seem slightly more prone than moms to engage in what researchers call "pressure-to-eat behaviors." The literature says that fathers are particularly prone to pressuring sons, though not exclusively, and Kyle Ganson, the University of Toronto researcher, speculates that it may relate to fathers wanting sons to perform athletically in specific ways. "If the dad is pushing the kid in a certain direction with sports, or if the dad is their coach and heavily influencing their exercise plans, that can lead to disordered eating," he says.

On the flip side, fathers of kids with eating disorders may resort to pressure because they are confused by a child's inability to comply. "Anecdotally, the phrase I often hear from male caregivers is, 'Why can't they just eat?' They may also be more likely to think their child needs to 'grow up' or 'deal with it,'" Ganson says. "Female caregivers tend to be doing a lot of the emotional processing around the eating disorder, while fathers are much more driven by logistics; how do we move to the next phase of treatment, when do we see results?" And when progress isn't evident—as it often isn't in the circular recovery process of eating disorders—dads are more likely to disconnect from the process. "This isn't really my territory" is another comment Ganson and his colleagues often hear from dads.

This is not to say that men can't engage emotionally with a sick child, or that the labor of managing treatment logistics isn't valuable. But this conditioning—to push away from feelings and move toward action—intersects powerfully with the "no pain, no gain" messaging of male diet culture. "Something I haven't told him is that I constantly do think he looks at me differently," says Zoe of Cody. "I think he's silently judging me all the time, like thinking, 'Hmm, that's not good for you' about what I eat." And the hard thing is, she's not entirely wrong. "I do always want to say, 'Just get up and do it, just take a walk. I understand it sucks and it's not easy, but just do it,'" Cody says. He's trying to accept the idea that Zoe's depression manifests differently than his did; that meal prepping and weight lifting might not be her solution. But tangled throughout these conversations, for both, is Zoe's belief that she needs to lose weight to be happy—and Cody's tacit endorsement of that. "If you want to lose weight, I do think there's something to be said for starting that process and taking that responsibility and ownership," he says. "Yes, because you'll feel better if you're stronger and healthier and at whatever weight. But even more because you'll get to come back to yourself every day and say, 'This is what I'm doing to help myself. This is how I'm moving forward.'"

This means that Cody is never challenging Zoe's premise that her body is wrong and needs to change to secure her happiness. He's never saying to his beloved stepdaughter, "You are already enough as you are." And when I ask Zoe what she needs from Cody, weight loss assistance doesn't come up at all. She's adamant that she doesn't want meal plans or workout schedules. "I think, sometimes, all I need is his support," she says. "I don't need you to tell me how to live. I just want to hear, 'Hey, it's going to be okay and whatever you need, I'm here.'" Cody is trying. "I don't understand it when she says, 'It doesn't work like that for me.' That's completely foreign to me," he admits. "But I'm okay not understanding it. I don't have to understand. I just have to accept it."

Kenneth is also striving for acceptance, as he and Tracy support Francine through her eating disorder recovery. Soon after Kenneth's realization of just how sick Francine had become, she was admitted to an inpatient recovery program for nine days. When she came home, Kenneth and Tracy began following a common eating disorder treatment protocol known as family-based treatment or FBT, where parents take full responsibility for feeding their child with the eating disorder—planning and preparing every single meal and snack and monitoring every bite. FBT is, in some ways, the opposite of Satter's Division of Responsibility, but it's a necessary intervention when an eating disorder has become so entrenched that a child can no longer hear hunger cues or make decisions around food. It's the mental load of family meals on steroids. And it can be brutal.

There were many nights when Francine cried at the table. Tracy bore the brunt of making the food and talking Francine through the process of eating. "A lot of nights, I could see, she just could not eat unless Mom was there to support her," Kenneth says. Those were the days he felt most helpless, watching impotently from the outside, just as the eating disorder literature has so often painted fathers. But he began to look for ways to contribute, getting out board games for the family to play after dinner, when Francine had finished eating but still needed some help and distraction from the eating disorder voice in her head. In a weird way, it helped that it was 2020 and their early weeks with FBT happened in lockdown. "All the kids were home, and we could all just be there with her," Kenneth says. "We'd all sit at the table every night and play games and just let her work through those post-meal feelings."

Just being there—without judgment, without trying to fix it—may feel impossible to a lot of dads, because men have always been taught that they need to have the solution; that their voice should be the loudest in any room. "I still believe it's my job to be the protector of my family, but I've had to sort of rethink what that looks like," says Kenneth. Even men in less traditionally gendered family roles struggle with how to be present but not necessarily in control of the situation. "I do sometimes hate being a dad and a dietitian," admits Flores, who has fourteen-year-old twins. At work, Flores is often in the position of providing FBT-style meal support to an eating disorder patient; working them through the process of finishing a plate of food despite the voice in their head screaming at them not to eat it. At home, he plays a very different role. "I say to my family all the time, I'm not a dietitian for you, I'm a parent and a partner," he explains. "And that means I shut up around food. Because I know, the more I try to control my kids' food, the more out of control the experience will be."

Instead of micromanaging the nutritional balance of every plate, Flores focuses on cultivating a home environment that lets his kids build trust in food and trust in their bodies. "It starts with doing my own work," he notes. "If I present to my kids that I think my body is bad, they will pick up on that message. So, it's having this really strong intention of not creating a culture of body shame in our house." Instead, Flores tries to make their house the place his kids can let out their feelings about the messages they're getting around food and bodies from the rest of the world. "They're going to get all of it from school, from friends, from a dance teacher," he notes. "This is the place where we can talk about why that's hard."

I check in with Kenneth again just after Thanksgiving in 2021. He is thrilled to report that Francine has been accepted to art school, and even more thrilled that she enjoyed a big plate of food at their holiday feast, including multiple desserts. Nobody compensated with a workout or made plans to start a diet the next day. They celebrated with his in-laws, who do still engage in the kind of weight and calorie talk that Kenneth has worked so hard to quit. And hearing some of those comments made him realize what a relief it's been to stop engaging with the world in that way. "I like not judging people's food and bodies," he says. "I'm just neutral now. I like neutral."

PART 3

. . .

TAKING UP
SPACE

CHAPTER 10

Diet Culture in the Classroom

CAIT O'Connor, now twenty-seven and an eighth-grade English teacher in Westchester County, New York, remembers precisely where she learned it was bad to be fat: at school. O'Connor was in second grade and attending her school's aftercare program while her mom was at work. The teacher running the program served saltines for snack and seven-year-old O'Connor asked for seconds. "This woman looked me dead in the face and said, 'It's like your hobby is eating. Why don't you ever stop?'" O'Connor recalls. "That was my entry point into understanding that my body was wrong."

It's also one of the early experiences that pointed O'Connor toward becoming a teacher herself, in large part because she wants to change the way educators talk to kids about food and weight. Because twenty years later, not much has changed. Every September when kids go back to school, readers fill my inbox with reports of the confusing and often downright harmful messages about eating habits, exercise, and fatness that their children are encountering in the classroom. In the fall of 2020, I interviewed Julie Ralston, a mom of two in Denver, Colorado, for a story for the *New York Times*. Julie had contacted me about the assignment to keep a food diary that her daughter Katie, then fifteen, received in the strength training class she was taking to meet that year's physical education requirement. For two weeks, Katie was supposed to write down everything she ate, and then tally up how many calories and grams of protein, carbohydrates, and fat she had consumed. The class would then use these food logs to develop their own nutrition plans.

And that's what worried Julie. She's a thin, athletic blonde who spent years tracking her own food and exercise habits, even working a stint for Beachbody, a diet where anyone can sign up to be a self-styled health coach and sell their friends shakes and meal plans. Later, she trained with the Primal Health Coach Institute, which pushes a version of the Paleo diet, and went down the Whole30, sugar-free rabbit hole. "I thought I was super into health and wellness, but I was really just doing it to feed my own insecurities and fears," she says now. In 2019, Julie began to learn about intuitive eating and decided to stop tracking and deleted MyFitnessPal and a few other food and exercise apps from her phone. But then Katie asked her mom how to figure out how many calories were in her breakfast—for school. Julie took a deep breath and showed her how to download one of the same apps she no longer used, to make the assignment easier. "To show my daughter how to count calories felt like the most horrible, dangerous thing," she told me. "It was like, 'I'm just handing my kid the needle and the drugs.'"

Julie also told Katie that she could opt out of the assignment, or have Julie call the physical education teacher and talk about it. Because the assignment's harm was clear and immediate: "She said, 'Every time I go to eat something now, it makes me not want to eat it because I'll have to write it down,'" Julie explained. But Katie didn't want to rock the boat. She liked her teacher, and she already felt weird enough as one of only two girls in a class of twenty-three boys. So, Julie emailed her concerns to the school guidance counselor and didn't get much of a response, but left it at that. When I first talked to Julie in 2020, the assignment had been over for a few weeks, and she was hopeful that Katie had left it behind her. "I think she has walked away not a lot worse for wear," she said then. "But things do come up," things like Katie checking nutrition labels more often. One day, when Julie asked what she wanted for lunch, Katie said, "What can you give me that's not going to make me fat?" But she laughed, and Julie thought, *Well, okay then.*

Three months after the *New York Times* piece ran, Julie sent me another note. Katie was not okay. She was going days without eating, sleeping as much as possible so there would be fewer opportunities to eat food. "Even the word 'meal' scares her," Julie wrote. When I talk to Katie, she says anxiety about her weight predated the tracking assignment. "I've always been pretty self-aware of how I look in comparison to everyone else," she notes. Her mother's years on diets were part of it. "And even now that she's not dieting, she still talks about food all the time," Katie tells me. "It can be a lot." (Julie, to her great credit, tells me several times before my Zoom chat with her daughter that she's told Katie, "Feel free to throw me under the bus.") Being stuck at home for months during the 2020 COVID-19 lockdown didn't help. The isolation coincided with Katie's depression and anxiety and left her with little else to do except obsess over how she looked and what she was eating. But the strength training class assignment met her where she was—and gave her the tools to take her eating disorder farther. "After we did that, it was hard to get out of the food counting mentality," Katie says.

Food diaries, as well as exercise logs, are "very commonly used in health and physical education classes across the country," says Christopher Pepper, a health educator, curriculum writer, and teacher consultant in San Francisco. Such assignments have been a cornerstone of nutrition curriculums for years and became even more popular when the United States Department of Agriculture put a nutrition calculator tool called SuperTracker on its website in 2011, as a companion educational tool for the government's 2010 dietary guidelines known as MyPlate. SuperTracker recently retired, in part because the popularity of slick food and fitness tracking apps like MyFitnessPal have negated the need for the USDA's much-clunkier tool. Those apps have also made the assignment even easier for teachers to assign and for students to complete. And so, they do, even though the potential for harm is so high.

Schools should be our children's safest spaces outside our homes. So why do they so often turn out to be incubators of diet culture and anti-fat bias? The answer to that question lies in how these beliefs have become embedded in our education system, which all too often only engages with the concepts of nutrition and fitness through a weight-centric lens. Anxiety about the childhood obesity epidemic is deliberately written into formal nutrition curricula taught in health and physical education classes across the country, thanks to guidelines from government public health offices. "I can't think of any movie shown more often in health class than *Super Size Me*," notes Pepper, referencing the 2004 documentary that followed filmmaker Morgan Spurlock gaining weight as he ate only McDonald's for a month. The film is still shown regularly even though, in 2017, Spurlock admitted to sexually harassing his female assistant and has been accused of other sexual misconduct. Weight anxiety also shows up in a formalized way for the 40 percent of kids who live in states where schools weigh them regularly and send "BMI report cards" home to parents, according to data published in 2020. Such weigh-ins and BMI calculations are sometimes conducted as a stand-alone screening program and sometimes as one part of a more comprehensive fitness evaluation, the most well known of which is the President's Physical Fitness Test. It's clear on school cafeteria menus that teach kids to classify food as traffic lights that correspond to "go, slow, or whoa!"—a strategy also employed by Kurbo, the Weight Watchers–owned weight loss app for kids. And these official assignments and policies reinforce the informal ways that anti-fat bias spreads through a school's culture, in casual, off-the-cuff remarks from both students and staff—and in what teachers so often *don't* say or do to challenge this status quo.

O'Connor and Pepper are both advocates of a different, less stigmatizing, and more weight-inclusive approach to education, which is slowly gaining traction. In reporting this chapter, I interviewed half a dozen teachers across the United States and Canada who were trying to call out the anti-fat bias endemic to their curriculums and school cultures. There are also many pediatric dietitians advocating from the outside for this kind of change. But these folks are the minority. "I think the kids are ready to have these conversations in schools, but the adults around them are not," says O'Connor. "Among teachers, I see an almost-universal recognition that something is broken, but it's like nobody can find the broken part. And the broken part is fatphobia."

TRACING THE BIAS

Another mom I interviewed for that 2020 *New York Times* story was Caitlin Kiarie, RDN, a mom of three and a pediatric dietitian in Montclair, New Jersey. When we spoke, most American school districts were still remote, and so Caitlin was juggling the needs of her newborn with the virtual education of her older kids, then in third and first grade. One morning, while listening to six-year-old Emerson's morning Zoom meeting, Caitlin heard the conversation take an unexpected turn: Emerson's teacher asked the class to share what they ate for dinner the night before. After every child had responded, Caitlin heard the teacher say, "I had turkey and vegetables for dinner last night. My husband and I are trying to eat less carbs, so we didn't eat any bread." Caitlin, who specializes in family feeding, was alarmed. "I know it's a seemingly harmless conversation, but these teachers are role models," she said.

But the problem with expecting teachers to role model a healthy relationship with food is that teachers, much like doctors, are immersed in diet culture just as much as anyone else. Diet culture and weight stigma aren't part of their formal education—in fact, nutrition and fitness are often not part of their training at all, even though, especially in elementary schools, regular classroom teachers are often the people instructing kids in those subjects. And so, teachers cobble together their understanding of these topics from their personal experience, internet research, and colleagues. And they inevitably hold biases against their fat students: As noted in Chapter 4, physical education teachers may have lower expectations of students in bigger bodies in terms of both their physical abilities and their social skills. And a student's weight has a bigger impact on a teacher's assessment of their academic ability than their test scores, according to a 2013 analysis of data collected on kindergartners.

In 2019, Sarah Nutter, PhD, the weight stigma researcher at the University of Victoria, published a systematic literature review in the journal *Current Obesity Reports*, on the prevalence of anti-fat bias in educational settings. She collected evidence that teachers were likely to assume that girls in larger bodies read at a lower level than thinner peers, and that boys in larger bodies were worse at math. Teachers across all specialties were also likely to agree that "children with obesity are a burden and have control over their body weight." And Nutter reviewed strong evidence of this bias among student teachers, suggesting that most folks are coming into education with these preconceived notions about their future fat students already on board. Unfortunately, their teaching education isn't doing anything to combat those assumptions.

Nutter did find one piece of good news in her literature review: Even though teachers may not see how their own biases contribute, they do identify weight-based bullying as a problem that needs to be addressed in schools. "There is a lot of unlearning to do, whether you're a thin teacher who can't see the harm of fatphobia you don't experience, or a teacher in a larger body who is dealing with your own marginalization," notes O'Connor, who describes herself as small fat. "Mostly what I find is that there is some awareness [of the problem], but no awareness of what to do next."

Emerson's teacher's comment about her no-bread diet is the kind of casually derisive "fat talk" that we encounter everywhere in our culture, but especially in women-dominated spaces, which many school staffs are. "It's that chorus of 'Why did you bring in cupcakes, I'm trying to be good!' in the break room," notes O'Connor. When "good" is unconsciously synonymous with "thin" and "abstains from sugar," it's easy to see why Emerson's teacher likely didn't even register that she was giving diet tips to six-year-olds. But that implicit bias may play a role in the finding that more than half of six-to-eight-year-old girls and a third of boys that age think they should weigh less, according to research by Common Sense Media. A 2017 study of 169 Korean children found that, by sixth grade, 63 percent of girls engage in "fat talk" at least once a week, even though it left 50 percent of them feeling dissatisfied with their bodies and 20 percent reported a drop in self-esteem.

This insidious normalization of body shaming also plays no small part in the fact that weight-based bullying remains so pervasive in schools, despite years of anti-bullying interventions. Of course, what kids learn from weight-based bullying is exactly what the adults around them often reinforce: that if your body is the target of teasing and cruelty, you should change your body to be less of a target rather than demand better treatment from, or consequences for, your abusers. This raises children's risk of body dissatisfaction and disordered eating. And it also teaches some fat kids to *be* bullies, as we saw in Chapter 4. "We're supposed to self-protect as fat people at all times," notes O'Connor. And that might mean going on offense. "Because it's understood that we deserve people being mean to us. If we're not self-preserving, then we better be ready to get punched in the face."

Even when fat kids aren't bullied for their weight, they are told, in dozens of implicit ways, that school is not a place where they fit in. As Aubrey Gordon recalled in Chapter 4, classroom chairs with desks attached are "a special kind of hell" for fat students who may not fit in the seat. "Flexible seating like bean bag chairs shouldn't be a fad, it should just be how we're designing classrooms to be inclusive," says O'Connor. The limited accessibility of size-inclusive uniforms or stigmatizing practices like team weigh-ins keep fat kids from playing sports, as we'll explore more in Chapter 11. O'Connor also points to high school theater department casting, which often relegates fat kids to playing sidekicks or working quite literally in the wings.

Dress codes also reinforce fatphobic, as well as racist and sexist, ideas about which kids' bodies are allowed to be visible. At the high school where Elizabeth DePriest teaches English in Maryland, dress code rules specify that a student's shirt can't reveal any cleavage or midriff. "If you're gaining weight—and they're teenagers, they're all supposed to be gaining weight—and your pants don't fit anymore, you might suddenly be wearing a crop top when you didn't mean to wear a crop top, but your back shows when you sit at your desk," she explains. Many of DePriest's students live in poverty and can't afford new pants, and DePriest and several of her colleagues refuse to penalize them for this. "I think it's understood, there is a secret network of non-fatphobic teachers here," she tells me. "We will not write you up for dress code if your pants are tight because you gained a few pounds."

But DePriest says that's not every teacher at her school—and it's certainly not every teacher in every school. In 2016, a nine-year-old girl in Brookhaven, Mississippi, was given in-school suspension because school staff thought her T-shirt was too tight, according to the school's dress code, which stipulated that students' shirts must be "size appropriate."

When her mother brought a replacement outfit to school, they vetoed that one as well. But how many fast-growing thin kids show up to school in too-tight or too-short clothes without penalty?

"I've noticed how my friends have gotten dress coded on stuff because they have bigger hips, bigger breasts, or bigger butts, yet I have worn similar things, but I did not get dress coded because I'm skinnier, and it is less noticeable on me," sixteen-year-old Ayiana Davis told researchers for the National Women's Law Center in 2018 for a report on dress code policies in Washington, D.C., schools. The report focused on how Black girls are disproportionately punished for violating dress codes compared to their white peers, finding that Black girls are 20.8 times more likely to get suspended from D.C. schools than white girls. And they are specifically subjected to more dress code violations because "adults often see Black girls as older and more sexual than their white peers, and so in need of greater correction for minor misbehaviors like [. . .] wearing a skirt shorter than permitted," the study authors wrote. And we see anti-fat bias intersecting with these racist assumptions, as several girls interviewed for the report note *which* Black girls get the dress code write-ups. "Like the little skinny girls can just wear whatever they want. I'm just being honest. And then the girls with curves, like really curvy, they just [say], 'Oh, you're showing too much, you're revealing so much,'" said Essence Kendall, eighteen. Concluded Ayiana: "That kind of thing teaches girls to be ashamed of their bodies."

FORMALIZED FATPHOBIA

Rules around what kids can wear are one way that the informal, and often unspoken, anti-fat bias of a school community becomes, quite literally, codified. But fatphobia is built into the formal structures of a school in other ways as well. The most visible example occurs in the twenty-five states where schools are legally required to monitor students' BMI, and in the eleven of those states that send a "BMI report card" home to parents. This practice began in 2003, as an extension of the Presidential Physical Fitness Testing protocols that I grew up with, when Arkansas became the first state in the nation to introduce

BMI tracking in its public schools. "We saw such a lack of awareness. So many children had become overweight or obese that these kids looked relatively normal to their parents," says Joseph Thompson, MD, MPH, president and CEO of Arkansas Center for Health Improvement (ACHI), a health policy center housed in the University of Arkansas for Medical Science in Little Rock, which helps manage the state's BMI program. "It's like if you put a frog in a pot of water. It doesn't know when to jump before it's boiled alive."

Thompson said he knew the Arkansas program was "starting to work" the day he was out mowing his lawn and saw a mother in his neighborhood power walk by with her three children "pretty much on a forced march." He stopped her to say hello and during their conversation, she thanked him for his efforts: "She said, 'My mother just died of diabetes, I just got diagnosed, and I'm not going to have these kids going down the same path.'" When I asked Thompson if he worried about fearmongering to parents or making kids overly anxious about their eating and exercise habits, he said he did not, though he knew why I was asking. "Everyone worries about eating disorders, but I think eating disorders are relatively rare events. And they are largely psychiatric issues," he said. "The obesity epidemic is an environmental problem. It's everybody's concern." In other words, you can't bake a cake without breaking a few eggs. Also, don't let your kids eat cake.

But more recent research on school BMI programs shows that they both don't work and do cause some measurable harm. When Arkansas launched their program in 2003, 17 percent of American children had a BMI in what we now consider the obese range; by 2018, the rate was 19.3 percent. Defenders of BMI screening might argue that without them, that percentage would have risen even higher. But when researchers tracked BMI screening efforts across seventy-nine public schools in California over three years, they found no evidence that the letters themselves resulted in weight loss for the over 28,000 students involved. "But we did see that these letters are having unintended negative consequences," says Hannah Thompson, PhD, an epidemiologist at the University of California at Berkeley and a lead author on the paper. Thompson studied how the experience of being weighed and having a "BMI report card" sent home made kids feel about themselves—and found that the higher a child's weight, the more likely they were to report feeling ashamed and stigmatized by the experience. "These kids are already feeling bad about themselves," she notes. "And getting weighed at school doesn't make it better." Indeed, 30 percent of parents with children aged six to fourteen reported noticing at least one worrisome new behavior in their child (like suddenly refusing foods or otherwise restricting calories) after participating in their school's obesity prevention programming, according to a 2012 poll by researchers at C.S. Mott Children's Hospital in Ann Arbor, Michigan.

ACHI's Joseph Thompson acknowledges the risk for shaming and self-esteem issues if school weigh-ins and fitness assessments are done insensitively. "We came up with a standardized protocol to ensure a student's privacy was protected and avoid any kind of embarrassment or pressure on students," he says. This includes weighing students privately, with their backs to the scales, and mailing the BMI letter home directly to parents rather than putting it into students' hands. "I have to be honest; I think there were some schools that cut corners," he admits. "But when we had an independent evaluation done of our program, they did not find any negative repercussions for students."

It's possible that Thompson's evaluators weren't asking the right questions or following students long enough to document harm. As we've seen, when researchers themselves carry weight bias, it informs the quality of the work they do. And it's certainly not hard to find anecdotal reports from families who have found BMI screening stigmatizing. When then nine-year-old Maggie came home from her elementary school in Philadelphia, Pennsylvania, carrying an envelope, her mom, Fran, says, "She looked like she thought she was carrying her own death warrant." Her daughter handed over the envelope and said, "They weighed us today, and the nurse said I need to give this to you." And then: "Does it say something bad?"

What the letter said was that Maggie's BMI was in the 84th percentile, putting her right on the line between the "normal" and "overweight" categories, which wasn't news to Fran, who knew her daughter's weight because she was required to have a physical to be enrolled in school. Fran told Maggie that the letter didn't say anything bad. "But my daughter is not an idiot," she says. "Her next question was, 'Well, then why did only me and Melanie get the letters?'"

Fran called Maggie's school to complain and threw the letter in the trash, which is what Diana, a mom in the Philadelphia suburbs, now wishes she had done. She received a similar letter when her daughter, Clara, who is now thirteen, was in fifth grade and the school nurse calculated her BMI to be in the obese range, above the 95th percentile. "They told us to see our pediatrician, and our pediatrician sent us to the 'Healthy Weight Program' at a local children's hospital," Diana says. At the first appointment, a dietitian started to talk about meal plans and workout programs and gave Diana lists of "go foods" and "no foods." Clara was upset, so Diana never made the next appointment. But over the next year, Clara started to "slim down," as her mom put it. "We chalked it up to, 'Well, she's getting older, she's more concerned about her appearance,'" Diana says. But then one night, Clara cried when her mom offered her a piece of pie. "We realized she was eating less and less with every meal." Clara was diagnosed with anorexia in June 2020 and has since been hospitalized four times, including a six-week stint on a feeding tube, and nineteen weeks in a residential treatment program in Denver. Because of COVID restrictions, Diana wasn't even allowed to visit after sending her child across the country. "This is the hardest thing we've ever done," she says.

When I talk to Diana, Clara is newly back at school after her treatment in Denver and working closely with an outpatient team. Diana is clear that Clara's struggle wasn't solely caused by her BMI report card or the visit to the Healthy Weight Program. "I believe that her eating disorder was there all along and was going to get triggered somehow," she says. "But I also now believe that schools should not be weighing kids. That was the first thing that should never have happened."

BMI testing isn't the only way that schools cause this kind of harm. Samantha, a mom of two in Los Angeles, says she wonders all the time if her now nineteen-year-old daughter Greta's anorexia has its roots in the FitnessGram, a program that tracks BMI as well as a student's performance on various fitness challenges, which California schools conduct in fifth, seventh, and ninth grade. Defenders of the FitnessGram say that it offers a holistic assessment of a child's health that goes beyond a weight measurement; kids also do push-ups, sit-ups, and other strength and flexibility challenges. But in Greta's case, it was her fifth-grade experience with the mile run test that felt the most stigmatizing: "She ran too slowly and failed the test," says Samantha. "And the teacher was encouraging kids who finished first to line up and cheer for the kids still running—which sounds like a great thing, but it ends up feeling pretty rotten for the slower students." I feel this one in my bones because I was the slowest kid to run the mile in my gym class every year when we did Presidential Physical Fitness Testing. And I will never forget ninth grade, when two boys from the football team decided to jog alongside me, their long legs loping easily as I huffed and puffed and tried not to cry. I still wonder: Did the gym teacher not notice? Did she not understand that they were jogging to mock me? Or did she think, on some level, that this was the kind of motivation I needed to get faster?

Things get even more twisted when the same teacher measuring mile times (and ignoring or encouraging this kind of bullying) is teaching the school's nutrition curriculum. In the 1980s, my fellow elementary school peers and I studied a "food wheel," which was replaced by the Food Pyramid in 1992 and with the MyPlate system in 2011. All these food guides were developed by the United States Department of Agriculture to communicate our federal dietary guidelines, which were originally designed to ensure nutrient adequacy in the American diet. In 1979, with anxieties rising about Americans' body sizes, this shifted to include the goal of "moderation." Ever since, nutritional guidelines have been synonymous with "obesity prevention," which makes it increasingly difficult for schools to teach nutrition without enforcing ideas about good and bad foods, and good and bad bodies.

School nutrition curricula are written at the state level and must be in accordance with the National Health Education Standards set out by the Centers for Disease Control and Prevention. While the standards themselves are open-ended, the CDC also created the Health Education Curriculum Analysis Tool, known as HECAT, to help school districts make sure their curricula meet the national standards. For nutrition, HECAT details specific curriculum objectives by age: By second grade, for example, students should be able to "demonstrate effective refusal skills to avoid unhealthy food choices." By eighth grade, they should be able to "explain various methods available to evaluate body weight."

"HECAT is a disaster. We should not be teaching children to weigh themselves or eat to maintain or lose weight," Sarah Ganginis, RD, a dietitian who specializes in eating disorder treatment in Maryland, told me when I interviewed her for the *New York Times* in 2020. Ganginis began advocating to change Maryland's health curriculum after her then kindergartner came home saying, "You can't pack me potato chips for snack anymore, they're not healthy!" Ganginis was disturbed by her daughter's shame for liking a food that her teacher had criticized as unhealthy. "Of course, we want kids to learn to enjoy fruits and vegetables," she says. "But first we have to help them understand that foods can have different nutritional values but still be emotionally equivalent."

Critics of school nutrition curriculums also take issue with a fifth-grade goal that children should be able to "state personal beliefs to improve the food and beverage selections of others" because of the pressure it puts on kids to police peers (thereby paving the way for weight-based bullying), as well as their caregivers. "Kids don't do the grocery shopping, and they don't control family finances," says Katherine Zavodni, MPH, RD, a dietitian who works with families in Salt Lake City, Utah. "It's very fraught to have a public health strategy rely on sending children home to educate the parents."

Such objectives also fail to acknowledge the socioeconomic diversity of students and can be culturally and racially insensitive. "The vast majority of our multilingual students are the first in their family born in America, so their parents have very different ideas about nutrition and cooking. I think they often see the nutrition information coming home and don't know how to even begin to cook that way," said Megan Reikowski, a federal title program coordinator for a large school district in Minnesota's Twin Cities, when I spoke with her for the *New York Times*. They may also have different ideas about "what a healthy kid looks like," which can make lessons around body weight fraught. On the flip side, Reikowski discourages the teachers she works with from making a patronizing fuss about the food traditions of students of color because this makes them other and exotic. "You can't read *Too Many Tamales* and call on the one Latinx kid in class and ask him to tell everyone about tamales," she told me. "If kids always feel like what they're eating at home is either being judged as unhealthy or held up like it's in a museum, it's hard for them to talk about what's actually important to them about food."

These are all nuanced distinctions that many adults, including educators, struggle to grasp because every form of diet and food marketing we encounter tells us that there is one right or best way to eat. But Ganginis, Zavodni, and others advocating for nutrition curriculum reform say it's developmentally even farther out of reach for most kids, who tend to be concrete thinkers. "Educators are trained to tailor their messages to a student's cognitive readiness in every subject except nutrition," says Zavodni. "We can teach kids facts about food—like how apples grow— without teaching moralistic value statements, just like we can teach kids the names of different religions without teaching them to believe in one religion."

One barrier to making that kind of systemic change is the fact that the format and quality of nutrition education varies wildly from state to state. "Health education has not been well supported or respected, frankly," notes Pepper. It's a lower priority because it's not a subject tested by the state to assess a school's performance, which means it happens in a patchwork way around the country: Some states require health education for high school graduation, but most do not. In middle school, health may be a required course taught by a trained health educator, or it might just be a movie thrown on by a science teacher on a Friday afternoon. In elementary school, nutrition may be taught by a grade's main classroom teacher or folded into physical education class. "You often see teachers who are teaching something else and get asked to pick up a health class on the side," Pepper explains. "It's not necessarily the thing they wanted to do when they became a teacher."

All of which makes it difficult to improve teacher training in any one area of health education. Gwen Kostal, a dietitian in Ontario, Canada, and owner of Dietitians4Teachers, an organization that trains educators and creates anti-diet classroom resources, says that the limited bandwidth of teachers is a huge piece of the puzzle. "Teachers inherit resources from whoever taught the class before—or they're googling online on their own time, looking for things, and up comes a free resource, and they might be like, 'Well, that looks good,'" she explains. "And because they're not dietitians, they may not have a way to vet it."

Pepper, who has taught health education since 2002, says that the field has nevertheless made huge strides in some subject areas, thanks to the efforts of advocates and progressive-thinking curriculum writers. "We teach a lot more about healthy relationships and consent now," he notes. "And many states have moved away from the abstinence-only model to a more comprehensive and LGBTQ-inclusive approach to sex ed." Substance abuse prevention has seen a similar overhaul from the disastrous "Just Say No" lesson plans of the 1980s to an evidence-based harm reduction model. But the best way to teach nutrition—and by proxy, the best way to teach about weight, body image, and eating dis-order prevention—is still a subject of intense debate. "There is a lot of movement around incorporating body positivity and recognizing that some of the ways we've addressed this in the past were either not super useful or may even have been harmful," says Pepper. But nobody has settled on a better replacement model. "There is not yet a place that I feel like, 'Oh, this is a really great, trusted source with great lessons that are engaging, and trauma-informed, and culturally aware,'" he says. "And it doesn't make sense for every school district in the country to try to figure this out for themselves."

But the local school district is where most advocates have to start. Ganginis brought her concerns about her daughter's potato chip shame and the school's nutrition curriculum to her child's classroom teacher and principal. She also testified at a board of education meeting, where she was then advised to find out who wrote nutrition curriculums at the state level. She found the state's health education specialist, who wel-comed her suggestions, and two years later, Maryland's newly revised state health curriculum included no mention of weight and had adopted an "all foods fit" approach to nutrition, where all foods are kept neu-tral rather than labeled as good or bad. "The tough part now is waiting for this to trickle down, because whether the curriculum says it or not, teachers will talk about their own experiences," Ganginis told me. "We need to educate teachers directly and establish more rules, like we are not allowed to talk about weight or dieting in the classroom."

And all of this advocacy only addresses the way nutrition is officially taught in schools—it doesn't touch the way anti-fat bias shows up in the curriculums of other subjects. "There's a presupposition among many educators that, if it's not my content area, it's not my job," says O'Connor. "There's an ongoing sentiment among math teachers, for example, that teaching anti-racism isn't their job, that's for humanities to handle. But the idea that any content area is politically neutral is a fallacy." Word problems assigned in math class may ask kids to calculate how much pizza someone has eaten when they "should" have had apples, or the number of calories in a fast-food meal. Social studies assignments or reading comprehension texts may include newspaper articles about the dangers of the obesity epidemic, presented without further context. English class reading lists may lack positive fat representation or feature books that reinforce anti-fat stereotypes. Every time a thin child encounters this kind of offhand stigma, it reinforces their understanding that fat is a bad way to be. Every time a fat child encounters it, it reinforces their understanding that they are a problem to fix.

O'Connor makes sure that books displayed in her classroom include fat protagonists and looks for opportunities to put a book like *Fat Angie* or *Love Is a Revolution* into a student's hands. "I've had a kid email me at nine p.m. on a Friday night to write a page about how much a book like that meant to her," she says. DePriest says when she does teach books from the white, heteronormative canon, she makes sure to highlight the representation problems in the text. "I fought for years to get *The Scarlet Letter* off our curriculum because the message is awful, and the book is just not accessible to kids anymore," she says. "But when I did teach it, we talked about the way Hester Prynne is seen as sexually available because she's thin and lots of students wrote about the book's lessons on bodies." Diversifying book lists or subbing out a math problem about calories for one less stigmatizing isn't difficult—but it is asking teachers, already stretched beyond capacity in so many ways, to do even more.

OPTING OUT?

It's important, when considering the myriad of ways that diet culture shows up in schools, to do a little triage. The "not eating bread" comment that Caitlin Kiarie overheard on Zoom doesn't require the same response from a parent as a calorie-tracking assignment or an experience of weight-based bullying from a peer or teacher. But sometimes sussing out that difference can be difficult because once you've started to spot fatphobia, you can't unsee it. And it all feels potentially harmful to your child because, well, it is. It can help to remember that one primary goal of education at its best is to teach kids to be curious and critical thinkers. And that doesn't mean protecting them from every potentially harmful comment or demanding that textbooks be scrubbed clean of every insensitive reference. It means helping them learn to identify these problems and start to advocate for change themselves.

This is a gradual process. When my four-year-old came home from preschool to inform me we had to stop eating cookies because "they have sugar bugs that eat my teeth," I wasn't about to tell her that her beloved teacher had food-shamed her or suggest she go back in and announce that she was always allowed to eat cookies, sugar bugs be damned. Instead, I explained that cookies are delicious, that we would not stop eating them, and that brushing our teeth would take care of the "sugar bugs." I wondered if I should have done more or engaged the teacher (who I knew to be otherwise excellent, caring, and quite overworked), but I didn't. And four years later, when this now eight-year-old looked up from reading *Harry Potter* to say, "Oh, you'll hate this part, they've got Dudley on a *diet*," I realized she was learning to identify bias, even in an otherwise-beloved book. If I had steered her away from reading those books or jumped in with a red pen to edit them, I would have deprived her of the opportunity to use and build those skills.

This doesn't mean teachers shouldn't try to assign more books with fat protagonists, or by fat writers, or that there isn't a case to take texts with offensive stereotypes and slurs of all kinds out of curriculums. But as parents, we can assess when these instances present clear harm to children—in which case, of course, we should intervene and advocate for them—and when they present an opportunity to have a conversation and to be curious about how our child is interpreting things. "Ask some questions. Try and understand what's going on before jumping to conclusions because we know that impact and intent are different," says Kostal, who often advises parents on how to respond to fatphobic microaggressions at school. "Remember that no teacher is intentionally doing harm. They're stuck with some unlearning to do, or some policies that they may not even like and have to find ways to work around."

If you do decide that a situation warrants your direct involvement, either because the potential for harm is so high or because your child is too young or otherwise not ready to advocate for themselves, Kostal advises asking for a phone call rather than sending an email. "Email is the land of misinterpreted tone and miscommunication," she says. "Have a conversation and just listen to understand first. You might say, 'Here's what I'm seeing,' and then, 'I'm curious because I'm concerned about . . .' Describe your feelings and stay focused on your kid. And remember, you are in a parent-teacher partnership with this person for the next year." That might feel daunting if the teacher is starting from a very different place than you—but it also means you don't need to solve it all in one conversation.

But sometimes, the potential for harm is so clear-cut that opting your child out of the assignment or experience is your best and only option. "Tracking food and weighing kids at school are dangerous," Kostal notes. "I would be a lot more apt to let something like a comment on your kid's lunch slide and do some home-coaching with my kids. But when it comes to a dangerous practice, I would say, 'I'm worried because this promotes disordered eating and body dissatisfaction. I'm giving permission for my child to not participate in this. Can you provide an alternative assignment they can complete?'"

Not every teacher will be thrilled when a student opts out of BMI screenings, fitness testing, or another stigmatizing assignment. But the more parents do this, the more educators will begin to question why such assignments exist in the first place. "If kids show up to school in a body, it's our job to keep them safe in that body," says O'Connor.

That's the support that O'Connor's second-grade self needed and didn't get that day in the cafeteria. But she's determined to do better by her own students. "Every person who works at a school is responsible for helping children to know that the body they come to school in is okay and that they deserve to learn, grow, and thrive in that body."

CHAPTER 11

"I Got Taller and Gymnastics Got Scarier"

"I started running when I was sixteen, because a girl called me Fatalie," says Natalie, now twenty-nine. "But I kept running because I loved it." She still does. These days, Natalie lives with her husband in Fredericksburg, Virginia, and works full-time in impact finance but also volunteers as an assistant coach for a local high school running team and runs on an elite team in Washington, D.C. Altogether, she spends at least thirteen hours a week running, cross-training, or coaching. Running is her main passion in life. And it's complicated. Throughout Natalie's running career, she has had to contend with the underlying anti-fat bias that motivated her into the sport in the first place.

I should clarify here that Natalie is, and always has been, straight-sized. As we're going to see repeatedly in this chapter, "fat" is defined much more broadly in running, and many other athletic pursuits, and "thin" much more narrowly. If the rest of the world is Old Navy, running is Prada. For years, Natalie wanted running to make her thinner, but it also seemed like she wasn't ever thin enough to be a runner. Intentional weight loss and disordered eating behaviors were common on her college running team. "My thing was bulimia," Natalie says. But she didn't lose much weight doing it. And that meant that Natalie didn't take her eating disorder seriously for years, and neither did anyone else.

But during her senior year, Natalie and her teammates did get worried about one runner whose eating disorder manifested in far more classic symptoms—namely, extreme thinness. "We knew she was having break-downs in the middle of the night about how hungry she was and bringing her own food to restaurants and skipping meals," Natalie recalls. "And she looked sick. You could see it in the hair all over her body, and how thin she was." Natalie spoke to an athletic department administrator about her concerns, who relayed them to one of the team's coaches—who gathered the whole team for a lecture. "He thought she had the ideal runner's body, and so there was no problem," Natalie recalls. "He said, 'Maybe if more of you ate like Steph, you would be national champions, too.'"

By 2015, Natalie's running had been derailed twice by stress frac-tures. "I had a little bit of a 'Come to Jesus' moment of realizing that running and eating the way I was would not be sustainable," she says. She found a therapist who took her disordered behaviors seriously and explained that eating disorders don't have to result in emaciation to be severe. Two years later, Natalie had recovered enough to join her current running team, which she describes as an outlier in the running community. "They have a zero-tolerance policy toward eating disorders because they know how highly transmissible those behaviors are on a team," she explains. "The messaging I get from this coach and the other runners is: Your body composition doesn't matter. We have short, tall, big, small runners, and we're all world-class athletes."

But that is not the message that the high school runners she coaches are getting from most of the adults around them. And the farther Natalie gets in her recovery, the more this disconnect frustrates her. "Our head coach writes off any kid who isn't what he calls 'long and lean,'" Natalie says. Last season, Natalie was concerned by how often one runner demonized food around her teammates. "There was a lot of 'Ugh, I ate chips, I'm so gross!'" Natalie says. "She was a kind of a toxic presence on the team in lots of ways." But the girl was also "long and lean," and so the head coach treated her as the team's star. "He would say, 'We need to develop this girl, she looks the part!'"

Meanwhile a talented member of another team, who Natalie sees often at meets, came back a few pounds heavier than she'd been the previous season and Natalie says the head coach's disappointment was palpable. "She ran four seconds slower at a meet this season, and it was still the second-fastest time ever run at that meet. But he's like, 'Well, she's in her head now,'" Natalie says. "It's almost like, 'We can't be as proud of you, if you can't perform at 110 pounds the same way you did at 105.'"

Until a few years ago, I didn't think of running as a sport with a ton of body pressure attached. Or rather, my own anti-fat bias led me to assume that most elite runners were naturally, effortlessly that thin. But in 2019, runner Mary Cain went public about her experiences on the Nike Oregon Project, which she joined at age seventeen, making her the youngest American track and field athlete to make a World Championships team. At the Oregon Project, Cain says she was coached to lose so much weight, she lost her period for three years and broke five bones. Cain had developed a disorder originally called female athlete triad, and now known as relative energy deficiency in sport or RED-S to acknowledge that it happens in athletes of all genders. In addition to lack of periods for menstruating athletes, the hallmarks of RED-S are low bone mineral density, which increases an athlete's risk of injuries and future osteoporosis, and what doctors term "low energy availability," meaning athletes aren't eating enough to support their caloric output. Not eating enough can happen intentionally or unintentionally, but RED-S is often diagnosed alongside eating disorders, to capture their physiological impact. And both can have long-term impacts on health.

"I joined Nike because I wanted to be the best female athlete ever," Cain says in a video on the *New York Times* website. "Instead, I was emotionally and physically abused by a system designed by Alberto [Salazar, the team's coach] and endorsed by Nike." Cain quit the team after finally telling her parents that she had become suicidal.

For decades, coaches and athletes alike have accepted the loss of periods and other RED-S symptoms as necessary prices for their sport, but Cain's story exposed the lie in that "naturally thin athlete" narrative. In fact, dangerous body ideals and training goals are common in many physical activities, especially those involving women and girls. And it happens at every level. Camille, now thirteen, fell in love with gymnastics at age five and joined a team that had her on track for a Division 1 college team. But she quit just before the start of eighth grade because, as she puts it: "I got taller, and gymnastics got scarier."

At five foot one, Camille, who lives in Boise, Idaho, isn't particularly tall to the rest of the world, but the standards in gymnastics are different. "I always wanted to be four foot seven in gymnastics and stop growing and never get bigger at all," she says. Her coaches began to comment on her growth spurt, though mostly in a friendly way. And Camille knew exactly how she compared to her teammates. Then, she started to fall more often or hit her feet on the bars. She was sure her changing body was to blame. A month before Camille quit, one of those falls resulted in a concussion. And while she was home recovering, she realized something: "I was kind of happy about it." Not going to practice for a few weeks gave Camille a chance to notice how different she felt without gymnastics looming over her. "It had gotten to the point where, whenever I had practice, I spent the whole day feeling stressed and anxious about how it would go," she says.

In addition to worrying about their height, Camille and her teammates often talked about how their stomachs used to be smaller before they hit their sixth-grade growth spurts. "You're in a leotard, and it's just very uncomfortable," Camille notes. How kids' bodies look in uniforms turns out to be one of the most common ways that anti-fat bias manifests in kid sports. "We're auditioning for summer ballet sessions, and one studio's application asked for height and weight on a program for eight- to fourteen-year-olds," says Helen, mom to thirteen-year-old Edith in the San Francisco Bay Area. Edith is in a larger body and has been dancing since she was three years old. "I just wrote 'This is concerning' on the application, so I don't think we'll get in," Helen says. "Honestly, without a long, lean body type, I doubt she'd get in there anyway." Helen also grew up in a larger body and played fullback and goalkeeper on her high school soccer team even though those uniforms didn't come in her size. "I remember having to shop in the men's section to find a goalie shirt that kind of fit," she says. She's determined that Edith be spared the same stigma, so she pays to have custom leotards and dance skirts made for Edith because the standard options don't come in her size, and she recently started designing her own line of plus-size kids' athletic clothes.

But she knows it's a privilege to have that option; the added expense of custom uniforms keeps many more kids from participating.

Katie, a mom of three in Pennsylvania, ran into the same issue when shopping for a softball uniform for her then eight-year-old Luna. "Why are they only selling 'slim-fit' softball pants for kids?" she asks. "When did softball become a sport that you have to be skinny to play?"

The answer lies somewhere between "in the last twenty years" and "maybe it always was." Many parents think of participation in dance or sports as an essential rite of childhood. We see these activities as a chance to make friends, learn about collaboration, develop healthy habits, and get good and sweaty. And sure, maybe we also hope to discover that our child has what it takes to become the professional dancer or college scholarship–winning athlete we dreamed of becoming ourselves. But pursuing youth sport and dance in our larger culture of fatphobia means you are very much also pursuing thinness. "Weight stigma is normalized and embedded into every part and every thread of youth sport," says Eva Pila, PhD, an assistant professor in the School of Kinesiology at Western University in Ontario.

Pila, who directs Western University's Body Image and Health Research Lab, is one of very few exercise scientists studying the impact of anti-fat bias on kids' experiences of sports and other physical activity. She says we don't have good data on the prevalence of weight stigma in these spaces both because "that literature is still almost nonexistent" and because so many sport and exercise researchers don't identify their own thinking about weight and health as stigmatizing. But Pila has traced how often experiences of weight stigma come up in the past twenty years of qualitative research on athletes and coaches. "We see fatphobia happening constantly, we just weren't able to recognize it for what it was at the time." Too often, we still aren't. "If you want to be a good athlete, the expectation is you will train hard and that means you will maintain or control your weight," Pila explains. "This is normalized to the point that kids may not even recognize that they are experiencing stigma."

But we need to start to grapple with the reality of anti-fat bias in kids' sports and the harm it causes. "Sport is one of the most amazing opportunities for kids to have positive, health-promoting, high-quality experiences in their bodies," says Dana Voelker, PhD, also a kinesiologist and associate professor of sport and exercise psychology at West Virginia University. "But right now, it's also one of the greatest risks to children's health and development because of how we have constructed the environment and experience for kids." Competitive athletes are more likely to engage in excessive exercise and to meet criteria for an eating disorder, according to a 2018 survey conducted by the National Eating Disorders Association of 23,920 respondents (most of whom identified as white, female, and between the ages of thirteen and twenty-four). Anti-fat bias encountered in sports and dance also reinforces stereotypes about who gets to be an athlete or a dancer that kids are already encountering elsewhere in their lives. This bias determines who joins the team, who excels on the team, and who drops out. And it underpins all the other ways that child athletes are told their bodies don't belong to them.

"IT'S JUST PHYSICS"

Before we dig into the very real harm caused by anti-fat bias in youth sports, we need to deal with the most obvious counterargument: that it's not fatphobia to say that being thinner improves athletic performance—it's science. "Weight is an easy target because it's visible, and we've tied it to every performance marker," says Pila. "I've had so many conversations with coaches and high-level trainers where the argument is, 'Well, this is just basic physics.'" Consider a sport like rowing, where athletes compete to see who can push a boat through the water the fastest. Pila has worked with coaches who argue that weight management is a critical component of their athletes' training regimens because the more the boat weighs (and by "the boat," we mean both the inanimate object and the people sitting inside it), the harder athletes will have to work to push it along. "Nobody asks, 'Should we build a better boat?'" she notes. Voelker, who has studied weight stigma in figure skating, points to a commonly invoked "eighty-pound rule," which dictates that a female figure skater must weigh at least eighty pounds less than the male figure skater who must lift her.

"Why eighty pounds?" she asks. "It's used as a proclamation of science, but where is that science? And why do we emphasize the female skaters losing weight but focus less on male skaters getting stronger?"

"It's just physics" also assumes fat athletes can't bring other skills to a sport beyond their physical presence. But fat people can be strong, fast, flexible, and graceful. And research on the relationship between weight and physical fitness, much like the relationship between weight and health outcomes, is largely correlative and clearest at the extreme ends of the BMI scale, both high and low. "When you look at everybody in the middle, it's not so clear," says Christy Greenleaf, PhD, a professor of kinesiology at the University of Wisconsin in Milwaukee. "There are people in bigger bodies that can do all kinds of physical activities at high levels." Many have cult followings on social media: The fat activist and writer Ragen Chastain has won ballroom dance competitions and run marathons; Mirna Valerio, known as "the Mirnavator," is a fat ultramarathon runner and hiker; Jessamyn Stanley is a fat yoga celebrity, author, and fitness influencer; author and influencer Meg Boggs is a fat powerlifter; and Louise Green, author of *Big Fit Girl*, runs the Size Inclusive Training Academy to help personal trainers work with folks in all body sizes.

But few fat people compete at the highest levels of most sports. And maybe, sometimes, this is physics. But stories like Mary Cain's teach us that "physics" has a very high human cost: "The body control piece is just seen as part of what has to happen at the elite levels," says Pila. "When shaving a second off your time makes the difference between getting a medal or not, folks will say we have to look at every possible way of optimizing performance. This is what must be done, and sometimes mental health must suffer."

And maybe, more often, it's not physics at all but rather the larger athlete's experience of anti-fat bias that keeps the doors to elite sports slammed shut. Because we see anti-fat bias emerge even in sports like shot put and powerlifting, where conventional wisdom holds that size equals strength, as well as football and rugby, where larger bodies are considered an asset, at least for certain positions. Across the sports spectrum, fat athletes can expect to encounter locker-room teasing, size-based nicknames, and differential treatment. "Fat athletes may excel" in certain sports, writes Frankie de la Cretaz, a journalist who covers sports, gender, and queerness, in a 2022 article for *Global Sports Matters*:

> But they are still overlooked when it comes to getting sponsorships. [. . .] Even in sports where fat athletes may contribute to a team's success—like a touchdown made possible by the blocking of a lineman—it is never those players who are allowed to be the face of a team. The glory and renown goes to quarterbacks or running backs.

In this way, assigning kids to sports by body types doesn't eliminate bias; it only narrows our understanding of what kids in different bodies can do. Laura, an attorney in Oakland, California, says people started asking if her now seventeen-year-old autistic son, Thomas, would play football when he was four years old. Laura is tall; Thomas's dad is tall and bigger bodied, and Thomas, at seventeen, wears a men's 3XL. "He's been way off the growth charts his whole life," Laura says. And on many trips to the park or the grocery store, she could expect to hear a passing comment of "Get that boy signed up for football!" Laura remembers touring a local high school when Thomas was in eighth grade and already over six feet tall. "The assistant football coach spotted us walking in the door and gave us this jolly but uncomfortably hard sell the whole time," she says. Thomas was flattered but also confused. He has never had any interest in football and views the constant commentary as "just one of those weird things adults always say," much to Laura's relief. "The risk for head injuries in football really concerns me," she says. "But it is tricky because this is one of the few sports where a bigger body is celebrated and sought after. And that's a different experience from other sports, where you're just the big kid on the team."

Within the field of kinesiology, scholars are divided on the question of whether the experience of anti-fat bias has a bigger impact than weight itself on a person's fitness level and athletic performance. "Some people see this as a social justice issue because if we're not creating environments where all youth can feel empowered to participate, we are systematically keeping people from experiencing the benefits of the sport," says Pila. "But there is also a camp that recognizes that, sure, at the participatory level, sport can be for everybody. But at the elite levels, exclusivity is a normative part of competing. So, we don't have to change the system because only very exceptional people can get to that stage anyway."

The problem with that latter argument is that "very exceptional" has always been code for thin. "In many sports, we've never tried anything different," says Voelker. "We haven't allowed people of certain body types to excel and move forward to the next level. So, it becomes a self-fulfilling prophecy that is far more about social construction than science." We don't even know what fat athletes can do at elite levels in most sports, because they never get there. And our resistance to changing is rooted in culture and emotion. "There is often this sense that we have certain rules in place to protect the authenticity of a sport," says Greenleaf. Consider the expectations around form and line for dancers, or the conviction of the head coach Natalie works with that he needs "long and lean" runners. "We hold on to these things as sacred," says Greenleaf. "But rules change all the time." She draws a parallel with the long-running debate about the high rates of head trauma in American football: "We know football is dangerous for athletes. But when I ask students, 'Could we create a form of football that doesn't involve head trauma?' they can't wrap their heads around it," she explains. "These are people who care about health! But there's this huge disconnect."

These "rules," which are traditions and rituals borne out of bias, may only apply in theory to elite athletes, but they absolutely ripple out and down through every level of competition. Meghan Seaman owns the On Stage Dance Studio in Stratford, Ontario. Even when placing dancers on her competitive team, Seaman never factors in weight. "If you're willing to put in the work, I will find a place for you," she says. Her competitive dance team travels to five competitions and puts on two shows each year between September and May. At every competition, Meghan's team of just over one hundred dancers, some tall, some short, some thin, some fat, line up next to teams where virtually every girl is five foot seven and weighs one hundred pounds. "I feel like the impression of my team at dance competitions is that my studio takes it less seriously," says Meghan. "Which is kind of true if [body size] is your scale. Nobody on my team would make it onto their team."

Meghan grew up in the dance world, taking lessons and performing from the age of five to eighteen, and says she spent most of those years justifying her own disordered eating habits as necessary in her quest to be "a better dancer," which meant having the ideal thin dancer's body. "My experiences really shape the environment I strive to create for my students today," Meghan says. She prioritizes diversity when she hires instructors and trains the staff not to give compliments or corrections related to a dancer's body size or shape. "There is a big difference between saying to a child, 'Suck in that stomach!' and 'Your butt is sticking out!' or saying to a child, 'Lengthen your spine,'" she notes. Meghan also gently challenges students who make fatphobic comments. If a student says, "I feel so gross in my leotard, I ate a huge dinner," Meghan responds, "Good, you needed that dinner. You're going to dance for two hours." When she hears, "I'm too fat to be a ballerina, I can't get my leg that high," she explains why flexibility and endurance have nothing to do with body size.

To Meghan, this style of teaching feels worth it because it allows her to bring what she loves about dance to so many more students, even if she doesn't have the glory of winning more competitions or sending students on to Canada's National Ballet School. "The percentage of kids I teach that are going to have a career in dance is so minuscule, I would much rather focus on helping them have a good time, be active, and make friends and memories," she says. That's true of all kids, in all physical activities. No matter how much thinness matters or doesn't at the Olympics, most of our kids aren't going there. And yet the sports leagues and dance classes we sign them up for are structured around the possibility that one of them might. That helps to justify training regimens and messaging that perpetuate anti-fat bias. "You could say, 'Well, let's change the standards of this sport,'" Pila says. "But they land on, 'Let's change the athlete.'"

THE PROFESSIONALIZATION OF YOUTH SPORT

Greenleaf, the professor of kinesiology at the University of Wisconsin in Milwaukee, was a talented childhood figure skater. She was never interested in elite levels of competition, but the year she graduated high school, in 1990, she joined the Ice Capades, a circus on ice that toured the country from 1940 to the mid-1990s, featuring figure skating performances from former Olympic and US national champion skaters who had retired from formal competition. Greenleaf performed in the Ice Capades for a year, and every week she and every other skater stood on a scale. "We each had a goal weight we were supposed to maintain, and if you were over, you were fined a couple of dollars for every pound," she recalls. The goal weight had nothing to do with health or even athletic performance: "They based it on how tall you were and how you looked. If they wanted you to look thinner, they would lower your goal." Let's change the athlete, indeed.

The pressure of those weekly weigh-ins resulted in lots of dieting and other disordered behaviors, Greenleaf confirms. But while the Ice Capades are long gone, figure skating and many other youth sports are a bigger business than ever. And that concerns Greenleaf and other researchers studying athletes' experiences of weight stigma. "When adults are spending a lot of money on kid sports and making a lot of money on kid sports, we see greater expectations placed on kids to conform to those adults' ideas about how they should look and behave," she explains. "A lot of money" is putting it mildly: 27 percent of parents with at least one kid playing a sport said they spent $500 or more on related expenses each month, according to a 2019 survey commissioned by TD Ameritrade. Travel baseball can run parents up to $3,700 per season and travel volleyball anywhere from $1,500 to $10,000, according to Next College Student Athlete, a company involved in the college sports recruiting process. A website with advice for parents with kids who play travel hockey says that sport can cost around $6,000 per season.

One reason that youth sports have become so professionalized, and so expensive, is the shrinking budget for such activities at public schools and town park and recreation departments. These are the fields and gymnasiums where many kids kick their first soccer ball or do their first cartwheel because the activities are low cost or free. But such programs are often only available at younger ages; by the time your child is in upper elementary school, there will be both fewer options for them to play sports in a noncompetitive way and the expectation (especially in wealthier communities) that they need to be on a special team to receive the best coaching and opportunities. "For-profit sport and activity programs come in to fill that need for those who can afford it," Greenleaf explains. "But this leaves by the wayside any families who can't pay, as well as kids who don't have the skill level or body that fits the expected mold."

For kids who can participate in for-profit youth sports, the expectations often rapidly change. With five-hour practices, five days a week, Camille, the thirteen-year-old who quit gymnastics after getting taller, says it felt like she spent more time with her coaches than she did with her own parents—and much of her anxiety about the sport was related to how her coaches would treat her on any given day. In practice, if a gymnast fell, she would be assigned fifteen extra routines. And there was emotional stress on top of the physical ordeal. "During competition season, one of my coaches would get really, really mean and sometimes wouldn't even talk to us," she says. Camille and all her teammates were upset about it, so she finally wrote him a letter saying, "Everyone is kind of scared of you right now because you're so serious. We do this sport to have fun." She says the coach was nicer after that, but Camille didn't feel better. "I got anxiety every time I went to the gym," she says. "And I had no other life outside of gymnastics."

Neither Camille nor her parents blame the coaches, even though things got so intense. "This was a really great gym that did a lot to prioritize kids' health over competition," says Camille's mom, Ann, who is herself recovering from an eating disorder and identifies as small fat. But she does think the sport's all-consuming culture dimmed her child's light. "We knew she was exhausted and anxious all the time, and that she never wanted to try new things or talk to new people. Gymnastics had a very negative impact on my child's mind and body."

At the high school level, Natalie, the running coach in Fredericksburg, Virginia, reports that many of the star athletes on her team and others in the area pay for private coaching outside of school. "They join these clubs so they can get personal coaching, and the training regimens are very, very intense," she says. But the part that bugs Natalie is that the coaches running such programs—"almost always these former college runners who are now guys in their forties"—promote their services on Instagram using photos of their female athletes. "It's all these photos of these girls in their sports bras, with captions going off about how fast they are because they've had this training," she says. "So even if these girls are keeping their own social media accounts private, it's their thin, fast body that the coach is using to sell their product."

The message these kids receive isn't just that their weight needs to be low. It's also that their body isn't entirely their own. "Other people have ownership of your body because they have invested in it and because what you do with your body reflects on them," says Greenleaf. It's hard to argue that the professionalization of youth sport has been good for anyone's health. "Can you really be well when you are training and pushing your body to its absolute limit, physically and emotionally?" asks Pila. "My personal opinion is no."

All this conditioning, at its most extreme, leads to experiences like Mary Cain's. It also leads to the numerous incidents of emotional abuse and sexual misconduct by coaches documented in an investigation into the National Women's Soccer League, as NPR reported in October 2022, after several former players came forward with allegations. "Abuse in the NWSL is rooted in a deeper culture in women's soccer, beginning in youth leagues, that normalizes verbally abusive coaching," former acting US attorney general Sally Q. Yates wrote in her report on the investigation.

And it leads to a similarly toxic culture enabled the abuse of the 250 girls and young women (and at least one young man), many of whom were USA Gymnastics national team members, by renowned sports doctor Larry Nassar. For decades, we now know, team coaches normalized Nassar's behavior, brushing off why Nassar would prescribe (and perform) a procedure involving vaginal penetration and other forms of genital manipulation under the guise of necessary "sports massages" and pelvic floor physical therapy designed to treat hip or back pain. Olympic gold medalist Aly Raisman told *Time* magazine that while Nassar made her uncomfortable, it took years to understand that his actions were sexual abuse because the sport's "culture of success at any cost" trained athletes to keep quiet and not ask questions. "These girls

are groomed from an incredibly young age to deny their own experience," Joan Ryan, whose 1995 book *Little Girls in Pretty Boxes* explores
the physical and psychological toll gymnastics takes on girls and young
women, told the *Guardian*. "Your knee hurts? You're being lazy. You're
hungry? No, you're fat and greedy. They are trained to doubt their own
feelings."

IT'S ALL AESTHETIC ATHLETICS NOW

Here's where I need to confess that the world of youth sport and dance
is almost entirely foreign to me. When I was four my parents put me in
a ballet and tap class, and I sat down onstage for the entire recital. At age
seven, I played one season of Little League and sat down in the outfield
during every game. We are not a family of natural athletes, and nobody
except my dad cares about professional sports, so it was easy to lean,
instead, into my passions for books and art. Plus: I was a thin kid, so my
lack of interest in physical activity was greeted with amusement rather
than alarm. Since I didn't have to lose weight, I didn't need to like exercise. By middle school, it was a given that I would not be signing up for
basketball or track. There was one week in eighth grade when I thought
I might be a secret field hockey star—we played in gym class and I
somehow, accidentally, scored a goal. I showed up for the first practice,
realized they had to run sprints and only wore the cute skirts on game
days, and quit. Now I realized that at thirteen, I'd internalized the idea
that I only wanted to do sports if I could look good doing them—and I
believed this to such an extent that I mostly didn't do them at all.

Most of my memories of those early experiences with physical activity are of boredom or confusion because I never understood the rules,
the dance steps, or how to keep my eye on the ball. But I also remember
feeling intensely aware of how *watched* I was, as a child in a sparkly dance
costume, or wearing the heavy batting helmet to step up to the plate.
Watching kids' bodies isn't always about their appearance. It's often about
form, alignment, speed, and skill. But each of those concepts very quickly
comes back around to how a child looks and how big they are.

We have been taught to expect this in activities like ballet, gymnastics, cheerleading, figure skating, and synchronized swimming, which are known collectively as "aesthetic athletics." Showing off very thin bodies, especially female bodies, is core to the mission in these worlds. Aesthetic athletes are judged on their choice of costume, how they wear their hair, and on the lines and shape of their bodies; a competition can be won or lost on these matters of "presentation." We also expect the body to be under scrutiny in a sport like wrestling, where athletes compete according to their weight class. As a result, all these activities have a long history of asking athletes to use extreme measures to control their weight. This pressure cuts across gender (although women's wrestling has lower weight categories than men's): Remember Cody in Chapter 9, chewing tobacco all day in school so he could spit out his water weight for high school wrestling meets. We can consider him Exhibit A for why youth sport does not always promote health. "These are the sports where you'll see coaches recommending stringent weight control techniques under the guise of the athlete's 'well-being,'" says Pila. "Controlling weight is just part of coaching tactics."

But aesthetic athletics aren't the only activities with pronounced anti-fat bias. Whether your child wants to row, play hockey, or shoot hoops, it's a question of when, not if, they will encounter toxic messages about body size and shape. There may not be such an overt focus on weight loss, but Pila's research shows that these "less aesthetic" sports are still rife with implicit bias and opportunities for microaggressions. This may come in the form of the uniform discrimination that Edith and Luna encountered. Uniforms in some women's sports, especially, have also become increasingly revealing in recent years in ways that perpetuate and reinforce anti-fat bias by emphasizing how well athletes' bodies adhere to the thin ideal. "I definitely think our shorts are not great, I'm pulling them down constantly," says Naomi, fifteen, a high school freshman from Raleigh, North Carolina, of her school volleyball team's uniforms, which feature very short shorts and a tight top. "There are lots of camel toe incidents. And we have a photographer who takes pictures at all the games, and you don't want to be caught with your shorts up your bottom."

In a misguided effort to compensate for the skimpiness of the uniforms, Naomi says the athletic department adopted a new rule: Female volleyball players (and only female volleyball players) had to wear athletic shorts over their uniform anytime they walked out of the gym, especially when their route to the school parking lot took them by the football team. "It's so weird. If the uniform is so 'inappropriate,' we should be wearing something else," says Naomi. "They made it sound like we were trying to show off our bodies or something, when we're literally just walking around in what they told us to wear." She's not imagining the double standard. One day when Naomi was on her way to take a team photo in front of the school, she heard one of the athletic staff members say to another girl on the team, "Pull your shorts down! I wouldn't let my daughter walk around like that."

This is where anti-fat bias intersects with sexual objectification, especially of female athletes. Naomi's uniform favors smaller bodies and sexualizes them in a sport that is ostensibly just about how well you can hit a ball over a net. Some proponents of such uniforms argue that they boost athletic performance: "If you're talking about aerodynamics and elite athletes, okay," says Voelker. "But when men and women's uniforms are different for the same activity, then you start to go, 'Well, this is a social construct that would better serve young people if we deconstructed it.'" I check with Naomi and indeed: "The boys' sports teams just wear regular athletic shorts," she reports. And when girls are penalized, as with the rule about covering up off the court, it teaches kids that bodies that look visibly female are somehow dangerous to have. This reinforces anti-fat bias since thin bodies tend to be less readily sexualized than fat ones, as we saw in the discussion of dress codes in Chapter 10.

Anti-fatness can also show up when other kids who use "fat" as a casual insult (one of Pila's qualitative papers is titled, "Can You Move Your Fat Ass off the Baseline?") and engage in the kind of food shaming and body comparisons that Natalie has observed in her runners. Parental anxieties and debates over the "right" snacks to serve at sport practices, or the best food to eat before games and meets, are another opportunity to reinforce to kids that the main reason they should play sports is to stay or become thin. A common rant on any online mom group is about the "junk" served at sports practices, and how Gatorade, protein bars, chips, and cookies have too much sugar and, thus, could undermine the benefit of the kids' workout. But you'd only draw that conclusion if you think of your child's soccer practice as a weight management program.

And all of that is just what happens when you're allowed to play. Natalie recalls that last season, a girl in a larger body showed up at cross-country practice a few times and then just disappeared. She wasn't cut; Natalie notes that her team doesn't make cuts in cross-country because most meets let teams bring as many runners as they want, but only score the top seven athletes. But she stopped coming to practice. "I wonder if we just didn't even have a singlet in her size," says Natalie. "Or if it's because she wasn't getting individual attention or coaching because we don't expect a kid who looks like her to be a great runner." Kids learn fast that sports are about winning and that coaches want to coach the kids they think can win. Natalie says she has spent most of her own running career ranking tenth or eleventh on a team where only the top seven runners matter. "And whether I was tenth or eleventh directly impacted how much conversation I'd have with my coach," she notes. "It was painful and discouraging and made me not want to try."

Kids who don't have the "right" body for their sport are subjected to the same aesthetic scrutiny as thinner athletes but get none of the potentially mitigating (if also complicated and objectifying) affirmation and validation. "Kids know when a sport has an idealized body type because they see what the Olympic athletes look like, but they also see what their friends on the team look like," explains Greenleaf. "This influences their ideas about where they might fit and be welcomed."

I wonder if the larger girl who tried to join Natalie's team did so because she, or someone in her life, thought it would help her lose weight—because all too often, this is the only reason fat kids are encouraged to be athletic at all. Exercising for weight loss, like dieting, is a risk factor for the development of future eating disorders. And while this shouldn't be the point, it also rarely works: Research has shown that physical education classes are ineffective at reducing student BMI, though scholars are unsure if that's because kids don't exercise all that much in a typical gym class or because of other factors.

There is similar evidence that youth sport participation rates do not correlate with lower childhood obesity rates. A 2011 evidence review of nineteen studies found "no clear pattern of association between body weight and sport participation." Again, researchers aren't sure why playing sports doesn't make kids thin. It could be because, like gym class, the average team practice doesn't involve that much movement: "There's a lot of standing around in that hour session, especially when coaches are only playing their best players," notes Voelker. But it may also simply underscore that the relationship between weight and exercise is murkier than we think. And we do know that it's very possible to improve fitness levels through exercise without losing weight. So even measuring the success of youth sports in terms of their impact on childhood obesity only reinforces their inherent anti-fat bias.

The long reach of aesthetic athletics and the ripple effects of anti-fat bias through youth sports almost certainly contributes to the complicated, uneasy relationship that many kids will continue to have with exercise well into adulthood. After all, when we think of working out primarily as a tool to make our body conform to aesthetic ideals, we're far more likely to stop exercising when it doesn't. Middle-aged women who listed "weight loss" as their primary motivation to exercise were the least likely to do it, in multiple studies conducted by Michelle Segar, PhD, a behavioral psychologist who studies health habits at the University of Michigan. "We stick with habits when we're internally motivated to maintain them," she explains. "Weight loss is always externally driven—and the bar is forever changing on what constitutes 'success.'"

But finding an internal motivation for exercise can feel impossible, because the most popular workouts right now are all exercises in self-objectification: We're watching ourselves in the mirrors at barre or spin class or CrossFit, wondering if we look too flabby or too sweaty. Even if the mirror isn't there, we're mentally floating outside our bodies, assessing our stomach rolls when we go into shoulder stand. Or whether we're able to open our hips so fully that our triangle pose could be held flat "between two panes of glass," as a yoga teacher once instructed me. We're checking the Peloton leaderboards or comparing our times on Strava to every other runner we know (and many we don't). We don't move our bodies to be in our bodies. We might talk about wanting to have more energy, or self-care, but mostly, we do it to look at our bodies and to be looked at. And this has severe consequences for our physical and mental health.

A BETTER WAY

What would youth sport and dance look like, if their priority shifted from athletic performance to athletic well-being? And how would this translate to a generation of kids who grow up to be adults who find intrinsic value in movement and the ways physical activities can reduce stress, build strength and flexibility, and otherwise benefit our lives without any weight loss agenda? These are the questions that Greenleaf, Pila, and Voelker are all asking in their academic research, but that don't yet seem to be on the radar of many coaches or trainers. Greenleaf notes that traditional kinesiology education is at least partially to blame: "We've always taught these future coaches and physical education teachers that obesity is bad and to be avoided at all costs," she notes. "We must shift away from thinking of the body as a machine and weight as a matter of calories in, calories out. We know that's overly simplistic."

That alone will be an uphill battle. But an even trickier shift may be what needs to happen in the culture of coaching, which still rests on the belief that athletes prove their commitment to a sport by toughing it out no matter what. When Greenleaf teaches first-year students, she talks about her research on the reality TV show *The Biggest Loser*, which critiqued how the show's personal trainers verbally abused its contestants. "I explain that screaming and yelling at people is not an effective strategy for long-term behavior change even if it gets a short-term result because you've intimidated them," she says. "But many students can't contemplate how they could ever coach a sport like football without screaming at their athletes. That was their own experience with youth sport, and they've decided the outcome was worth it."

Comprehensive anti-bias training could help those same students identify the harm caused by abusive coaching methods. But it's also true that most of the coaches whom the average parent encounters when we're signing our kids up for basketball or soccer don't have any specific training. They're just teachers who happened to have played the sport in college, or local parents or people like Natalie, volunteering for the gig. More likely than not, nobody is looking too hard at how the coach operates, let alone how they talk about food and weight. But that also means there is more of an opportunity for other parents to get involved, ask questions, and offer other perspectives. "If your child is just beginning a sport, do some homework," suggests Greenleaf. "Chat with the coach or the organization's leadership [if you're looking at a for-profit program] and ask, 'Hey, what are you doing to be inclusive of different body shapes and sizes?'" You can also ask about protocols around snacks at practice and pregame fueling, as well as the available size range of uniforms or costumes. Especially with aesthetic athletics, it makes sense to ask how they think about eating disorder prevention and whether there are ever weight requirements to progress to the next level. "Any coach or studio owner who has actively grappled with this issue should have answers at hand," notes Meghan Seaman, the dance instructor. "I actually love when parents ask me these things because it gives me a chance to share what we do differently."

It may make sense to encourage kids in bigger bodies to try sports where their bodies are more likely to be viewed as an asset: Laura reports that Thomas has had wonderful experiences doing kung fu and shot put. "He doesn't feel like he's the biggest kid on the team," she says. She liked kung fu, especially, because people enter the sport at all different ages. "I never encountered body issues, it's just about skill." Finding a sport safe space like this could be essential for many kids who wouldn't feel welcome in other activities. But we also shouldn't steer fat kids away from their passions. And so Thomas, who has always loved the water, also plays water polo on both a club team and his school's team. He's one of the biggest kids—"and they wear Speedos, it's all out there!" notes Laura—but so far, the experience has been a positive one.

If your child is older, or already deeply passionate about a particular sport, you should still ask these questions any time they join a new team or program. But you'll also want to start fostering their own awareness of the risks of their sport. If your child doesn't have the kind of body idealized by their sport, you can discuss that with them honestly. Acknowledge what they love about the activity, but also bring up the problems: "Ballet is such a beautiful art form, but it has a really problematic history around body size." Then you might say: "You have a bigger body, and we think that's amazing. But it might get hard in this world. Do you want to do this?" suggests Zoë Bisbing, a therapist who specializes in eating disorders in New York City, who is herself a former child ballerina. "You need to name it and set some boundaries. 'I know you love to dance, and I want to support you in pursuing this passion, but I'm not going to let you starve yourself or try to manipulate your weight. Eating enough to support your growth is a condition of participating.'"

For my own kids, I've opted to steer clear of aesthetic athletics, beyond one adorable and very low-pressure kindergarten ballet class. But my older daughter is passionate about riding horses and rock climbing—and I know that small, lean bodies are prized in both of those sports (which are also expensive and not readily accessible to many families). So, I look for opportunities to name and discuss anti-fat bias if it comes up and seek out examples of climbers and equestrians in bigger bodies excelling at their sport. (We're fans of @TheStrongSarah and @DrewClimbsWalls, two fat climbers on Instagram who post videos of themselves excelling, but also falling and messing up, on rock walls.) At eight, Violet also opted not to join a local rock-climbing team precisely because she didn't want the pressure to have to climb faster and win at meets. She may decide in the future that she does want to compete—but making competition optional helps her understand that her own enjoyment of the sport matters more than what other people think of her body and her performance. If your child adores a team sport (where competition is built-in), consider whether the elite travel team is necessary or beneficial to their experience. Can they just play pickup basketball at the park or go on family bike rides? Can you join a community pool and let them have fun swimming there on weekends instead of taking on the intensive schedule and pressure of a swim team?

Bisbing thinks of conversations like these as eating disorder prevention. And parents need to have them even when a child does appear to have the ideal body for their chosen activity, especially if they are still prepubescent. "Be clear: We can't interfere with puberty. It's not normal to lose your period, and I will step in to protect you if that's a risk." After all, while thinness may open doors to a sport, it doesn't guarantee a trauma-free experience. Greenleaf suggests opening a conversation with, "Your body is your calling card in this sport, and you might take a lot of pride in that. But it also gives people permission to comment on and evaluate your body." Talk with your child about their right to refuse to be weighed, or to set boundaries with a coach about body comments, and role-play those conversations so your child can practice advocating for themselves.

Helen has taken this approach with Edith and so far, it seems to be working. When I meet Edith over Zoom, she's aware that she's one of the biggest kids in her dance class: "I feel like I look different from the others," she tells me. "And I'll think, like, 'Do I stand out in a weird way?'" But she doesn't question her fundamental right to be there. She knows that her dancing adds value. "I don't think anyone else thinks [about my weight]," she says. "And if we only showed one type of body, that might be discouraging to other people."

It's also important that the kids know that they always have an out, and that you'll support them quitting the activity (yes, even if you paid for it, even mid-season), if the pressures around body and performance get too intense. Every expert I spoke with for this chapter cautioned against letting kids specialize in activities too early, or even at all. "It's fine to be an elite X kind of athlete, but you better have other things in your life that make you feel like you," says Bisbing. "Because this will inevitably end, and probably while you are still pretty young."

For Camille, the benefits of quitting have been immediate and clear-cut. She's grown a few inches and her periods have gotten more regular. And she's turned into a different person. "In seventh grade, I didn't talk to anyone, at all, at school," says Camille. She spoke only when a teacher called on her and made just one friend the entire year. In some ways, she barely noticed how isolated she was in school; the conversations and concerns of other kids seemed so removed from Camille's life. Because all day, every day was consumed with worry about how that afternoon's practice would go. "But now, in eighth grade, that's changed completely," Camille tells me, and she can't help smiling as she says it. "I talk to everyone. I'm friends with everyone in my classes. Without gymnastics, I can just be me."

CHAPTER 12

Normalizing Puberty

ONE day, in the middle of math class, Josie needed to go to the bathroom. She asked the teacher for permission, wrote her name on the blackboard, and went. But when she got there, "instead of normal pee, there was blood," Josie, who is now eleven, tells me over Zoom from her home in Minneapolis. Her mom had told Josie about periods, but Josie wasn't sure what she was seeing. "You know how, when you download a new app on your phone, it takes a long time to load and can be quite slow because your phone has a lot of random stuff you don't need?" she says. "My brain was, like, going through that process of slowly downloading this knowledge."

Also, she didn't have a pad. But Josie is a resourceful kid. "I took a bunch of toilet paper, rolled it up, and made this really thick piece," Josie explains, demonstrating with her hands. "And I stuck that in my underwear." She went back to class, hoping to just get on with her day. But the next time she had to go to the bathroom, the bleeding was worse. This time Josie told her teacher she needed to see the school nurse. As she walked down the hall to the nurse's office, she says, her brain finished connecting the dots. "I realized what this was," Josie says, "and I was quite embarrassed."

She was also seven years old.

The nurse gave Josie a pad and told her how to use it, then called her mom to come pick her up. On her way to the school, Josie's mom, Magen, stopped by the nearest drugstore to get supplies. And in the aisle where she was used to picking up her own tampons, she found a shelf of "tween" menstrual pads promising to "fit smaller bodies." "I just thought, how does this even exist as a product?" Magen told me when I interviewed her for a *Scientific American* story about menstrual taboos in 2019. Magen was anxious that Josie had started menstruating three weeks shy of her eighth birthday, but she was not completely surprised. When Josie was six, she noticed her daughter's body odor. By the time Josie turned seven, she was getting blackheads on her nose, slamming doors, and sleeping late. And she developed breast buds. "I had to buy her bras because she couldn't wear certain shirts without it being obvious," Magen said then. "It was the summer before second grade. So that was traumatizing for both of us."

Josie's first period lasted three days. She had painful cramps and was acutely aware that this was uncommon for kids her age. "She kept saying, 'Nobody else in my class does this!'" recalls Magen. When I ask Josie at age eleven to look back on that time, she remembers that embarrassment and confusion most. "I didn't really know if it was a good thing or a bad thing," she says. "I knew how babies are made and that getting your period is your body saying, 'Okay, we're not going to have a baby this month.'" So, Josie was relieved the period meant she wasn't going to have a baby. But she didn't understand why her body was doing such a grown-up thing in second grade. And neither did Magen, whose own period didn't start until she was twelve. But Magen is white, and Josie is Black, and many of the Black women on her father's side of the family were also early developers. "When we started to hear from some of them, 'Yes, this happened to me, too,' it helped Josie a lot to hear about their experiences and realize maybe this isn't that unusual," Magen says. Josie agrees: "It would be even better for your kid if you can show them, like, a famous YouTuber who has been there," she suggests to me. "Nobody wants to be the only one."

Josie's experience is what's known medically as "precocious puberty," when a child develops secondary sexual characteristics before the age of eight for girls and nine for boys, although I'll be focusing on the experiences of people assigned female at birth in this chapter. That's both because precocious puberty is more common for people who menstruate, and because the pubertal development of their bodies more directly intersects with anti-fat bias. Media reports on "precocious puberty" frequently include hand-wringing rhetoric tying it to the "childhood obesity epidemic." And indeed, the Centers for Disease Control and Prevention's records show that the average age at first menstrual period for American women has dropped from 12.1 years old in 1995 to 11.9 years old between 2013 and 2017, a period in which the rate of childhood obesity rose from a little over 10 percent to around 19.3 percent. The onset of breast development, a stage of puberty that tends to precede menstruation, now occurs eighteen months to two years earlier than it did a few decades ago, according to Frank Biro, MD, who studies problems related to pubertal maturation at Cincinnati Children's Hospital. His research, published in the journal *Pediatrics* in 2013, put the average age of breast development at 8.8 years old for African American girls, 9.3 for Hispanic girls, and 9.7 for White and Asian Americans. "The age of breast development has clearly dropped, while the age of menarche has drifted down," he told me in 2019. "They are both concerning."

This concern is rooted in the belief that earlier puberty is a by-product of kids getting fatter. Estrogen and other hormones rise with body fat percentage, and in Biro's research and many other studies, a higher BMI is the strongest predictor of early breast development and earlier pubertal onset across all racial groups. I'll own it: My first reaction upon reading Biro's data was to think, "Okay, well, this seems like the one unequivocal problem with kids having bigger bodies today." Girls who start puberty early don't also finish puberty early, so they tend to stay in the stage longer, researchers are finding, meaning their growing bodies spend more time in what's known as a "window of susceptibility," a time when the human body is in a particularly critical stage of development, so environmental chemical exposures and other experiences are more likely to have an impact on their future health.

"We know that for every year you delay menarche, you decrease the risk of pre- and postmenopausal breast cancer by 4 to 8 percent," said Biro. "On a population basis, that's really important."

There are also concerns about how early pubertal development affects kids socially and emotionally. "We know that early reproductive development is not matched by early cognitive development. Their brains don't keep up. So how do we teach children to manage sexual urges and other realities of puberty?" said Marcia Herman-Giddens, DrPH, an adjunct professor of maternal and child health at the University of North Carolina's Gillings School of Global Public Health when I interviewed her for the *Scientific American* story. And because the end of puberty corresponds with most of us reaching our full adult height, going through puberty too young can cause issues with bone development and may mean that kids end up shorter than they might otherwise have been.

But we can't separate our understanding of the risks of early puberty from the way thinness and whiteness inform how we research and think about "normal" puberty, as well as normal sexuality and normal bodies. The traditional timeline for breast development and other body changes explored in books, and in the movies shown to giggling fifth graders, is based on the experiences of thin, white, cisgender bodies. The fact that Black girls like Josie have always started puberty earlier than white girls is usually not much more than a footnote in puberty education. American research on puberty and race also rarely looks beyond three broad categories (white, Black, and Hispanic), ignoring a multitude of other experiences, including those of Asian and Indigenous children. When earlier puberty onset among kids of color is discussed by researchers and healthcare providers, it's often stigmatized and framed as a symptom of larger perceived dysfunctions in marginalized communities and tied to higher body weights.

And, as with most questions around weight and health, the existing data on puberty age and weight has only established a correlation, not causation. "The focus quickly becomes, 'How do we get kids' bodies to be smaller at eight, nine, or ten so they don't go through puberty too early?'" says Maria Monge, MD, director of adolescent medicine at Dell Children's Medical Center in Austin, Texas. "But we're not asking, 'Why is this happening in the first place?'" We're also not asking if early periods and breast development should be treated like a medical crisis—we're jumping straight to panic. But by "we," I mostly mean researchers, healthcare providers, and the media. Anecdotally, Monge reports that the families of patients she sees in early puberty are not usually all that worried about their child's health. "This feels very much like something that privileged white people are telling other people to be concerned about."

The families Monge works with *are* worried about the social ramifications of helping a child manage periods in third grade. They are concerned about how their children will be perceived by the wider world as they gain weight and if developing breasts will make them vulnerable to sexualization and harassment. And these fears are well founded. As we've seen, kids in bigger bodies are more likely to experience bullying and to be policed for what they wear. And regardless of puberty status, Black girls like Josie experience "adultification," where they are seen as sexually more mature than their white peers, according to the research by Georgetown University Law School's Center on Poverty and Inequality we also discussed in Chapters 4 and 10. "Adultification is a form of dehumanization, robbing [Black girls] of the very essence of what makes childhood distinct from all other developmental periods: innocence," the study authors wrote. But the solution to these problems is not weight loss. Trying to fight early puberty by making kids' bodies smaller sends the clear message that it's their bodies that are the problem—not a society willing to demonize and sexualize a seven-year-old just because she's wearing a bra.

These problems are not limited to early puberty. No matter when it happens, puberty is a phase of life too often experienced as being at war with your body. And that's because this cultural conversation—around the development of breasts and the onset of menstruation for cisgender girls, of voice changes and wet dreams for cisgender boys, and of so many other transitions for gender-nonconforming kids—has always been fraught. We frame puberty as an experience to dread, and to stave off for as long as possible, as an abrupt end to the idyllic innocence of childhood. And it's true that the physical changes and emotional growth that happens during these years can be painful. But it's also true that our fear of unruly bodies—especially fat bodies, Brown and Black bodies, and female or gender-nonconforming bodies—is the framing for our conversations about what kids' bodies are supposed to do during these years. "Puberty is this time when kids often feel like they're along for the ride, and this is a train that is going faster than they're comfortable with, and to places they can't anticipate," says Kate Morris, LICSW, a clinical social worker in private practice who previously worked as a therapist for a middle school and high school in Vermont. "And all of that is hard. But what breaks my heart is that their bodies so often can't be a place of safety during that time. And that's where anti-fat bias comes in."

It took another year before Josie's periods became regular. During that time, she grew three inches and gained forty pounds. When Magen took her to the pediatrician, she says their doctor was calm about Josie's early menstruation: "She said, yes, this happens, she likely won't be regular for a while, but she'll get another period in a few months to a year and then you'll see it get more frequent," she explains. But she did zero in on Josie's growth spurt. "That's when we started to hear, 'Well, her BMI is a little high, so maybe she should be eating less and exercising more.'"

Magen paid no attention to the doctor's advice. But Josie was already there. She began training herself to ignore her hunger for as long as she could during the day. Then at night, especially at her dad's house, she would sneak into the kitchen, fill a plastic baggie with bread and sugar cubes, and hide in her closet to eat it all. "There was a voice in my head saying, 'You're so ugly, you're so fat, you're not hungry, you don't need to eat,'" Josie says. "My brain just slowly taught itself weird things until I couldn't hear anything else. It's like you're drowning in an ocean, and every time you get to the surface, another big wave comes."

In November 2021, Josie dropped twenty pounds in one month. Magen was alarmed. "But the doctors were like, 'Oh, whatever, she's finally shooting up, because she also got taller.'" Magen pushed to get Josie into therapy, and both her eating and her weight have since been restored. But she's still angry at how our traditional puberty narratives—both in terms of the "right" age for bodies to change and the expectation that kids are always supposed to "lean out" as they get older—kept everyone from understanding how and why Josie was in crisis. And unpacking these traditional narratives isn't just helpful in cases of precocious puberty. Every kid, in every body size, of any gender, charts their own course through this phase, which rivals infancy for the amount of growth and development that must occur. Identifying how fatphobia and other biases show up in our conversations around puberty is the first step toward removing those barriers. If we can begin to reframe this phase as a time to embrace rather than avoid, we could do so much to lessen the stigma our kids encounter, just for growing.

WHY WEIGHT MATTERS DURING PUBERTY

When Holly, now forty-one, and a postpartum doula in Pittsburgh, got her period at age eleven, she didn't tell her mother for an entire year. "I would clandestinely steal pads from her, but I did not want her to know this had happened," she says. "I think I had some shame about growing up. I wanted to be older, but from my parents, I got the message, 'You're our little girl,' and it just didn't feel okay to mature and age."

Experiencing puberty growth as a form of loss is a common theme when I ask adults to reflect on these years. Isabel, now forty-seven, from Montreal, remembers looking in the mirror at age fifteen and not recognizing the body in the reflection. "I saw a young woman with curvy hips, flaring out from my waist in a way that was just unrecognizable to me," she says. "The dissonance is what I remember most vividly. This body was attached to me, but it didn't feel like it belonged to me. I used to hide it under loose clothing." Jaden, now twenty-four, from Columbus, Ohio, remembers the educational video shown at school claiming, incorrectly, that girls got their periods when they weighed over one hundred pounds. "That became seared in my mind because I was not ready to 'grow up,'" she says. "After that I was always freaked out when my weight went up."

For Rae, a twenty-nine-year-old trans nonbinary person assigned female at birth, the experience of gaining weight during puberty was especially disorienting. "My body just felt like it was wrong in every way," says Rae, who lives in upstate New York. "That was when I began disassociating the majority of the time." From age eleven to thirteen, Rae remembers avoiding in-person interactions as much as possible; they spent most of their free time online in various fandom communities. Rae thought fatness was the root of their body dysphoria and that weight loss would solve everything. "My mother was always on some sort of diet, so that made sense. I would lose some weight and then gain it back, then start again—but it never resulted in my becoming comfortable with my body like I assumed it would," they say.

It wasn't until they met a trans man in college that some of the dots began to connect. Rae realized they were more comfortable wearing men's clothes and came out as nonbinary in their early twenties. "It's been a struggle in my adult life to separate the two experiences of being trans and being fat," they explain. "Getting top surgery last November was a revelation. I am one hundred times more comfortable in my body."

Even cisgender kids whose bodies don't develop early are stressed when the changes eventually come and challenge the ways their identity has been tied to a smaller, more childlike body: Carly, now age thirty-two, was a "late bloomer" and didn't develop hips or breasts until she was sixteen, when she suddenly weighed more than her older sister. "I was the younger sister and was supposed to be small," she says. "Puberty was stressful because I was starting to take up space."

But taking up space is exactly what should happen during puberty—both in the metaphorical sense of learning who you are and in terms of physical weight gain. Girls accrue 90 percent of bone density mass by age eighteen, and boys by age twenty. Heavier bones are less prone to injury and future osteoporosis; they also provide more protection for our spinal cord, heart, and other vital organs. And those vital organs also grow during puberty: "Remember—every organ in the body starts out as this teeny, tiny little thing," says Monge. "They have to get all the way to adult size, and they have to last your entire life." Cardiac muscle thickens as kids grow, and doctors can see that muscle mass decline on echocardiograms when kids aren't getting enough nutrition. "This happens with every organ in the body, though others are harder to measure," Monge says. "When adolescents are getting adequate nutrition, their weight should continue to rise because all of these organs are getting bigger and denser."

But organ and bone growth are gradual processes. The body doesn't equally distribute every calorie consumed to enlarge every organ at once. And so, it's normal for kids to store weight as fat until their bodies are ready to use it. "This often scares families because they see kids getting a bigger stomach or hips," Monge explains. "But that's just how bodies accrue mass over time." Diet culture has taught us that a higher body weight is only okay if you're gaining muscle—but to make muscle, the body needs fat.

Bodies also need fat to stimulate hormone production, so hormonal processes like menstruation are one of the first things to go awry when kids aren't eating enough or start losing weight, as we saw in Chapter 11. And inadequate nutrition for weight gain can mean that kids don't attain their final adult height. The good news is that most of the growth lost during a period of interrupted nutrition (whether that's caused by an eating disorder, sports participation, or another medical condition like irritable bowel syndrome) can be recovered. But height is often permanently impacted. Monge is bemused by how often that last detail is the one that grabs parents' attention. "That one piece of information often seems more motivating than even, 'If your kid doesn't eat, their heart will stop,'" she notes.

When parents, coaches, and pediatricians focus on keeping kids thin during puberty, they increase the risk for the kind of disordered eating that causes inadequate nutrition and stalls critical growth. And they also increase the odds that underlying health issues will be missed, as Josie experienced when her doctors were relieved by her weight loss rather than curious about it. That response is particularly common—and particularly toxic—when weight loss happens to kids of color or kids in bigger bodies; remember how both of their famous parents, and the entire country, discussed the slimming of Malia and Sasha Obama during Michelle Obama's "Let's Move" campaign. "We stop questioning and start applauding," Monge says. "It's 'You're growing up, but your weight hasn't gone up, that's good!' And we have missed thyroid problems, IBS, all sorts of things because a kid grows up, but stops gaining weight, and everyone focuses on how their BMI 'looks better.'"

Growing isn't just a privilege for thin, white bodies. Everyone should be getting bigger during puberty—even kids who were big to begin with. Not every kid is going to lean out. And if those kids are going to feel safe in their bodies, that has to be okay. "Some people's ultimate adult body shape is really different from what it was at twelve or thirteen, but for a lot of folks, it's not," says Monge. "We reinforce a really damaging message when we say everyone is supposed to grow out and then up. No, you just grow."

Some of us also grow up first, and then grow out; think of every skinny teenager who experiences the "freshman fifteen" weight gain when they go to college. We tell kids to avoid this kind of "accidental" weight gain at all costs, but pediatric growth charts continue their curves until twenty-one for a reason. A hundred-pound teenager may have started menstruating and reached her full adult height by age fifteen but still not be done growing. "Once kids stop getting taller, the messaging from the medical community is, 'Now your weight should stop,'" notes Monge. "But it shouldn't." We know that a teenager's hormone signals are continuing to mature, that their bones are still building mass, that their brain development isn't finished until their early twenties. Why would their jeans stay the same size?

POP CULTURE PUBERTY

If weight gain during puberty is physiologically necessary, why do kids learn, so early, and so often, that it's wrong? Because they are usually getting their information about puberty from sources with high levels of anti-fat bias. Noa, an eighteen-year-old in Evanston, Illinois, says that most of her formal education around puberty and sexuality has come from school health and physical education classes, which, as we saw in Chapter 10, are often centered around "obesity prevention." During her sophomore year, a health teacher lectured at length about "good foods" and "bad foods," as well as her personal preferences for a plant-based diet, coconut water, and elderberry gummies. "I cringed through that class," Noa says. "I had a visceral feeling that she was wrong and not supposed to be talking about this to us." Conversations like those establish firmly that good health requires thinness (and, in this case, enough disposable income to cover coconut water and elderberry gummies). Kids carry that understanding with them when the curriculum moves on to body changes or safe sex.

Noa also chafes at how much her formal puberty education has focused on everything changing, but without normalizing those changes or supporting kids through the potential psychological discomfort they can involve. "It would be really nice if educators used reassuring language like, 'You will always be you,'" she says. Instead, the takeaway from such curriculums is that kids' bodies are changing dramatically, likely in problematic ways, and all they can do is try to keep up or stave it off.

Meredith Guthrie, PhD, a lecturer in the Department of Communications at the University of Pittsburgh, studies youth and girl culture in media. She analyzed puberty manuals and related media for her dissertation and says that Noa's classroom experience is not uncommon. "The movies shown in schools are almost always a little out of date, and corporate-sponsored," she notes. "They normalize menstruation and puberty as experiences that need to be tied to a constellation of products." It's not unusual for schools to hand out goody bags of sample pads and deodorant, sponsored by Kotex or Always. And while these products have practical value (getting caught without a pad, as Josie learned, adds to the stress of your first period), they are also marketing tools. The movies, product packaging, and accompanying pamphlets are all designed to sell, and have been carefully cast to show kids (usually professional models) who align with beauty ideals. The better films, much like college websites, may make a nod toward racial diversity, and maybe even show a token kid in a wheelchair. But body size diversity is rarely featured. This tracks with most of our popular culture depictions of puberty: Teen movies from *Ferris Bueller's Day Off* and *Pretty in Pink*, through *She's All That* and *10 Things I Hate About You*, and even the much more recent Netflix shows *13 Reasons Why* and *The Baby-Sitters Club* certainly show kids wrestling with very real challenges of growing up and feeling out of place in their bodies. But the actors are uniformly thin, predominantly white, and cisgender—and all "marketably beautiful," a term I learned from culture critic Sarah Marshall as a more precise way to discuss the benefits of this kind of culturally conventional beauty.

Books on puberty do marginally better showcasing of body diversity, in the sense that they usually feature photos or illustrations of bodies that don't belong to teen fashion models. But here again, we often see a reluctance to embrace fat bodies as normal, even though 16.2 percent of kids between the ages of ten and seventeen had a BMI in the obese range in 2019. *The Care and Keeping of You: The Body Book for Girls* by Valorie Lee Schaefer was first published by American Girl in 1998 and remains one of the best-selling puberty books on the market. It includes a chapter called "Belly Zone," which takes care to emphasize that "there's a wide range of weights that doctors consider normal for any girl, depending on her height and basic body type." But when they warn girls away from dieting, they add, "Talk to your doctor first to find out if it's necessary," which implies that for some kids, it just might be. "You can tell they're trying to thread the needle," says Guthrie. "They might talk about the dangers of dieting, or say, 'Don't skip meals!' But they also talk about BMI and choosing the right food groups. The message is, 'You're going to get bigger, that's normal—just don't get *too* big.'"

This awkward dance around staying the "right" size during a time when your body is growing at warp speed is accompanied by frequent metaphors of failure. "Even in really progressive books, there is a discussion of the menstrual cycle as the 'failed factory,'" notes Guthrie. "You have a period because your body failed to get pregnant. The egg failed to become fertilized. Why are we selling this metaphor of failure to every kid with a uterus?" When she says that, I flash to Josie, whose first understanding of her period was that of an absence; that she wasn't going to have a baby. Which she greeted with relief, of course, as a not quite eight-year-old. But what does it mean that kids' understanding of this essential biological function is entirely rooted in a lack of something else happening?

Menstruation is, of course, crucial to human reproduction and, therefore, survival. It's also one of the biological processes that makes us special, because humans, chimpanzees, bats, and elephant shrews are among the only species on Earth that do it. And yet: "We know so little about menstruation," said Tomi-Ann Roberts, president of the Society for Menstrual Cycle Research and a professor of psychology at Colorado College, when I interviewed her in 2019 for the *Scientific American* feature on menstrual taboos. "So, our attitudes toward menstruation are overwhelmingly negative. This has real consequences for how we can begin to understand healthy menstruation, as well as menstruation-related disorders and the treatment options available. And that's why it's so alarming when an unused tampon falls out of a purse."

Indeed, we teach kids to discreetly hide pads and tampons from public view, even when they are unused and still in their packages, and even though everyone, of all genders, can manage to see toilet paper every day without revulsion. The 2022 Pixar film *Turning Red* included a scene of a panicked mother rushing into school with pads and other menstrual supplies to the understandable horror of her thirteen-year-old daughter. Much less understandable was the backlash online, when conservative parents complained that this was supposed to be "a family movie" appropriate for their young children, who they felt should be shielded from such a bloody reality. (Whether those same kids have seen any Disney movie where a parent dies a bloody death is, I guess, a question for another day.)

Our cultural taboo around the practicalities and physicality of menstruation is so intense that it's determining what kind of research gets done on women's health. And that means that when things really do go wrong, we don't have great treatments or support available. Ninety-one percent of female college students reported at least one menstrual problem, in a 2018 study by Saudi Arabian researchers. Some got their periods irregularly or not at all; others reported excessive levels of bleeding and pain. And as many as one in five women experienced menstrual cramps severe enough to limit her daily life. Meanwhile, one in ten worldwide suffers from endometriosis, a disease where menstrual blood and tissue grow outside the uterus and form painful lesions in the pelvic cavity. And one in ten women has polycystic ovarian syndrome, a hormonal imbalance that disrupts a woman's cycle and is a leading cause of infertility. None of those health conditions receives anything like the research funding of, say, male erectile dysfunction. When menstrual issues are identified, they are usually treated with Advil and hormonal birth control. And there your options end until you're deemed old enough for a hysterectomy.

Most of the mothers I interview tell me they are trying to break this cultural silence around puberty, to talk more openly with their kids about body changes, to use the anatomical names for genitalia, to show bloody tampons to kids of all genders (even if one four-year-old did ask her mom, "Why did a mouse come out of your vagina?"). And this is a crucial first step, because when we don't name and challenge these taboos around bodies, kids assume that their body is what's wrong. And that desperation to make their body "right" is what makes them so vulnerable to diet culture and to believing that the solution is shrinking.

REFRAMING EARLY PUBERTY

Josie and Magen don't draw a straight line from Josie's early period to her eating disorder, but they are both things that happened during a time of upheaval and change in the family. Some of those changes were about Josie's body and some of them were unrelated, as she was also navigating what she and Magen both describe as an emotionally fraught situation with her father, from whom they are now estranged. "He would say, 'What do you want for dinner,' and if I didn't answer, I didn't get dinner," Josie tells me. "That's when I started to teach myself not to feel hunger during the day." She began skipping meals and sneaking the bread and sugar cubes after bedtime at her dad's house when she was six, about a year before her first period even began. When I hear this, I'm reminded of my conversation with Biro, the Cincinnati Children's Hospital researcher who studies early puberty. Although his work documents a correlation between population increases in BMI and the prevalence of early breast development, Biro was far more concerned with finding the root cause of that relationship. "What we need to ask is, 'Why has BMI gone up?'" he said. It's possible, for instance, that rising estrogen levels are driving weight gain, rather than weight driving hormones. Or an unrelated common denominator may impact them both. One potential explanation is the kind of trauma that Josie experienced. "Stress can change your hormone levels," Biro told me. "A parent's divorce, moving to a new house, the death of a family member—any major life event could trigger menarche." In all these scenarios, focusing on a child's weight at best won't help, and at worst, will actively do harm. Josie needed support navigating her depression, her changing body, and the difficult home environment at her dad's house. The last thing she needed was a diet.

Another focus of Biro's research is our ubiquitous environmental exposure to endocrine-disrupting chemicals. EDCs are a class of chemicals, including phthalates, bisphenol A, and others, used in many consumer products (shower curtains, plastic bottles, couch cushions), that have been shown to mimic estrogen and other naturally occurring hormones in the human body. Biro theorizes that some of these chemicals may promote weight gain or contribute to early puberty even more directly, by leading to higher levels of cortisol and adding to the collective estrogen in a girl's body. In the early 2000s, I was an associate health editor at a now-defunct women's lifestyle and wellness magazine called *Organic Style*. We were a kind of proto-Goop and the nascent research on EDCs was a major focus of our reporting. We wrote about how to choose phthalate-free nail polish and baby bottles and encouraged readers to write to their senators demanding an overhaul of industrial chemical regulation. In one of our final issues we also ran a weight loss story, operating on the premise that if EDCs accumulate in fat, the best way to protect yourself from potential harm is to have less fat.

I think about that weight loss story often. It's not that we were entirely wrong to be concerned about EDCs. Twenty years later, the impact of these chemicals in our environment is still not well understood, although the amount we're absorbing through consumer products like cosmetics and couches, which we neither inhale nor ingest, is likely not enormous. And it's possible that kids like Josie are paying the price, though we have made some progress toward increased industry oversight and reform. But at *Organic Style*, we linked our concern about these chemicals to our body size because our culture ties everything back to fatness. We think of body size as the factor we can and should control. And as we saw with athletics and classroom design, focusing on a problem in that personal way once again feels easier than fighting for larger societal change.

But making weight loss a personal responsibility project virtually always fails. Framing environmental safety this way lets the corporations responsible for these issues off the hook. And none of that helps Josie or any other kid navigating these changes. We do need to understand the root causes and potential long-term impact of puberty starting sooner. We also need to better establish how we're defining "sooner" and whether we just mean "sooner than white girls used to do this." But focusing on the body weight piece of the early puberty puzzle only increases the shame and stigma kids feel when their bodies get breasts or bleed sooner than the adults around them think is okay.

And that's the crux of this issue: Virtually no matter what age it happens, our culture is uncomfortable with the transitions that kids' bodies must make as they grow from children into adults. We don't know how to talk about it, and so we don't talk about it enough, or we talk about it in ways that cause harm. Audrey, a mom of two in the Seattle suburbs, was alarmed by how her kids' grandparents responded to their changing bodies the first time they reunited for a visit after the long separation required by the COVID-19 pandemic. Audrey's older daughter, Bea, had gotten noticeably taller and had begun to develop breasts. "One grandmother said, 'Oh, you have such a sexy body now!'" Audrey says, "To my nine-year-old." Bea was wearing shorts and a T-shirt. "Not that there's any outfit that would deserve that comment," Audrey adds. "But there was no attempt at or interest in looking sexy. She's a kid in a kid's body."

The problem is that Bea's grandmother, and most adults, have a too-narrow definition of what "a kid's body" should look like. In my conversation with Kate Morris, the former school therapist, she referenced a fifth-grade student she worked with who had begun puberty early. She started to describe the girl's body and then stopped. "I wanted to say, 'She looks like a woman,'" Morris told me. "That was my default. But no. She looks like a fifth grader because some fifth graders have breasts." Elementary school and middle school kids can also have sexual curiosity and desire—but that doesn't make it okay for adults to sexualize or adultify them just because we view their larger bodies as "adultlike."

What kids need is our radical acceptance of their bodies, even when those bodies are changing in seemingly unexpected ways.

For Morris, that has meant buying her own daughter a bra even though she's likely a few years off from developing breasts. "I remember getting my first bra after I had developed, and it felt like, 'Cover that up! You're too much now!'" she says. "So, for her to be excited about it, and let her choose, 'I'm going to wear the bra today' or not, feels really good." Holly, who lied to her own mom about her period for a year, has worked to have dramatically different conversations with her child, Sukie, who is now eleven and gender nonconforming. Sukie has always been tall, began developing breasts at eight, and "got bigger all over the place," as Holly puts it, from there. "We read books about puberty starting when they were six or seven, and they've always felt comfortable asking questions, which is a relief," she says. Sukie got their period at ten and "after some initial embarrassment, is just yelling around the house, 'I need pads!'" Holly reports. She does notice Sukie wearing baggy sweats most of the time and isn't sure how much of that is related to body shape anxiety or their gender identity, or just Gen Z fashion trends. But at least Holly knows that she's broken the silence.

Magen also notices that Josie tends to prefer sweatpants and baggy shirts these days. "I bought her workout clothes for her running club, and she said, 'These are too tight,'" she notes. But for Josie it seems less about hating her body and more about just wanting to coexist with it, after those five years of feeling so conflicted. "I don't really care about my body," she tells me. "Sometimes I look at myself, and I'm like, 'Huh, I look unique. And I'm going to take that as a compliment!' I'm not saying I don't like the way I look. It's more like, I'm here, I'm alive, I'm not dealing with self-harm, so this is A-OK." And at eleven, she's also found that being the first to get your period now brings a certain street cred. "It is known that I am the kid, if your period starts, you go to me," she tells me. "I'll give you a pad, I'll tell you what to do with the blood, I'll bring you chocolate. I'm the one who is like, 'It's cool, you guys. We'll deal.'"

CHAPTER 13

Social Media's Tipping Point

SIERRA, now fifteen, has been on Instagram since she was ten. Neither she nor her mom, Jaime, can quite remember why she got it so early. "We had to lie about her age to make her account, and it was like, ehhhh, lying? But to a huge, faceless corporation, so . . . okay?" says Jaime. "We basically bowed to peer pressure and let her have it." Except Sierra says none of her friends were even on social media yet: "It was before a lot of my friends got it," she recalls. "I was mostly just using it to keep up with family members who didn't live near us." And, they both agree, to follow cute dog accounts.

It makes sense that their recollections are slightly different because these were tumultuous years for Jaime and Sierra, who live in Portland, Maine. Jaime divorced Sierra's dad when their daughter was eight years old. Then he died, quite suddenly, just before Sierra turned eleven. "That's when we switched from her using an old iPod to getting a phone," Jaime notes. "Because she needed to always be able to reach me." Jaime and her ex-husband had laid down some ground rules around how such devices could be used. "The main thing we said was, 'You're still learning how to use this, so we have the right to look at what you're doing on here at any point.' And I would occasionally check Sierra's DMs and look at her activity," Jaime explains. "But it never occurred to me to check who she was following."

And since not a lot of Sierra's friends were on social media at that point, she began following influencers. She was a serious dancer at the time, so along with the dogs, she began following dance accounts. Which led her to fitness influencers. Her favorite quickly became Cassey Ho, a Pilates instructor who goes by @Blogilates on TikTok, Instagram, and YouTube, where she has been posting videos since 2009. Ho, who is thirty-five, has over eleven million followers across all three platforms, many of whom are teenagers or younger. They do Ho's 21 Day Tone Challenge, which features videos called "Waist Whittler Cardio" and "21 Minute Total Arm Tone Workout," or get recipes from her "Cheap, Clean Eats" series. But they also follow her for more personal content, like the story she tells about training for a bikini body builder competition at age twenty-four. "I had just started weight lifting a little bit, and I was really getting into it," Ho explains in a TikTok video from January 2022. "And somehow, through Google or Pinterest or whatever, I had found out about bikini competitions. I was so intrigued by the muscle, the glamour, the rhinestone bikinis, and just how confident these bikini girls were. And I wanted to be like them." Ho manages to be both earnest and peppy at the same time, with a tone and delivery that reflects the same longing that her young followers now feel—to be like Ho.

Ho goes on to describe how she began working out four hours a day while eating a dangerously low number of calories. "I am so ashamed to say this," she says before describing the diet in specific, and potentially triggering, detail. "But I didn't know any better because I thought that's what it took to get a body like a bikini body builder. [. . .] My head was, like, so cloudy. But every day I woke up and saw my body change, and I was so motivated by the progress! So, I kept going."

Ho is clear that her draconian training regime was unhealthy. She says it led to a restrictive eating disorder and body dysmorphia that stayed with her for years: "I wanted to get boobs because I didn't think I looked good enough," she recalls toward the end of the video. "I was scared of apples and bananas." To Ho, there is a major distinction between that type of disordered thinking, and the plans she promotes to followers, which, presumably, permit apples and bananas, even if there is one titled "Natural Belly Slimming Water Detox Recipe." This taught Sierra to make the same distinction. "I remember thinking, 'Oh my gosh, what she went through was so terrible and extreme,'" Sierra says now. "It kind of didn't even ring a bell in my brain that some of the thoughts I was having could be considered 'disordered.' I thought, 'Well, I'm just working out to be healthy!' But I was a ten-year-old doing daily YouTube workouts."

When I watch Ho's videos about her bikini competition–fueled eating disorder next to her workout content, all I see are the similarities: They both feature shots of her posing with perfect hair and makeup, muscles flexed. The diet she describes for the bikini competition is not far off from a 2022 TikTok where she films herself eating plain canned chicken and lettuce straight from the bag because she wants to stick to her clean eating plan even when "I have no time" to cook or meal prep. And she uses the same rhetoric of "motivation," "progress," and "goals" to describe her disordered behaviors as she does when teaching her followers how to sculpt their "best butt." This glamorizes Ho's eating disorder and makes it a key part of her influencer origin story. "Look, I don't regret doing the competition," she tells her followers. "Because the recovery taught me how to become the strongest and most resilient version of myself." But making her fitness brand all about this kind of strength and resilience lets Ho normalize what is disordered about the way she appears to live now.

Inspired by Ho, Sierra started to make her own fitness content during the pandemic lockdown in 2020. She began by offering dance classes for little kids via Facebook Live. She called her page "Move with Sierra," and it was immediately popular with families in her community, who were all desperate to give their kids something fun and physical to do while trapped at home. The local newspaper covered it, and she would get as many as two hundred views per Live, which felt both like nothing compared to Ho and other professional influencers, and like enough to start obsessing over how to get that number higher. Sierra started posting the videos on YouTube as well, and then she added yoga and other kinds of workouts. "It was less dance, less kid-friendly," she says.

"I would always make sure to say, 'This is for fun, this isn't about what your body looks like!' But I didn't believe it myself."

Sierra also jumped on various social media fitness trends, participating in a challenge to drink a half gallon of water per day, and trying out dances and workout moves that were popular with bigger influencers. In the process, she began to think a lot about how her body looked in her content. "If I made a workout video and didn't like how I looked in it, I would refilm the whole video," she says. "It was super tiring for my body. And nobody should be looking at themselves for that long."

Jaime became concerned that Sierra was working out seven days a week but also struggled to articulate why that was unhealthy. "I talked to her about how even pro athletes need rest days," she says. "But it was also like, 'Oh, look at my kid doing workouts twice a day while I'm just lying on the couch!'" Then Sierra became a vegan. It wasn't the first time she'd restricted with food: Even in preschool, Jaime recalls, Sierra would get stomachaches and decide, "Sweets make my belly hurt" and make a rule not to eat them for a while. "I both sort of saw this all coming and then didn't recognize it when it appeared," Jaime says.

By the summer of 2020, though, Jaime was concerned enough to get Sierra into eating disorder treatment. They worked with a therapist at home without much success for the next five months. Sierra's mental health continued to decline and, in the fall of 2020, she was admitted to a residential eating disorder treatment facility in Virginia. Neither Jaime nor Sierra see social media as the cause of her eating disorder. But they also know that Sierra didn't reach a turning point in her recovery until she went to residential treatment—where one of the first things they did was to take away her phone. "Other kids complained about that a lot," Sierra says. "But I thought it was kind of really nice. I did not miss looking at other people's curated versions of their lives."

SOCIAL MEDIA AND OUR ILLUSION OF CONTROL

The way social media enables us all to be content creators has long been both its great strength and its most insidious flaw. We can tell our own stories, elevating marginalized voices. But we can also share dangerous information; we can harass and harm one another; we can lie. And we've only started to grapple with how much control social media companies have over the kind of content we both consume and create on their platforms. The proprietary algorithms of Facebook, Instagram, YouTube, TikTok, and every other platform are shrouded in mystery. But what we do know is that they all work by showing us more and more extreme versions of whatever content we initially choose to see. If you share a video of an influencer making a tasty salad, you'll soon be inundated with vegan recipes and "What I Eat in a Day" videos. Like someone's workout selfie, and it will be followed by increasingly dramatic before and after pictures documenting people's weight loss journeys. In this way, social media has become a place where kids learn the customs, vernacular, and rules of diet culture and anti-fat bias. And this happens far more quickly and intensely than many parents want to imagine.

In September 2021, the *Wall Street Journal* published internal documents from Facebook (now called Meta), which owns Instagram, showing that the brand's own researchers have long known that the content kids find on Instagram can increase their risk for body image struggles and eating disorders. Facebook immediately challenged the story: "Many teens we heard from feel that using Instagram helps them when they are struggling with the kinds of hard moments and issues teenagers have always faced," they wrote in a press release. But they couldn't dispute their own findings: "We make body image issues worse for one in three teen girls," reported one slide by Facebook researchers from 2019.

This issue is not limited to Facebook and Instagram (which is depressing news since kids are increasingly done with both of those platforms anyway). In January 2021, journalists for Insider.com reported that they had created a TikTok account for a fake fourteen-year-old— and it took just eight minutes for a plastic surgeon's promotional video to appear in their feed. And it's not only girls who are vulnerable. When researchers analyzed a thousand Instagram posts made by or depicting men and boys, they noticed that pictures of men with lean, muscular bodies received more likes and comments, and that most messaging around food, exercise, and other health-related behaviors was tied to this idealized body. "My kids are not going to find anything on social media that will ever validate the bodies they have now or who they will become," says Thu Anh, a Vietnamese American mom of two boys ages ten and eleven in Gaithersburg, Maryland. "They aren't going to see men like my father with his Buddha belly, or my uncles and brother who are all on the short side, a bit gangly, and dark-skinned. If they see Asian men at all, they are only ever warriors doing martial arts."

Thu Anh hasn't let her kids on social media yet and is hoping to delay if she can. She was an English teacher and department chair at prestigious private schools in Washington, D.C., for over fifteen years, which gave her a front-row seat to all the ways that kids learn to weaponize social media against themselves and each other. But she may be an outlier. Social media use is starting younger, with 38 percent of kids aged eight to twelve in 2021 saying they've used it at least once (up 7 percent from 2019) and 18 percent saying they use it daily (up 5 percent from 2019), according to data collected by Common Sense Media. Granted, they're only using it for an average of eighteen minutes per day, but they spend much more time (an average of two hours and forty minutes) watching TV and online videos on sites like YouTube. And when the same researchers studied teenagers, they found that kids averaged almost ninety minutes of daily social media use, plus over three hours of videos.

Reading those numbers, I, too, feel a panicked urge to delay my kids' entry to social media for as long as I can. It's overwhelming to think about teaching them to navigate the messages they'll encounter there when giant technology companies have designed these apps to work against us. But I also know that banning screens works out about as well as banning sugar. When researchers followed five hundred adolescents and their parents from age twelve to fourteen, they found that parental attempts to control social media made no difference to the amount of time their kids spent there. "It was actually the opposite," says Jasmine Fardouly, PhD, a psychologist who studies social media, body image, and weight stigma at the University of New South Wales in Sydney, Australia. "We found that the amount of time that kids spent on social media predicted how much control parents thought they had."

In other words: The parents of kids who naturally spent less time on social media felt like they had a lot of control over the situation. And parents of kids who spent a ton of time online felt like they had very little control over what their kids were doing. But in both scenarios, the kids' inclinations were driving the bus. One more twist: Fardouly's team also looked at how much time parents spent on social media and found that our habits are a strong predictor of what our kids do online and how much time they spend there.

This makes sense because we already know, on some level, that the whole concept of parental control is a fallacy, especially as kids reach their teenage years. "There may be benefits to screen restrictions when kids are younger," notes Fardouly. "But the teenage years are all about becoming independent. Having discussions with kids about what they're doing online may be far more important than just trying to control it." And to navigate those conversations, we need to understand more about how social media promotes diet culture and anti-fat bias and how it increases kids' risk for harm. Then we can think about how and whether to change their (and our own) relationships with it.

THE INFLUENCERS AND ME

On YouTube, a video from influencer Alana Arbucci from March 2019, about the $1,600 makeover she got for her twenty-first birthday that included under-eye and lip filler injections, has over 277,000 views to date. A top-ranking Google result for boob job videos, posted by then nineteen-year-old Alyssa Kulani, has been watched 881,000 times. These influencers are open about the grisly details of their beauty rituals and procedures, taking their iPhones into dermatology appointments and plastic surgery operating rooms. But somehow, this only serves to make such procedures seem more accessible. In their sweats and messy buns, beauty influencers look a lot like the kids who follow them—in most cases, they're only a few years older, after all. And that makes the level of glam they can achieve seem within reach to the average middle or high schooler.

Indeed, Johns Hopkins researchers found that people who use YouTube, Tinder, and Snapchat photo filters had an increased acceptance of cosmetic surgery compared to those who didn't, according to findings published in the September 2019 issue of *JAMA Facial Plastic Surgery*. In another study, published in the journal *Sex Roles*, researchers asked 604 tweens and teenagers about their social media use and interest in future plastic surgery, and found that the kids who spent more time on social media sites were also more invested in their appearance—which led to an increased desire for cosmetic work, compared to their less social media–oriented peers.

The confessional nature of influencer videos teaches kids to think of the people they're watching less as unattainable celebrities and more as peers, something the parasocial relationship–building facet of online media encourages. Kids feel both like they are friends with their favorite influencers, and that they can and should be influencers themselves. And they are quick studies of the form, because as much as these platforms give everyone a voice, they also foster a certain homogenization. Influencer after influencer adopts the same tropes of this communication style; filming themselves in the front seat of the car, posing in front of any multicolored wall, starting videos with phrases like, "I wasn't going to post this, but so many people are asking me to talk about . . ." Even as she was doing it, Sierra acknowledges that she was aware she was studying other influencers to decide what kind of content she would put on You-Tube herself. "It was about me producing what seemed like popular content, it wasn't necessarily what I wanted to do," she says. "It was because I wanted to be an influencer, and I thought this could be something I did as a job."

I can relate. Now that a social media platform is a job requirement for being an author and journalist, I've also had to get comfortable taking and posting selfies and filming myself from the front seat of my car to answer a follower's question or share a random hot take about a diet culture trend of the week. It's fun and I like connecting with readers in such a direct way. But it's also work. I find myself strategizing when to film based on when I plan to wash my hair in a week. I rarely wear makeup, but I will think much harder about outfit choices on those days. And followers notice. It's not at all uncommon to have the message of a video all but ignored but receive a flurry of DMs asking where I got my top. And once when I posted a selfie of myself voting (to . . . encourage voting), a flood of comments came in thanking me for showing my "unfiltered face," break-outs and all. I hadn't intended to make a statement about normalizing adult acne (although, sure, let's do that). I didn't think my skin was part of the story. But when you're in influencer mode, how you look (and how much time and labor you are or aren't investing in how you look) is always the story. And I can't blame my followers for noticing—I've also sent the "I know, not the point, but where did you get those leggings?" DM. When I'm following other people, I can't help but notice these tiny details about their faces and bodies, too.

This complicated influencer-viewer-influencer relationship is one of the aspects of social media that researchers like Fardouly worry about the most in terms of its impact on kids' body image and mental health. For starters, it teaches kids to engage in what researchers call "upward appearance comparison," where we follow celebrities, influencers, and other people we perceive to be more attractive, and then focus relentlessly on how our own bodies and faces fall short. Several studies have shown that kids' body image concerns are worse when they compare themselves to these seemingly perfect strangers than when they compare themselves to family members and close friends. "We've only found a correlation because this is not easy to test," says Fardouly. "But we do know that view-ing images of influencers and celebrities is associated with worse body image. I think part of it may be that you don't have a real-world refer-ence. You know what your best friend looks like offline, without makeup and filters. But with influencers, it can be hard to tell how enhanced the image is." Even when we know intellectually that images have been Photo-shopped or otherwise altered to look as perfect as possible, we don't grasp it on an emotional level. Studies on both kids and adults have found that applying a label like "this picture does not portray reality" does not stop us from negatively comparing our bodies to the unrealistic bodies we see.

A newer area of study for media researchers is what happens to body image when kids are creating their own content, especially in the beauty and fitness spaces. Fardouly's research shows that taking videos or photos of yourself and editing them is more closely linked to heightened body image concerns than just posting frequently. Again, it's important to note that researchers have only documented a correlation. It may not be that editing your selfies causes body image issues, but rather that people already vulnerable to body angst are more likely to obsessively retouch their photos. But the pressure to have content perform well on a social media platform certainly doesn't help. "These kids are learning that there is an ideal 'look' of fitness, and it just so happens to be absolutely identical to the ideal 'look' of sex appeal," says Lindsay Kite, PhD, cofounder of Beauty Redefined, a nonprofit that raises awareness about body image issues online. "And they get caught up in how they look in these posts because they think their content has to live up to that ideal or nobody else will look and pay attention." This tracks with Sierra's experience: She wasn't just watching her content to make sure her explanation of a workout move was clear. She was also analyzing her body, dissecting it for flaws, and then editing or reshooting to make it look closer to the ideal in her head. She powered through soreness and exhaustion to make more workout content, ignoring how her body felt to stay focused on how it looked to others. "This is the essence of self-objectification," notes Fardouly.

Influencer culture also brings self-objectification to boys, who can get just as readily caught up in the diet and fitness messaging that they find online. "Boys are sold the lie that they need to take up more space in the world by having bigger muscles, just like girls are told to take up less space by being thin," explained Kite, who is also the co-author of *More Than a Body: Your Body Is an Instrument, Not an Ornament*, when I interviewed her for *Choices* magazine in 2017. "Both are harmful ideals that can lead to unhealthy behaviors like purging, overexercising, or the use of diet pills and steroids." For that *Choices* magazine piece on the trend of "fitspo," or "fitspiration" content, I also spoke with Ian Irby, then seventeen. Ian talked to me about the pressure he felt following fitness accounts on Instagram. "These people are just on another level," he said then. "It's easy to see this stuff and be like, 'Man, what will it take for me to get there?'"

Social media also teaches boys to view girls' bodies as objects. After we'd chatted for a while, Ian admitted, "I do think it's influenced what I find attractive in girls." Real teenage bodies come in every shape and size; they have extra body hair and zits; they are every race. Influencer bodies are, almost uniformly, thin, tanned, toned, hairless, and pore-less. They have more in common with the equally unrealistic images that teenagers see in online porn than they do with the kids sitting next to them in math class. "Fitspo sexualizes fitness," Peggy Orenstein, author of *Girls and Sex* told me for the same story. "It becomes all about specific body parts and how they look, not how your body feels or how useful your body can be, regardless of its size and shape. And we don't talk enough about what it means for boys to be saturated with these images, or how it can entitle them to judge girls by these standards."

We also don't talk enough about how parents engage with this sexu-alized fitness content. When viral TikTok dances became a thing during the COVID lockdown of 2020, I saw lots of moms learning them and often dancing with their kids. It seemed an innocuous enough way to bond and stay active. But I also found myself studying the videos that went viral from celebrity moms like Jessica Alba, Victoria Beckham, and Reese Witherspoon, and noticing how interchangeable their bodies were with the bodies of their teen and even preteen children. "The dance videos that get the most shares are of very young girls, or women with very idealistic bodies," says Kite. "This is how social media fur-thers the objectification of certain bodies."

Kite isn't arguing that we should stop dancing with our kids—in fact, as we'll discuss shortly, engaging with the content your kids follow is one key strategy for helping to mitigate its potentially toxic effects. But she does wonder what it means to celebrate bodies dancing without ever thinking critically about why *those* bodies, why *that* sexy dance. "It looks so innocent and benign," Kite says. "But who is not in these videos? Whose videos are not reaching the 'For You' page?" Indeed, if a fat mom were to go viral with a TikTok dance, the response from many commenters would be to dissect her body in horror, or mine her con-tent for easy fat jokes. And any affirmation of her dancing would come in the form of "you're so brave," which sounds empowering—but only reinforces that we would rather her body not appear in public at all.

Influencer culture has learned to disguise its adherence to restric-tive beauty standards by co-opting the rhetoric of body positivity and self-acceptance. Although it has its roots in radical fat activism, "body positivity" has become a way for white, thin influencers to show their stomach rolls under the guise of "authenticity," in between posts about their ab workouts and favorite green smoothies. Phrases like "you do you" or "all bodies" have become a kind of shorthand for representing yourself as woke. And they enable influencers to continue to uphold beauty standards and beauty labor under a veneer of self-love that may be just as hard for our brains to detect as Photoshop. After all, "you do you" can be employed to justify dieting and excessive exercise as easily as it can be used to celebrate showing a smidge of cellulite in your bikini. Kite believes this happens because of a fundamental flaw in the body positive movement. "It's so easy to co-opt and commodify," she says. "If you tell people that you're beautiful just the way you are, you're still reinforcing the message that your body matters the most."

This is what Cassey Ho is doing when she shares her eating disorder history and then talks about "feeling strong" and "finding joy in my body and my food," while adhering religiously to her aggressive diet and exercise regimes. Themes of self-love and empowerment are also prevalent when influencers discuss their decisions to have cosmetic procedures. In 2017, YouTuber Jaclyn Glenn documented her decision to get a boob job and wrestled with what it said about her relationship with her body, as I later reported in a piece for *Elemental*. "I don't want it to come off as though I'm 'conforming to the beauty standards of society,'" she says in one video. "Because I've always kind of wanted everyone to love their body and accept who they are and things like that. [. . .] If I lived in a world where nobody had boobs, would I even have this insecurity to begin with? Obviously, the answer is no." And we can't discuss the commodification of body positivity without reckoning with the Kardashian family, who continually claim to challenge beauty norms—because Kim appropriated the sexiness of a big butt from Black culture, because Khloe's Good American jeans brand comes in plus sizes, because Skims, Kim's shapewear collection, "fits everybody"— while also profiting off and perpetuating those same standards.

In 2022, Kim Kardashian made headlines for wearing a vintage dress once worn by Marilyn Monroe to the Met Gala, and talking openly, and without remorse, about spending three weeks on a crash diet to lose the sixteen pounds she needed to shed to make the dress sort of fit. She showed up to the event looking gaunt and not any more marketably beautiful than she always is. And that is the real takeaway, says Jessica DeFino, a journalist who writes critically about beauty culture and once worked for the Kardashians' app company: "She looked fine. It wasn't a standout moment. And that makes it a pretty perfect parallel for mass beauty culture, because we're all taught that we must put that much effort into our appearance, just to exist in the world."

DeFino describes the Kardashians' impact on beauty standards as "aesthetic inflation" because they have so normalized beauty work, as well as the argument that such beauty work is a tool for empowerment and self-care. "Performing beauty *can* feel empowering, since acquiring beauty capital confers literal power," she wrote in a 2022 piece for *Vice*. But most of that power stays with the Kardashians and other massively profitable beauty and diet brands. "[The Kardashians'] beauty standards require outsized aesthetic labor from their followers," DeFino wrote. "Fans who adopt their aesthetic, purchase products from their beauty and clothing lines, and post to their own social media pages act as an army of (unpaid) marketers."

CAN ONLINE EVER BE REAL?

While reporting this chapter, I download a new social media app, called BeReal. "It's where the kids are going now," I hear from more than one interview subject (some teenagers themselves, some researchers who study how teenagers use media). And it is, kind of, the anti-Instagram or anti-TikTok. You are only allowed to post once a day (the app notifies you when it's time). You can't use filters or Facetune or shoot video. Posts are set to private by default (though you can opt to make them "discoverable," and when I do, I encounter the same anonymous men who seem to spend their time liking the photos of women they don't know in every corner of the internet) and there are no hashtags or other obvious tricks to boost engagement. You also can't easily like people's posts or share them. And, as of this writing, there are no advertisements or sponsored content. Scrolling the "Discovery" page, I see ordinary people, mostly teenagers, brushing their teeth, shooting random walls or street corners, or piles of laundry. Nobody is influencing. They are just living. And it is refreshing, and sort of oddly intimidating—do I just show people the messy inside of my car and my unbrushed hair? On BeReal, it seems, that's what we're there to do.

And yet—BeReal's format also requires you to shoot a selfie and a forward-facing photo at once. It's a move, I soon learn, that requires creative gymnastics to shoot both with any skill. It's often impossible to share what's in front of you and your own face without shooting your face from below, which creates the impression of many double chins. I don't think BeReal intends this as a fat positive celebration of chins. Although there is some social capital to be gained by showing how much you don't care by shooting the "worst" selfie possible, I think they know that influencers, and teenagers, are good at these gymnastics, at figuring out their angles. The app also allows for retakes, though it shows how many retakes you do on your final post, as a subtle callout of the performance. And so even if BeReal holds to its initial premise to be free of filters and sponsored content (and let's talk about how skeptical I am that they will stay that way—assuming they even still exist by the time you read these words), it still works by requiring users to consider their own face along with whatever other aspect of their life they want to share. In other words, the apps are not coming to save us.

Instead, we have to think about saving ourselves. And in our effort to do so, we need to not replicate the same scarcity mindset that we've learned from diet culture by piling on lots of rules about what and how much. Robyn, a lawyer, and mother of three kids aged eighteen, fourteen, and twelve, in Portland, Oregon, says that she waited until sixth grade to let each kid have a device tied to Wi-Fi and until eighth grade for phones. But she realized the futility of too many screen-time rules beyond that when her oldest, Alex, let slip that he had at least three Instagram accounts she didn't know about. "I realized that I had much less control than I expected," she says. She switched her approach to talking it out with each kid, and then letting them make their own decisions.

"We go over, 'What are the problems? What are the good things? How do you balance the need to protect yourself, both emotionally and in terms of privacy, with the desire of connecting with people?'"

When Robyn's daughter, Isla, turned thirteen, they had a long conversation about whether she now wanted to get on TikTok, and Isla decided, on her own, to wait. Now fourteen, she is on it, but still prefers looking up craft projects on Pinterest. "She's the kid who will come show me when she sees some really overt fatphobia on TikTok," says Robyn. In that way, experimenting with social media, and having open lines of communication with Robyn, has helped Isla connect more deeply to her own values. "If you have a relationship with your kids where they feel like they can talk to you without getting punished, they're going to come and talk to you about the things that worry them," Robyn says.

Robyn acknowledges that both of her sons spend much more time online than Isla and may each have a less tight handle on it. She does set time limits for her twelve-year-old, Benjamin. "He's the kind of kid who will otherwise forget he has homework, so we do make sure he's getting certain things done before he gets online." But even there, she's open to conversations about easing those limits. "I just feel, the tween and teen years are so hard," she says. "To whatever extent I can, I prioritize my relationship with them over having these set rules around how they need to be."

This approach might sound loosey-goosey in contrast to the standard parenting advice around screens, which has long told us that we should think in terms of minutes consumed per day. But screen-time researchers are increasingly shifting their focus from how much time kids spend on screens to what they do when they're on them. A 2022 study of 151 preteen girls published in the journal *Body Image* found that girls who spend time on appearance-focused social media had more body image concerns than girls who used social media for what the researchers called "communication engagement." "Liking other people's posts, direct messaging friends, just using social to stay in touch did not result in the same body image anxieties as, say, watching lots of makeup tutorials on YouTube," says Charlotte Markey, PhD, the study's lead author and a professor of psychology at Rutgers University. She notes that these activities are not easy to separate: "If kids are on TikTok to talk to their friends, they'll also see this other content. But parents can ask, 'Well, what are they mostly doing? If it's mostly about communicating with friends, even if they see #Fitspo and other body-focused content, it's likely not destroying them.'"

Markey's study is among the first to look at how kids as young as ten are using social media. "There's been a misconception in the research community that you're supposed to be thirteen to use these platforms so we don't have to start thinking about ten-year-olds yet," she notes. "But when you start studying younger kids, you see that around half of eleven- and twelve-year-olds are starting to use these platforms. They are here, and they're more vulnerable, and the research we have on seventeen-, eighteen-, nineteen-year-olds is not helping us understand this group." This lack of research makes a compelling argument for waiting till thirteen to let kids on social media—but age limits alone won't help if kids aren't also learning media literacy skills.

One trend that has emerged in the past few years, especially among privileged parents whose employment status doesn't hinge on 24-7 availability to a boss, has been the "digital detox." Some families practice a weekly Screen-Free Saturday or Sunday; others unplug monthly or quarterly or only during vacations. A total digital detox raises clear practicality questions especially now that so many of us live without landlines. And it borrows both the language and the pro-deprivation mindset of diet culture. So yes, some of us might be able to live within the parameters of screen restrictions. But most of us will quickly find the workarounds or make up for a day or a week off screens with more hours on screens as soon as we get back. And as Fardouly's research shows, kids are much less impacted by our attempts to control their access to screens than we'd like to think.

There may be some benefits to both parents and kids, however, in taking breaks from whichever social media platforms we spend the most time on, just as Sierra found when she went to eating disorder treatment. "It can be crucial to take a breather from social media— especially if that sounds really hard to do," says Kite, who recommends deleting the apps in question from your phone for at least three full days. The goal in coming back isn't necessarily to make you use your phone less or post less often; it's to "resensitize you" to what you're seeing. "The content that's fake and harmful will be more obvious because you're no longer inured to it," Kite explains. "Now you're looking with eyes wide open as you scroll, and you'll be able to see which kinds of content inspire those feelings of 'I need to quit sugar, I need to go shopping, I need to know her skincare routine.'"

The next step would be to unfollow any accounts that elicit such anxieties, because you can't recast your favorite Netflix show with fat actors, but one real asset to social media is that you can curate your feeds. When Fardouly and her colleagues randomly assigned 195 women aged eighteen to thirty to view Instagram content that was either body positive, body neutral, or promoting the thin ideal, they found that participants who got the #BoPo posts scored more highly on body satisfaction and body appreciation. They've found similar benefits in #NoMakeupSelfies, though any kind of body-focused content still seems to increase users' level of self-objectification. Turning down the volume on toxic body messages, and body messages of any kind, seems to be so beneficial that it has become a standard protocol in most eating disorder treatment programs that work with teenagers, says Lauren Muhlheim, PsyD, a psychologist in private practice in Los Angeles who specializes in adolescent eating disorders. "Every time I start talking about body image with any client, I always say, 'We must look at your social media feed and see what you're exposed to.' We talk about the way media idealizes thin bodies, but also the stigmatizing ways we see larger bodies."

Muhlheim doesn't tell parents to put phones away altogether, though. "We don't want parents to overcontrol kids," she says. "I'd rather see parents help kids create body positive feeds. Or if you're going to do a TikTok dance, make it a duet with a body positive creator." The fat acceptance communities on social media can also offer a critical counterbalance to the messages kids are getting about bodies from other places, like school. Melora, a mom of two in Huntsville, Alabama, says she's made a point to show her ten-year-old, Harriet, "music videos that are probably not appropriate for young kids," because Harriet went through puberty early and now describes herself as "more on the chunky side." Melora wants her to see a more diverse definition of beauty than the bodies shown in most children's media. "I like Lizzo and Megan Thee Stallion," Harriet tells me. "It makes me feel better, like I'm doing fine. Because they're super famous and nobody's judging their weight. Or maybe some people are, but those are just mean people." Following celebrities also helps them talk about the realities of anti-fat bias: "Remember when Tess Holliday wore that really expensive strawberry dress to the Grammys?" Harriet asks. "It went on the top ten ugliest outfits list. But then a bunch of skinny white girls started wearing it and wow, it's the best dress ever. That really bothered me because it's like, anybody can wear anything."

Harriet also tells me that "maybe once a year," she cries because "I'm fat, and I want to be skinny." And even on a normal day, she admits, "I'm so very insecure about that and wish I was skinny, because I think skinny people are pretty." When her mom tried to reassure her that being fat doesn't matter, Harriet was having none of it: "That felt like I was being babied, and I didn't like it." But talking about fat celebrities they see on social media—even when they're talking about their experiences of anti-fatness, as with the Tess Holliday example—seems to give them a different language. Melora and Harriet can bond over their admiration for these influencers and their outrage at the backlash they experience just for existing in fat bodies. This helps Harriet build her media literacy skills—and maybe even more important, to know that she's not alone.

I saw similar potential in the summer of 2022, when TikTok influencer and former American Idol contestant Jackie Miskanic released her viral hit "Victoria's Secret." Miskanic, who goes by Jax, wrote the song for Chelsea, a twelve-year-old girl she babysits, after Chelsea came home from the mall crying because a friend called her "too flat and too fat" when they tried on bikinis. In the song, Jax talks about how the rigid beauty culture of Victoria's Secret and magazine covers had helped fuel her own teenage eating disorder: "I stopped eating, what a bummer / Can't have carbs and a hot girl summer!" And then she explains that

Victoria's real secret is that she's "an old man who lives in Ohio, making money off of girls like me," in reference to Les Wexner, the billionaire now in his eighties who founded L Brands (now known as Bath & Body Works, Inc.), which used to own Victoria's Secret as well as Abercrombie & Fitch and Express.

Jax released the full version of the song via a TikTok of herself and a team of dancers, several of them plus-size, doing a flash mob performance on the sidewalk outside a Victoria's Secret store. As of this writing, the video has over thirty-two million views; the song also made Billboard's Hot 100 list and was one of the top three best-selling songs on iTunes. And it has inspired many, many, many tribute videos from little girls singing it, but also from millennial and Gen X moms and Gen Z influencers of every body size and shape.

"Victoria's Secret" is not a perfect song. I winced, watching Jax talk to Chelsea about her mall shopping incident because Jax expresses outrage at the "too fat and too flat" comment but doesn't clarify that there is nothing wrong with being fat or flat-chested. I also don't love that people who make tribute videos tend to do so in bikinis or lingerie. This makes sense given that they're singing about Victoria's Secret. And yes, it's progress to say, "All bodies can be bikini bodies." But I'd love us to go even further and say, also, hotness is optional. You don't owe the world pretty. You can just show up—online, offline, at work, at school, to vote—in the body you have, with the skin you have, and still have every right to be there.

It's also complicated that the challenge to Victoria's Secret beauty standards comes from a young, thin, white, blond musician who checks most of those boxes already. We need to hear this message from influencers with non-idealized bodies because we need to see more nonideal bodies to reject the "ideal body" concept. But while thin, white women are overly centered in the internet discourse on body positivity, it's also true that they arguably have the biggest responsibility to dismantle beauty and diet culture instead of continuing to perpetuate and profit from it—and too often, they abdicate instead of engage.

So, I still teared up the first time I played the video for my kids. And

I added it to our summer camp drive playlist. We talked about what the song meant and whether a giant company like Victoria's Secret would change their marketing based on it (unlikely, but we agreed that we don't have to shop there). A few weeks later I heard my four-year-old singing it idly to herself while drawing, and I thought of Melora and Harriet. And when a mom friend texted that her fifth grader reported singing the song with her entire lunch table, I teared up again.

For Sierra, social media continues to be a world she navigates carefully. Before she left treatment, she went through her phone with her therapist and unfollowed any influencer who talked about weight, diet, fitness, and beauty. And even having curated her feeds, she didn't immediately jump back in. "We have a rule that the phone comes out of her bedroom at bedtime, which is ten p.m. now that she's a sophomore," notes Jaime. "But when she first came back, I would see the phone plugged in on the kitchen counter right after dinner. She was done for the day." Sierra says in her first month home, she didn't even redownload any social media apps. "I was a little scared of it, I think." But she ultimately did decide to bring them back, one app at a time. "I wanted to see how I could create a new relationship with social media," she says. These days, Sierra mostly uses Snapchat to stay in touch with friends and TikTok to post content. In one video, she talks about how she used to think thirty followers "was nothing," but has now identified that as a toxic mentality. "I was basically saying, thirty people is actually a lot. And it's not realistic to expect to have millions of followers; that's just the content we're being served," Sierra explains. Ironically, that video has over eleven thousand views—and Sierra gained around a thousand followers from posting it. "It's been a little weird," she says. "This is not the same situation as it was when my eating disorder was brewing. I know I don't have to be a content creator. I don't want to feel like I have to create [a certain kind] of content for my followers." She's also concerned that a lot of her followers are girls around her age, or a few years younger, who send comments like "You're so cool," or "You're so pretty, I want to be like you!" "It's such good intentions to say that to someone, but my brain is immediately like, 'Oh, people are noticing these things,'" Sierra says.

And she doesn't want to be the person making someone else compare themselves, either. "I used to think I was the problem for not liking how this stuff made me feel," Sierra says. "Now I know, it's a lot more normal than I realized to feel crappy about social media."

How to Have the Fat Talk

ONE night, toward the end of writing this book, as I was putting my then four-year-old daughter, Beatrix, to bed, she asked me to read *It's So Amazing* for her bedtime story. It's a kids' book by Robie H. Harris, with delightful illustrations by Michael Emberley, about "eggs, sperm, birth, babies, and families," just as the subtitle promises. And it includes many drawings of naked bodies at different ages, as well as different stages of pregnancy. A lot of it goes over a four-year-old's head, but she was newly mesmerized by the pregnancy pages. And so, we snuggled up in her bed with her thirty-seven favorite stuffed animals, and I read a few paragraphs about sperm meeting eggs, until Beatrix interrupted.

"Your tummy is fat now because you grew me inside of it," she informed me.

I paused. I felt about sixty-four different emotions in the span of one second and wondered if I was keeping my face neutral. And then I said, "Well, you helped. But I think my tummy was always going to be fat."

"Yes," Beatrix replied, a little dreamy now. "Some tummies just get to grow up to be fat."

Of course, I want this story to be my moment of victory. I'm proud that we've made "fat" a positive concept in our house; that my daughter sees my squishy, plus-size, fortysomething midsection as something to aim for rather than a fate to dread. I'm also proud that I didn't give her all the credit for its roundness—that I owned my fatness as mine, and not something I have to justify with, "Well, I had two kids." We need to normalize how pregnancy changes bodies. But we also need to be clear that pregnancy is not the only acceptable reason for a round abdomen. Some tummies just get to be fat.

But raising kids in diet culture means we never get one final moment of victory. The fat positivity I've cultivated in my kids now is a value we'll have to fight to protect and reinforce over and over again. And when my tweet about this moment went viral, I saw, in the variety of responses, just how far we have to go. Fat folks zeroed in, with joyful surprise, on Beatrix's use of "get to" because we know how rare it is for our bodies to be aspirational. Mothers shared their own stories of their kids admiring their stomachs and other jiggly parts. But many of those anecdotes were tinged with anxiety because we also know that the rest of the world judges a fat body quite differently. "I am literally sitting here like, 'Yes, all fat tummies . . . EXCEPT MINE,'" one person responded. "The way they can lay down a complisult . . ." wrote another. And of course, there was the inevitable trolling: "Some *lifestyles* grow fat tummies." (Emphasis mine.)

I shared the story online (even though quotes from precociously woke and wise children can be an exhausting Twitter trope) because I know how rare it is for a child, or anyone else, to speak positively, let alone reverentially, about fatness. But I also shared it because it doesn't have to be this way. We can rewrite these narratives about our bodies, and our children's bodies. We can untangle weight, health, and morality. We can teach our children and ourselves that "fat people are worthy of respect, safety, and dignity," as fat liberationist and public health scholar Marquisele Mercedes wrote in a 2022 article for *Pipe Wrench* magazine:

> If you want to challenge fatphobia, you have to start with the understanding that fat people are worthy of respect, safety, and dignity. A "but" cannot follow this statement. Fat people are worthy of respect, safety, and dignity. Fat people are worthy of respect, safety, and dignity no matter how fat they are. Fat people are worthy of respect, safety,

and dignity no matter how sick they are, no matter how much they eat, no matter how much they move, no matter how far they are from any notion of health, however defined.

We can make fat into just another body descriptor. And we can make fat good. Because once we know that to be true, we have no reason to keep pursuing thinness at any cost. We can stop judging how our kids' bodies grow. We can reject the premise that our worth, as parents or as people, should be measured by our weight. And when we do that, diet culture has nothing to feast on. Controlling your body size stops being the goal.

Changing these narratives and rejecting these assumptions happens when we change how we talk about bodies—to our kids, but also to everyone else. As I've spent the past decade divesting myself from diet culture, the past five years reporting on anti-fat bias, and the past two years researching and writing this book, I've realized that this kind of unlearning work is only phase one. If you've read this far, you've worked through the realizations that the BMI is a terrible measure of health; that diets don't and shouldn't work, that they do cause harm, and are particularly dangerous for children; and that weight and health are tangled together in our culture not because weight decides health but because powerful industries and social hierarchies want us to equate these concepts. All of that is a lot. It takes time and energy to wrap your head around these ideas, to sit with the feelings they bring up, to realize just how many lies you've been told about your body and your value. But learning how to talk about these issues with other people is where our real work begins.

These conversations can feel dangerous and potentially explosive. You often don't know the other person's context. Which biases and assumptions do they hold? Which premise are they taking for granted that you're trying to question? Or maybe you do know where they stand (because they are your carb-phobic parent, or your boss who talks about intermittent fasting nonstop), and that gulf makes it even harder to articulate your own perspective. This is especially true when there is a power differential: when fat people have to talk to thin people, when anyone more marginalized has to talk to a straight, cisgender white man, when any of us have to talk to doctors. And when we have these conversations with our kids, they feel extra loaded because we worry so much about getting them wrong.

The good news is that almost no conversation is ever finished, especially with our kids (as my poor children can attest). We can always request a do-over and try again. We can also, always, be honest about where we are with our own understanding of diet culture and fatphobia. No matter who you're talking to, but especially if you're talking to your kids, it's okay to say, *I used to think fat was bad, or unhealthy, but I'm learning.* Or even, *I'm still struggling with my own body, but I know I don't want fat people to be treated this way.* Kids can know we don't always get this right, but we're trying to do better. So can adults.

So how do we have these conversations? Just like we've learned that we can't expect our kids to get everything they need from one formal "Sex Talk," there is no one "Fat Talk." There are many conversations we need to have, quite deliberately, about fat, anti-fat bias, thin privilege, and the multitude of ways that diet culture infiltrates family life. And then there are so many other conversations where fat doesn't need to be the central theme, but we can continue, more subtly, to push the importance of body diversity and the value that how we look is the least interesting thing about us. Kids pick up on these themes in how they hear us talk explicitly about food, exercise, weight, and health. And when they see how much we care about how they look in family photos—or how we look in the mirror at ourselves.

I know it can feel daunting, even terrifying, to start talking about fat differently. You may feel like a hypocrite, or you may worry that the person you're talking to will knock the legs out of your argument with a well-placed statistic or the dreaded "but what about health?" To that concern, remember Mercedes's words: Fat people are worthy of respect, safety, and dignity, no matter what their health status. There is no "but" in that sentence. You may also worry that by talking about fatphobia, you'll teach your kids fatphobia. On this front, I can assure you: They already know. Studies show that kids start to equate fat bodies with negative traits between the ages of three and five. They need to hear your counternarrative to know that's not true. It may also help to remember that parents don't cause eating disorders or the other most severe conse-quences of diet culture exposure, even if you are struggling intensively with these issues yourself. Parents can teach behaviors and beliefs, and in kids already genetically or biologically vulnerable to eating disorders, this can have disastrous consequences. But we can also use our influence for good.

And we should, because we can't keep our kids in diet culture–free bubbles. The goal isn't to stop Grandma from ever saying a bad word about bread; it's to help our kids know her bread comment doesn't apply to them. The goal isn't to make sure our kids never watch a cartoon with a stereotypical fat villain or a YouTuber on a detox; it's to teach them to think critically about the media they consume and to call out those instances of harm for what they are. The goal isn't to raise kids who never experience a moment of body anxiety; it's to teach kids who to blame when our culture makes them think their body size is their value.

Here are some thoughts about eight Fat Talks that we should all start having more often. Some of what you'll read here repeats strategies dis-cussed in earlier chapters; I've gathered it all together to make it easy to reference these ideas when you need them. The rest, I hope, will give you some starting points for answering questions that may have come up as you've been reading.

1. HOW TO TALK TO DOCTORS

As we learned in Chapter 5, many pediatricians, family medicine doc-tors, and other primary healthcare providers still practice weight-centric medicine. This means we're asked to step on a scale at every visit, even when we've come in for a sore throat or an ear infection. Our kids' weight is plotted out on growth charts, and far too many pediatricians think of the 50th percentile as the goal for every child. And anyone who falls into the overweight or obese BMI categories is automatically counseled to lose weight. Doctors often dispense this advice without first screening for eating disorder risk factors or history, without definitively linking our body weight to specific health concerns, and without disclosing the high failure rate of intentional weight loss.

But here's the thing: You can refuse to be weighed at any medical appointment. "There is no obligation for a patient to be weighed, and they have the complete right to refuse," said Louise Metz, MD, a weight-inclusive internal medicine doctor in Chapel Hill, North Carolina, when I interviewed her for *Scientific American* in 2019. If you're thin, or otherwise privileged, you likely don't need to say anything more than "No, thank you" when they ask you to get on the scale. Another line I like, from anti-diet dietitian and author Christy Harrison: "Thanks, but I don't do scales!" If a healthcare provider says they need your weight for insurance purposes, you can tell them to write "patient declined." And for the record, Metz says not taking weights has never impacted her ability to get an insurance company to cover medical care.

Very often, thin and small fat folks find that getting the scale out of the visit completely changes their experience of healthcare; doctors are forced to ask different questions, to get to know us better and think more comprehensively about our health needs. This gives us an opportunity for advocacy. As we build this rapport with our doctors, we can and should explain why skipping the scale is so crucial for good healthcare. This is important because if we only decline to be weighed, without ever exploring why, we reinforce to our healthcare providers and to ourselves that fatness is a problem. And this does nothing to shift the reality that for fat folks, declining to be weighed may not improve your medical care—in fact, it could antagonize a provider already biased against you. "A medical professional does not have to weigh me to know that I'm fat," writes blogger and fat activist Linda Gerhardt. "This is because they have eyeballs and can see me." For Linda, and many other fat folks, declining to be weighed feels risky:

I'm already judged as noncompliant the moment a medical professional lays eyes on me. [. . .] Before I open my mouth at an appointment, I am perceived as *difficult*. Anything I do to advocate for myself is further evidence of my noncompliance. I just want access to competent medical care. That's all. I have to save my energy to fight for things that are important to my care.

If declining the weigh-in doesn't feel safe, or you try and receive pushback, ask *why* they want to weigh you: Are you taking any medications that are dosed by weight? Are you recovering from a restrictive eating disorder and need to weight restore to protect your health? Are you in heart failure and need your fluid levels monitored? Or are they concerned about a condition where a significant weight gain or loss may be a correlating symptom? Weight monitoring can be useful in managing diabetes or polycystic ovarian syndrome, as well as some mental health conditions. If you have a family history or other circumstances that increases your risk for these issues, weight may be a useful touchpoint, especially if it's a condition (depression, say) where you might struggle to disclose other symptoms to your doctor because they are difficult or stigmatizing to discuss. But this will only work if your doctor can look beyond the scale. Unequivocally treating all weight loss as good, and all weight gain as bad, will obscure the reality of what's happening with your health.

If you do have a medical reason to have your weight monitored, you can still request that healthcare providers take a "blind weight," where you stand with your back to the scale. And remember that even if they know your weight, and even if you have a weight-linked health concern, you still have the right to ask for weight-inclusive healthcare. "You do not need to accept a prescription of intentional weight loss as a first or last option. You can ask, 'How would you treat this condition in a thin patient?'" suggests Ragen Chastain, the fat activist and writer who specializes in anti-fat bias in healthcare settings. "Because we know when a thin person gets an evidence-based treatment for their symptoms and a fat person gets put on a diet, this delays the fat person from getting that evidence-based treatment, sometimes forever."

Should you also keep your kids off the scale? This is a little more nuanced, because kids are supposed to be growing and gaining—and a sudden weight loss, or even a failure to gain as expected, is often cause for concern. In infants, it may be a sign of malnutrition or a congenital heart condition; in older kids, weight loss can be a red flag for diabetes or an eating disorder. Knowing your child's weight is also useful when you're picking a car seat or trying to dose Tylenol or other over-the-counter medications. But the frequency with which we weigh kids in the United States is likely unnecessary. The American Academy of Pediatrics 2016 clinical report discussed in previous chapters recommends that healthcare providers talk to kids and families about healthy habits, rather than discussing weight. So, there's good reason to ask your pediatrician's office to do blind weights, and to save any discussion of weight and diet for when your child is out of earshot. Depending on the protocols of your medical practice, you may be able to email your pediatrician ahead of time or bring a note requesting this and ask the nurse who does your child's vitals to put it on the top of their chart for the doctor to see. (You can download a template letter at sunnysideupnutrition.com/a-letter-to-your-childs-doctor, or order cards printed with this request for your kids and yourself at more-love.org.)

What if the doctor ignores your request and talks about weight in front of your child anyway? Remember that what you say matters most, and what your child needs to hear in that moment is that you will advocate for them. When their pediatrician got worked up about her six-year-old's jump from the 60th to the 90th percentile, Fanny Sung, a mother of three in Nashville, Tennessee, refused to join in the anxiety. "I let her know that, at some point, my kids will be what her charts consider 'overweight,' because I was, and so was my husband," says Fanny. "And I told her, 'I am okay with that.'"

2. HOW TO TALK TO TEACHERS AND COACHES

After parents, teachers and coaches are often the adults who have the biggest influence on our kids' lives. In elementary school, they may spend more waking hours per week with a classroom teacher than they do with us. If they love a sport and become serious about it, their coach is likely shaping their relationship with their body for years to come. Which is why it matters when teachers and coaches bring diet culture into their work. And as we learned in Chapters 10 and 11, this is all too common. Messages about body size, health, and ability show up in obvious places like dance class, physical education, and health class.

But kids also learn about good foods and bad foods in the way their classroom teacher talks about what she ate for lunch. They learn to equate body size with certain character traits when their English class curriculum includes books with fat stereotypes and no counternarratives. They learn that eating less should always be the goal when a word problem in math class involves calorie counting.

But deciding when and how to fight these battles as a parent can be overwhelming. Your relationship with your child's teacher or coach is a complicated one. Teachers and coaches are underpaid and overworked, and parental communication is something they do on their own time. You may also be working with them to navigate your four-year-old's biting phase or your eleven-year-old's inability to complete homework on time. You need these people on your side. This is why Gwen Kostal, the dietitian from Ontario who runs Dietitians4Teachers, encourages parents to take a beat when our child reports something a teacher said or did that raises a diet culture red flag. "Ask some questions. Try and understand what's going on before jumping to conclusions because we know that impact and intent are different," says Kostal. "Remember that no teacher is intentionally doing harm. They're stuck with some unlearning to do, or some policies that they may not even like and must find ways to work around."

If your child mentions a teacher's passing comment, or encounters some fatphobic elements in a textbook, it might be more useful to use this as an opportunity to identify anti-fat bias to your child. Ask them what they think about the way a character's body is described or joked about in a book, then offer your own take: "I don't like that this author equates this character's stupidity with his fatness. That's such a harmful stereotype. Have you ever noticed that stereotype in other books or shows?"

But some assignments—like keeping a food and physical activity log—present a clear risk to our kids because they teach restrictive behaviors, and are often assigned in middle and high school, already the years when kids are most vulnerable to dieting and disordered eating. In this case, opting your child out of the assignment is your best and only option. Kostal suggests saying: "I'm worried because this promotes disordered eating and body dissatisfaction. I'm giving permission for my child not to participate. Can you provide an alternative assignment they can complete?"

One more note about schools: If your school is in one of the twenty-five states that does periodic BMI screenings, know that it is your right to opt your child out of that experience. (Not sure? Ask your school administrators or check your state's Department of Education website for the official policy.) Contact your school administrators or school nurse at the start of the school year; they may need you to write a letter or sign a form confirming that you've declined to participate. This is important to do even if your child is thin, or otherwise not troubled by getting on a scale, because when fat kids are the only ones who opt out of being weighed, sitting it out becomes just as stigmatizing as getting weighed. Talk to your kids about why you're having them skip the screening. You might say, "We know that healthy bodies come in all shapes and sizes, and it's unhealthy for kids to focus on their weight." If your child is thin, you can also explain that this is a good way to be a thin ally: "We're opting out of this to make it easier for kids who get unfairly teased for their weight to avoid such a stressful experience." If your child is fat, use this as a chance to reinforce that their body is never the problem: "We know your body is growing perfectly. We're not worried about your body, so there is no reason to do this."

With sports and other extracurricular activities, begin by doing your own homework, as dance studio owner Meghan Seaman advised in Chapter 11: What are their protocols around snacks and pre-workout fueling? How size-inclusive are their costumes or uniforms? And how do they think about eating disorder prevention in their sport? If this is a sport your child is already passionate about, you'll also want to spend some time talking to them directly about how diet culture shows up there. How do they feel about their body when they dance or play this sport? Are they worried that they need to be shaped differently to excel?

If your child doesn't have the kind of body idealized by their sport, discuss that with them honestly. Acknowledge what they love about the activity, but also bring up the problems: "Ballet is such a beautiful art form, but it has a really problematic history around body size." Then you might say: "You have a bigger body, and we think that's amazing. But it might get hard in this world. Do you want to do this?" suggests Zoë Bisbing, the therapist who specializes in eating disorders in New York City, who is herself a former child ballerina. "You need to name it and set some boundaries. 'I know you love to dance, and I want to support you in pursuing this passion, but I'm not going to let you starve yourself or try to manipulate your weight. Eating enough to support your growth is a condition of participating.'"

Bisbing says that hard conversations like these are eating disorder prevention, and that parents need to have them even when a child does appear to have the ideal body for their chosen activity, especially if they are still prepubescent. "Be clear: 'We can't interfere with puberty. It's not normal to lose your period, and I will step in to protect you if that's a risk.'" After all, while thinness may open doors to a sport, it doesn't guarantee a trauma-free experience. Christy Greenleaf, PhD, the professor of kinesiology at the University of Wisconsin in Milwaukee, suggests opening a conversation with, "Your body is your calling card in this sport, and you might take a lot of pride in that. But it also gives people permission to comment on and evaluate your body." Talk with your child about their right to refuse to be weighed, or to set boundaries with a coach about body comments, and maybe even role-play those conversations so your child can practice advocating for themselves.

3. HOW TO TALK TO YOUR MOTHER (AND FATHER. AND EVERY BABY BOOMER.)

I once stood next to a total stranger in line at a restaurant bathroom. She was a woman in her mid-sixties who had just come from a table of adorable grandkids. A fat woman went into the bathroom ahead of us, and the grandma turned to me with a sigh. "Well," she said softly. "No matter how bad I feel about being old and fat, at least I know I haven't let myself go like *that*." I was surprised that a stranger felt so comfortable making such a fatphobic comment to me. But I also wasn't: Our kids' grandparents are often one of their most explicit sources of diet culture exposure. And this is complicated because those grandparents are also *our* parents (or parents-in-law). Just in the time that I've been working on this conclusion, I've heard from a reader whose mother bought Barilla Protein Pasta when she picked up groceries for them: "This is her coded way of letting us know the kids aren't getting enough protein, I guess." And another whose mother makes it a habit to let her know, anytime she runs into a mutual friend, if that person has gained or lost weight. It's not just mothers, of course. Maybe your dad is the one who talks at length about the wonders of Paleo during Thanksgiving dinner, or your otherwise-favorite uncle gets weirdly competitive when you go for a run together and wants to compare stats.

Baby boomers have lived through modern diet culture in its entirety, from the advent of jogging and Jazzercise in the 1960s, through the fat-free 1980s, and the carb-cautious 1990s, and on and on and on. And as diet culture has evolved, many boomers have simply added in the new "what not to eat" rules rather than dropping older iterations or questioning the wisdom of the entire operation. Many women and people of color in their sixties and seventies now were also among the first in their professional fields, directly challenging sexist and racist societal norms. The pressure to champion the thin ideal probably seemed like the least of their worries while they were also facing sexual harassment and microaggressions in white, male-dominated workplaces. And this generation now deals with ageism, another chronic oppression we don't talk nearly enough about. Their bodies have always been a problem, and weight control has been offered again and again as the only solution.

We don't need to excuse or downplay the harm caused when older relatives make fatphobic comments. But putting their comments into this larger context can help us find compassion for the ways they've struggled to feel safe in their own bodies. It may also make sense to share some of that context with your kids, maybe as a debrief after a meal where a grandparent has engaged in a lot of diet talk: "Did you hear how Grandma isn't eating sugar right now? It makes me so sad she feels like she needs to shrink her body. Women in her generation have always been told not to take up space, but we want better for you." You don't need to blame or shame or put limits around their relationship with their grandparent, but you can offer your own take on what they're hearing. And remember that the comment that triggers you so deeply because it comes from your parent is likely much less loaded coming from their grandparent. Also: Your parents' unhappy relationship with their bodies is not your problem to fix.

But you can let them know, lovingly, that it's not a conversation you want to have. You might toss in: "Oh, let's not talk about weight! Having a body is so hard!" the same way you might say, "Oh, let's not get into politics!" and then quickly move on to another topic. If your parent (or other older relative) seems genuinely curious about why you're opting out of weight talk, you can share more about articles you've read, podcasts you've listened to, or the questions you're thinking about. If you are otherwise close, you might even be able to talk about your own experiences and why you've stopped dieting or become more weight inclusive. Personal stories usually do the most to change people's minds on controversial issues, especially when we can say, "I used to feel this way, too." But this kind of sharing is also a much more vulnerable way to engage. So don't feel bad if you sometimes just let the anti-fat comment sail by.

The comments you should be prepared to tackle more directly are comments about your kids' bodies or eating habits, especially those made within their earshot. One gentle way in might be to mention, before a visit, that you've noticed your child becoming more body conscious recently, so these are topics you're working hard to avoid, and you'd appreciate Grandma and Grandpa's help. Then when a comment inevitably comes up, you can jump in and say: "This is what we talked about. We're not doing diet talk around the kids." If you have a partner, co-parent, sibling, or friend who will be there, loop them in ahead of time so they can also help enforce the boundary and redirect the conversation. And when you do have to cut off a hurtful comment, stand in solidarity with your child: "We trust her to listen to her body." "We trust his body to grow." "We're not worried about their eating/growth trajectory/jean size."

4. HOW TO TALK TO YOUR FRIENDS

Steph, a thirty-five-year-old mom in Fort Worth, Texas, wrote to me in a panic before a fifteen-year reunion with her college roommates. They were planning to spend a whole weekend together, eating and talking nonstop. But Steph knew from past visits that would also mean a potentially endless onslaught of diet talk and body shaming. "In the past, I've generally just been silent when this happens," she told me. "But I'm feeling more empowered now." The question she was wrestling with was how much to bring that empowerment to the table when her friends start demonizing their bodies or talking about why they can't eat cheese. Female friendships, especially, are often built on a foundation of anti-fat talk. And it can be scary to consider how to change that dynamic. "I don't know what to talk to my closest friends about anymore," another mom told me. "Do we even have anything to say to each other if we don't talk about our diets?"

In some cases, you might not. And maybe that's a useful piece of information to have about a relationship as you consider the role you want it to play in your life. But you may also find that you have deeper, more meaningful, and certainly more fun conversations with friends once you move away from the shared misery of body and food shaming. Rather than putting them on the defensive by raising concerns about their welfare, share how skipping these topics is important for your own well-being. You might say, "If it's okay, I'd rather not go there. I don't feel good about myself when we have this conversation." This boundary is especially important to set if your friends are thinner than you, and maybe unaware of the harm caused when thin people ask fat people for support while dumping on their own bodies in a way that lets us know our bodies are their worst nightmare.

This may help steer the discussion toward safer waters for everyone. It may also create an opening for your friends to share how they're struggling in a more productive way. If they do open up to you, stay curious and compassionate: Yes, their diet, and feelings about their postpartum belly, are rooted in anti-fat bias. But they are also rooted in the reality that none of us feels safe in our bodies. Resist the urge to proselytize; it's rarely useful in interpersonal relationships. And it's straight out of the diet culture playbook to try to tell other people how to eat, move, or feel about their bodies. But you can share your own experiences, resources, and questions.

Of course, this kind of heart-to-heart only works with close friends and in situations (like a long reunion weekend) where you have time for a deep talk. Often fat talk between friends manifests far more casually: It's your co-worker explaining why she's only eating salad for lunch. It's another mom on the playground telling her kid they can't have any more "junk" unless they eat some "real food," or bemoaning how much chubbier one of her kids is than the other. And here we walk a fine line: Naming this kind of anti-fatness is the only way we'll ever dismantle it. But doing so in the moment doesn't always feel safe or kind. If the conversation happens in a context where you spend a lot of time (say, a workplace or even a monthly book club), you might do better trying to establish an official policy or sharing some general education rather than tackling individual comments one by one. If it's a casual one-off on the playground, you may have to let it slide in the moment. But make a note to stay open to another opportunity for the conversation.

And think about how you can model different approaches: Be the parent who unapologetically serves snacks with processed sugar on playdates and at birthday parties. Respond to comments about a child "getting chunky" with a friendly "I know, isn't body diversity so amazing!" You can offer empathy for the pressure they face as a parent of a kid with a bigger body but also put the blame where it belongs: On diet culture. And if you need to push back against a fatphobic coach or pediatrician, let other parents in your community know you're doing this work and would love their support. Post it on social media when you opt out of the school's BMI screening so other parents know they can, too.

The librarian at my children's school recently posted on Facebook that she'd gone to the school district's CPR training and realized they were only being taught how to perform CPR on thin dummies without breasts. She asked the instructor if there were different strategies for performing CPR on people with breasts or larger bodies, and it turned out, indeed, there are—but nobody had thought to include that information in the training. This is how fat activism saves lives. And sharing these experiences with our communities is how we work toward making respect for body diversity a shared value.

5. HOW TO TALK TO YOUR CO-PARENT

Midway through reporting this book, I asked my Instagram followers: "Who or what stops you from taking an anti-diet approach to feeding your kids?" The most common answer, by a landslide: "My husband." I also heard from many divorced, separated, or single moms, like Abby in Chapter 7 and Magen in Chapter 12, who struggle with a male co-parent they aren't partnered with. And I heard from queer couples who struggle with a mismatch of values around weight, health, and food, so this issue is by no means limited to heterosexual co-parents. But the ways in which straight cisgender men are taught to interact with food, exercise, and bodies do set them up especially to parent from an anti-fat mindset, as we saw in Chapter 9. One reason for this is that the intersections of white, male, and thin privileges enable many men to assume they are experts on the best ways to do a lot of things, but certainly on how to eat and exercise—and they haven't reckoned with how much of their health or thinness stems from winning various genetic and social lotteries rather than their own wisdom.

Another issue is that in most heterosexual relationships, men do far less of the mental load of meal planning, grocery shopping, and cooking. This means they also aren't keeping up with the changing cultural conversation around feeding families, so they remain attached to "old-school" ideas, like making kids clean their plates to earn dessert. Mothers do more of the research on how to feed children because we've been socially conditioned to feel responsible for it. And this means we're more likely to encounter the backlash against diet culture and responsive feeding strategies. Then we're put in the unfair position of having to get someone on board with these new ideas when he hasn't done the same homework.

What we need to do instead is ask our partners and co-parents (of any gender) to do this work. Start by sharing why these issues matter to you on a personal level, and why raising kids who love their bodies and don't obsess about food and exercise is a core parenting value for you. Your co-parent will likely have questions, and you can and should answer them, assuming the conversation stays open-minded and respectful. You should also listen to their own stories around food and bodies because their experiences of being pressured to clean their plate or getting bullied for weight are influencing their feelings about all this now. But if you start to feel like you're on trial, you can say, "This really matters to me, and I'd like you to read some things." You can put this book in their hands or share other resources. (See page 289 for a list.)

They may not be willing or able to do this work with you. But if that's the case, it means they must cede this territory to you and let feeding kids and talking about food and bodies be the areas of parenting where you take the lead and set the tone. They can't backseat drive your decisions and strategies; they have to back you up. And that means respecting boundaries like no anti-fat jokes and no diet talk in front of the kids. One other boundary I strongly encourage: Don't keep a scale in your house. It's almost never medically necessary to have one, and as we saw with Ava in Chapter 7, often becomes a tool for dieting and obsessive weight worry for kids and adults alike. If giving up the scale feels hard for you or your partner, at least move it to a closet or other very-out-of-the-way corner where your kids won't encounter it. And consider talking to a therapist who can help you work through what it would take to get rid of it altogether.

Remember that whatever your partner's current or past struggles are, they aren't yours to solve or change. A better approach may be to figure out where your values do align on these parenting questions. Maybe all you can agree on is how many nights to order takeout. But maybe you do share a few larger food values, like being vegetarian, or having certain traditional dishes on holidays and birthdays. Wherever you overlap, use that as a starting point to identify some shared family values about food and body. And agree to save conversations about how your values conflict for when the kids are in bed. In my house, that has meant Dan working hard to stay chill when one of our children decides to eat only a stick of butter for dinner, and then later deconstructing with me whether that was a reasonable or terrible parenting choice in our shared quest to keep foods neutral and honor their bodies. (I land on reasonable—isn't butter basically cheese?—but I do agree we should buy the cheap butter when they are in this phase.)

All of this is only a starting point. Your kids' bodies and eating habits will change and change again, you'll be perpetually reinventing the wheel on how you navigate these questions together, and there are going to be tough moments when it's hard to make a decision that honors both your feelings and your partner's feelings about a situation. Neither of you will get this right all the time, and that's okay.

6. HOW TO TALK ABOUT YOUR OWN BODY

One night at dinner, when my older daughter was about eighteen months old, I told Dan that I hated how all my clothes fit. I was far enough past the postpartum stage that I felt like I should have my body "back," and I was still working through the idea that I might just be larger from here on out. "I just don't like my body that much right now," I said to him. In response, Violet began patting herself all over saying, "My body! My body!" I realized she was listening—and that I was damn lucky that she didn't yet understand everything I was saying. But also: I absolutely couldn't say that anymore.

Deciding to stop talking negatively about my body meant that I spent the next year or so realizing just how often I had a negative thought about my body that I had to stop myself from verbalizing. It was a little horrifying to realize how much I'd normalized being mean to myself. But stopping myself from saying the thought out loud meant that I also had to take a minute and investigate the thought. Was I truly that frustrated with my stomach? Or was I feeling annoyed that I didn't have an outfit I felt good about wearing to a work meeting, or having anxiety about seeing friends who hadn't seen me in a while and might notice how my body had changed? For me, body shame is almost always rooted in social anxiety—and identifying this pattern has helped me, slowly, to start to break it. If doing that work alone is daunting, a trauma-informed, weight-inclusive therapist can help. But if that kind of support isn't accessible to you, check the Resources section on page 289 for more.

Stopping the habit of negative body talk in front of our kids is critical, no matter what gender or body size our kids happen to be. If you're a fat mom raising thin boys, shaming your body in front of them will help them learn that women's value is tied to our appearance—and that there is only one right way to have an aesthetically valuable body. If you're a thin dad raising fat girls, your perception of your body's flaws reinforces to them that their bodies are wrong, and perhaps unlovable. And research shows that even parents who are struggling with eating disorders can limit how they pass those struggles on to their kids by avoiding negative self-talk, as well as negative talk about their children's bodies and eating habits.

But saying nothing isn't enough, because the rest of the world talks about bodies so loudly, all the time. As a small fat mom, it's been important for me to reclaim "fat" and find ways to use it neutrally and joyfully around my kids: to let them know that I'm not afraid to be described that way; that I don't see my fatness as a failing or a problem to solve. My kids also see me wearing a swimsuit and expressing enjoyment about my appearance, which feels important, so their understanding of beauty can include a fat abdomen and a double chin. Whatever size you are, finding ways to appreciate your body without apology can be a valuable way to challenge the incredibly narrow definition of beauty they're encountering in other places. (But if you're straight-sized, I hope you'll also seek out positive representations of fat bodies and other forms of body diversity, in books, in music videos, in art.)

And when your kids do witness you struggling with your body (because it will, inevitably, happen), place the blame where it belongs: "I'm frustrated these jeans don't fit because clothing brands do such a bad job of making clothes in different sizes." "I'm feeling anxious about what I wear to this big party because our culture teaches us that how we look matters so much and sometimes it's hard to remember that I know that's wrong."

7. HOW TO TALK TO YOUR THIN KIDS

Most of the time, your child's own body size doesn't impact how you talk to them. Thin kids and fat kids need to know that all bodies are good bodies. Thin kids and fat kids need to know that they are more than their appearance, or eating habits, or athletic abilities. They need to know that weight isn't synonymous with health, and that neither weight nor health has a moral value. And kids of all sizes deserve to feel in control of their bodies. They deserve to be able to say whether they are hungry or full or in the mood to try broccoli tonight. They deserve to say if they feel uncomfortable giving Grandma a hug, or with the way their track coach talks about their "runner's body." They deserve to opt out of school assignments that teach dieting, and to have a doctor who looks at them as a whole person, not a point on a growth chart.

And every kid needs to understand that we live in a fatphobic culture, and that we can all work to change that. One easy way to explain this to kids: "A lot of people in our world say and do mean things to fat people. We call this fatphobia or anti-fat bias and it prevents fat people from living their lives the way they want and keeps thin people in line through the fear of becoming fat. And this is never okay because all bodies are valuable. Fatphobia is a big problem, and grown-ups like me are working on fixing it. I bet you'll have some ideas to help."

But thin kids not only need to understand the concept of fatphobia—they need to know how and when they might perpetrate fatphobia. Just like we know that white parents raise less racist kids when we talk to our white kids about racism, parents of thin kids need to make sure they understand their thin privilege and its potential for harm. The tricky part of this is that your thin child is, of course, still vulnerable to body anxiety. Having a socially acceptable body often means absorbing, in all sorts of ways, that your body—and how it looks in clothes or performs in a dance recital or a big game—is the best thing about you. And that can make the inevitable ways that all bodies change hard to navigate.

But helping thin kids recognize that their own body anxieties are part of a larger constellation of cultural issues can help. This starts early, by normalizing body diversity every chance we get. Choose art, books, and shows with fat people (I've listed some favorites in the Resources section). If fat characters are treated badly or portrayed as stereotypes, talk about why that's problematic. Resist the urge to correct your thin child for calling someone fat, especially if they are aged five or under: There's every chance they are using the word as a neutral descriptor, and you rushing in to say, "That's not nice!" will be what teaches them that fat isn't such a nice thing to be. If the fat person in question is in earshot, and you're worried they'll be offended, you can say: "Yes, that person has a larger body. All bodies are good bodies. But let's not talk about other people's bodies without their permission."

Approach fat jokes or anti-fat statements in much the same way you would if your child makes a racist or homophobic comment. If your thin child uses "fat" as an insult, you don't have to shame them or get angry. But do ask them why they've chosen to weaponize that word. Make sure they know and care about fat people in real life and talk frankly about how fat people are bullied for their weight, have trouble buying clothes or fitting in restaurant seats, and are often paid less and receive worse medical care. Frame these issues as *everyone's* responsibility to fix.

As kids get older and body worries are more likely to manifest, look for ways to connect their anxieties to the concept of fat justice. If your tween asks, "Do I look fat in this?" you can reply honestly: "No. But why would 'looking fat' be a bad thing?" Make space for their feelings: "Our culture makes it hard to have a body. And it's normal to want to look like everyone else. But when we decide that a thin body is best, we make it that much harder for people who don't have thin bodies to feel safe and accepted."

8. HOW TO TALK TO YOUR FAT KIDS

The first instinct of every parent of a fat child is to avoid describing their child as fat. This is perfectly understandable, deeply rooted in love—and entirely wrong. When we say something like, "You're not fat, you're beautiful," we are telling our fat kids two terrible lies: one, that we think their body is something other than what we both already know it to be (fat), and two, that fat bodies can't be beautiful.

What fat kids need is to know that we see them, we accept them, and we know they are worthy of respect, safety, and dignity. They need to know we believe this unconditionally; that we would not love them more if they weighed less because our love already has no limit. And they need to know that we trust them to be the experts regarding their own bodies and physical wants and needs. This requires us to do our own work, because our culture is so quick to judge us as parents of fat kids. And fat kids need to know that we know the world. They need to see us advocate for them with doctors, teachers, and family members who see their weight as a problem. One magic phrase you can use in almost every scenario: "I trust their body."

Perhaps most of all, fat kids need us to listen and support them when they tell us what they experience. In our rush to tell fat kids how much they matter, we can't discount their own experiences of fatphobia. Our fat kids are more likely to be bullied by other kids and by adults. They may have a hard time finding a sports uniform that fits or a dress to wear to prom, or just clothes, period, that don't invite unwanted commentary and sexualization. None of this is their fault. Making their body smaller isn't the solution. And these experiences are deeply painful. We can't rush past how hard and isolating it can feel to be a fat kid with our determination to help them love their bodies. Depending on what they've been through, loving their bodies may not always feel possible. So, if they tell us they don't want to be fat, we must hear it. But we can validate how hard it is to be harmed by anti-fat bias without upholding that same bias: "Our culture makes it so hard to be fat. But your body is never the problem. I never want you to make yourself smaller. I want you to take up all the space you need in the world."

We've been told that fat kids are failures and proof of our own poor parenting. They are not. Fat kids are just as smart, capable, strong, beautiful, and lovable as their thin peers. And every child deserves to grow up in a world that celebrates, protects, and respects their bodies, and their fundamental right to body autonomy.

THAT'S NOT THE world we give our kids right now. Anti-fat bias is a part of every cultural system we and our children encounter. It is the air we breathe. But we can change these systems if we hold ourselves and others accountable for making that change. We can work toward a world where panicked parents don't lock up the Oreos. Where fat kids have a place on every team and in every classroom. Where thin kids don't think of their body size as a status they must preserve at any cost. Where every person knows they alone can decide what feels good, or safe, or right in their bodies. Where thin isn't a privilege, just another way of having a body.

We can have a world where body size doesn't determine your access to healthcare, education, clothing, and public spaces. We can have a world where our children's changing bodies—and our own—are honored, supported, and nourished, no matter what. We start by making home the safe space. We start today.